Do-it-yourself Yearbook

Popular Science

Do-it-yourself Yearbook

1985

Popular Science Books   New York

ISSN: 0733-1984

ISBN: 0-943822-38-6

Manufactured in the United States of America

introduction

Welcome! You have just opened the third volume of the *Popular Science Do-it-yourself Yearbook* containing many more of the informative and helpful chapters you have come to expect in this series. This volume contains eleven chapters on house design, construction and remodeling, and five chapters on innovative yet practical insulating, water heating, passive solar, and heat leak information. The thirty woodworking projects for both inside and out are designed to meet a great variety of needs and run the gamut from simple weekend "put-together" to satisfying and complex wood construction. There are also chapters on woodworking tool and jig techniques, how-to guidance on plumbing and electrical wiring in your home, pouring concrete, and an excellent roundup of new tools.

Advanced technologies

The fruitage of today's advanced technologies in new materials and methods abound in this volume as you read about solid-foam construction and insulation, waferboard, and super-efficient solar water heaters. These are brought to you by techno-building experts V. Elaine Smay, Richard Stepler, Al Lees, Susan Renner-Smith, and others of the POPULAR SCIENCE editorial staff who constantly ride the crest of new developments in this field.

Is it possible to have a successful solar house in an area where the sun shines only one week in three months? Yes, by combining several alternate energy systems controlled by an advanced microprocessor system. See how it was done in southeast Idaho by Ronald Cordes in "Solar House for a Sunless Climate." Can you successfully build a home of solid foam? Check out the house with 12-inch thick walls in "Foam House" by V. Elaine Smay. What about fire in such a home? That question is amply answered, too.

Can the truss-framed home building technique actually save 25 percent in costs over the conventional "stick built" method? What are the problems? The details are in "Truss-Framed Construction" by Charles Miller. Can you get a kit-home that is both energy efficient and easy to build? Try "Foam-Core Walls" by Charles Miller.

Woodworking Feast

In the Woodworking and Tool Techniques section, R. J. (Cris) De Cristoforo, the foremost innovator of jigs for advanced woodworking techniques, brings you a new master drill-press jig. Incidentally, his book, *De Cristoforo's Complete Book of Power Tools*, is now being updated and expanded into two new volumes, one on stationary power tools, the other on portable and bench-top tools, to be published in mid and late 1985 respectively. The original book was the most successful one published on this subject, with print runs in the hundreds of thousands.

In the Woodworking Projects chapter John Capotosto, twin brother of Ro, brings several unique sets of plans to this volume with easy to grasp concepts in the special Capotosto style. Tom Jones, Monte Burch, Rich Day, A. J. Hand, and Mack Phillips, all expert craftsmen-writers and known to our readers, add projects, techniques and new ideas to make this volume a wonderful working reference for you.

Your ideas are welcome

Now that the *Popular Science Do-It-Yourself Yearbook* program enters its third year, our editors are gratified that you, the readers, have responded with enthusiasm to the information and projects in the first two volumes. We also welcome your thoughts as to what you would like to see in the forthcoming volumes of the *Yearbook*. Perhaps there is special information on building techniques that interests you, or a certain project you'd want to build to meet a special need, a problem that needs solving. Do let us know, it will be a pleasure to help in any way we can.

John W. Sill
Editorial Director
POPULAR SCIENCE BOOKS

the authors

Below is an alphabetical sampling of the authors for this issue. They include freelancers as well as members of the *Popular Science* New York and field staff.

Mark Bittman is a full time freelance writer who lives in New Haven. His hobbies are carpentry and cooking, and those are also the subjects about which he most likes to write. His work appears regularly in *Popular Science*. His food articles are published in newspapers on both coasts (and in between), and he also writes for magazines such as *Connecticut* and *Sports Afield*.

Paul Bolon took a humanities and science degree from M.I.T. before working several years as a cabinetmaker and carpenter. Later, in New York as an associate editor for *Popular Science*, he wrote and edited articles on science, consumer products, and do-it-yourself projects. He's now writing full-time, also renovating his Chicago condo and indulging in its basement workshop.

Monte Burch is a prolific do-it-yourself writer with extensive on-the-job experience in cabinetmaking and electrical work. For seven years he served as Associate Editor of *Workbench* magazine. His articles in this Yearbook are "Round Victorian Table," "Cane-bottomed Chair," and "Electrical Plans and Blueprints." In addition, he has written several books, including *The Home Cabinetmaker, Basic House Wiring*, and his newest, *Building Log Homes*.

James Calhoun is an architect who has won several awards and honors, including national recognition for his entry in a NASA/AIA competition to design a space station based on the shuttle deployment system. Back on earth, he balances his time between the practice of architecture and involvement with a youth group at his church. His contribution to this Yearbook, one of the "Kids' Backyard Play Centers," was designed for his two sons.

John Capotosto is a crackerjack woodworker, furniture designer, carpenter, author and do-it-yourselfer. In addition to numerous articles on wood projects and home improvements, he is the author of *Basic Carpentry, Residential Carpentry, Furniture Making and Finishing, Remodeling and Home Improvements* and *Making and Using Simple Jigs*. Many of his original toy and furniture designs have been converted to easy-to-follow plans used by woodworkers, novice and professional, nationwide.

Ron Cordes has a Ph.D. in chemical engineering and a J.D. in law, both from the University of California. He has worked for industry, and for government in the field of environmental conservation. Currently Ron is employed as an attorney for the high-technology firm EG&G Idaho, Inc. He has authored three books, including his most recent widely acclaimed sports book, *Lake Fishing With a Fly*.

Richard Day, contributing editor for home and shop at *Popular Science*, was the owner of an auto-repair shop before he turned to writing. Considered an expert in many subjects beyond auto repair, such as masonry, plumbing, housebuilding, shop work, and tools, Day is a prolific writer of magazine do-it-yourself articles and the author of over a dozen related books, including *How to Build Patios and Decks* and *How to Service and Repair Your Own Car*. He is also president of the National Association of Home and Workshop Writers.

R. J. De Cristoforo has long been one of the leading woodworking writers. He is widely recognized as a master of tools, a shop-work genius, a highly accomplished photographer, and a skilled draftsman. Besides serving as consulting editor for tools and techniques for *Popular Science*, he is the author of countless articles and over two dozen books, including *How to Build Your Own Furniture; Build Your Own Wood Toys, Gifts and Furniture;* and *De Cristoforo's Housebuilding Illustrated*.

A. J. Hand began preparing for a career as a writer-photographer at the age of six by assisting his writer-father, the late Jackson Hand, with photo setups. A.J. later served on the *Popular Science* staff, winding up in 1975 as the magazine's home workshop editor before he began freelancing full-time. His photos have appeared on many magazine covers, and his articles appear in magazines and in his syndicated newspaper column, "Hand Around the House." He is the author of *Home Energy How-to*.

W. David Houser, art director for *Popular Science*, has written up several of his home projects for the magazine. At home in upstate New York, Dave is usually working on some improvement or woodworking project. For this, Dave does his own designing. He also restores old MGs.

Thomas H. Jones is a full-time writer specializing in furniture making, home improvement, and woodworking techniques. Before taking up writing full time in 1970, Tom was an aerospace engineer. He has sold hundreds of articles on do-it-yourself subjects and is the author of three books, including *How to Build Greenhouses, Garden Shelters and Sheds*.

Alfred W. Lees, the *Popular Science* group editor for reader activities, is in charge of all do-it-yourself instruction. He built the Lockbox leisure home as the focus of 19 feature articles during the 1970s, and is currently renovating a loft shell in lower Manhattan. He also created the PS "Leisure-Home" and "Storage from

Scratch" series and the national design competition for plywood projects, which he judges annually. His books include *Popular Science Leisure Home* (with Ernest V. Heyn) and the forthcoming *67 Prizewinning Plywood Projects*.

Charles A. Miller formerly was associate editor at *Popular Science*, where he handled how-to, science, and consumer stories. Chuck has written a variety of well received articles on projects and innovative construction methods—some of which appear here.

Jeff Milstein is an award-winning architect. Educated at Berkeley, he now lives and works in Woodstock, New York. He has been designing home projects and writing on passive solar topics for *Popular Science* since the early 1970s, and his designs have been published internationally. He is coauthor of *Designing Houses: A Guide to Designing Your Own House*.

Susan Renner-Smith, a Senior Editor at *Popular Science*, writes and edits articles on all topics covered by the magazine, ranging from space stations and electronic home banking to tiling bathrooms and installing flooring. She lives—with husband, Norman Smith, and son, Eric—in a 60-year-old house that serves as a proving ground for the products and projects she reports on.

Daniel J. Ruby, an associate editor at *Popular Science*, writes and edits articles on technology, energy, physical sciences, house design, and home do-it-yourself projects. In recent years, he has honed his construction and home-improvement skills by converting a raw warehouse space into a living loft. He newest interest is his home computer, upon which he coauthored (with Ernest V. Heyn) the *Popular Science Book of Home Alternate Energy Projects*.

George Sears, whose article "25 Heat Leaks and How to Plug Them" appears in Part III of the Yearbook, is a freelance writer who covers a variety of subjects for *Popular Science* magazine.

Bryan Shumaker is a man of many talents. A physician by profession, he is also an avid amateur astronomer, an author, and a designer/woodworker. His articles on astronomy have appeared in *Astronomy* and *Sky & Telescope* magazines, and he has had two projects published in *Popular Science*. One of them is one of the "Kids' Backyard Play Centers," which his two children enjoy year-round.

Howard Silken has been inventive all his life and, at present, hold six patents on power tool accessories. He is the author of *How to Get the Most Out of a Radial Arm Saw* published by Black and Decker. He has written many articles on tools and new woodworking techniques for *Popular Science* and other handyman/how-to-publications. For many years, he demonstrated the radial arm saw in Pennsylvania and Grand Central Stations in New York City, and at hundreds of do-it-yourself trade shows.

Richard Stepler, group editor for consumer information at *Popular Science,* has written on a variety of home-improvement subjects, ranging from house design and construction to decks, roofing materials, lighting, and custom built-ins. He and his wife and young son live in a 100-year-old cast-iron-front loft building in New York's Soho, the renovation of which you can read about in his article, "Extra Living Space Within Your Walls."

Peter and Susanne Stevenson are the husband-and-wife team behind Stevenson Projects, Inc., a California company that supplies do-it-yourself plans for scores of projects ranging from furniture to sailboats. Many of their projects, which combine beauty and utility, have been featured in national magazines. Pete's the designer, builder, writer. Susie's the business manager and publications director.

David Vigren, late Copy Chief at *Popular Science* magazine, had a long and distinguished career in publishing. He was the editor, in the 1950s, for the original feasibility studies for reaching the moon and other space exploration; prior to that he had been a project editor on the Nike ICBM guidance systems. Before coming to *Popular Science,* he was an editor at McGraw-Hill Book Company and Managing Editor at *Fishing World* magazine. Among his other credits was the position of Visiting Professor of Journalism at New York University.

contents

solar home for a sunless climate

Designing a solar home for the Sunbelt is no longer a major challenge. But what do you do in an area of the country that during one recent (and all too typical) winter had only one week of sun in three months? This was the question I faced when planning an alternate-energy home for my property in southeast Idaho, two hours from Yellowstone Park. In this area the winters are cold and unpredictable. And although a good solar heating system can be a great energy saver, you must have another efficient source of energy for those long periods when solar simply is not available.

My solution was to combine several alternate-energy systems and their controls. Some of the systems are quite familiar; some are very new. Basically, the house I designed is passive solar with a rock bed for heat storage. Wood heat is the primary backup, and an electric furnace backstops that. An advanced microprocessor controls heat distribution from all of the sources.

CUPOLA FAN

FAN

INSULATED AIR PASSAGE

HOLLOW COLUMNS FOR RETURN AIR

FIREPLACE GRATE

SPILL DAMPER

AIR-COLLECTOR BOXES

GRAVEL HEAT STORAGE

HEAT-EXCHANGER COIL

RETURN AIR

Together, the systems make my home energy-efficient regardless of the weather.

Here's how the systems work together. When the sun shines, a south-facing greenhouse captures the heat and a series of blowers generates an "envelope" of warm air. This surrounds the main living quarters, insulating them from the cold while at the same time providing heat. Simultaneously, two solar collectors heat the hot-water supply.

At night or when cloudy weather sets in, water flows through a hollow fireplace grating to a heat coil in the ducting. There, the heat extracted from the wood fire is distributed through the house's forced air ducts. A small programmable controller and a series of automatic motorized dampers monitor temperatures throughout the house and direct the heat to where it's needed. If the fire isn't producing

enough heat to meet the demand, a small electric furnace kicks in.

Good weather or bad, night or day, this combination of energy systems and controls keeps the hot-water supply hot, the house warm, and the electric bills substantially reduced.

Despite the periodic lack of sun in southeast Idaho—or in any other sun-poor climate—the first task in designing an efficient alternate-energy home is still to use a system that capitalizes on solar energy when it is available. For my home, I decided on a passive solar collector and chose the classic south-facing greenhouse but with a somewhat unusual geometry.

The greenhouse has three sections of Thermopane glass surrounding three sides of a glassed-in, trapezoidal-shape dining room. The middle, and largest, section faces due south; the two remaining sections face southeast and southwest, respectively. These

three sections allow the capture of the sun's energy more effectively over a longer period of time than a greenhouse with only a south face. A tile floor combines with the generous air space to create a large heat-storage capacity.

Ceiling vents and attic fans circulate the warm air between the house walls and down to a gravel-filled under-floor plenum (see illustration). This modification of the classic envelope design creates a cocoon of warm insulating air that moves around the main living quarters of the house, transferring heat and storing excess heat in the rock bed for nighttime use.

The sunless solution

When the sun is cut off by clouds for extended periods of time, the envelope of warm air simply is not available. To provide heat during the long stretches of cloudy weather, I installed

Solar heating, Idaho style, starts with a three-sided, insulated greenhouse (above) designed to capture heat from the elusive winter sun. Three 400-cfm squirrel-cage blowers in the attic suck warmed greenhouse air up through ducts in the ceiling and into a six-inch, insulated passage below the rafters (left). The air exits into an insulated roof-peak chamber and is blown into the north side of the house, flowing along the vaulted ceilings until it's drawn down into a series of hollow columns along the north walls of the two rooms. The columns direct the air into a set of large, perforated wooden boxes buried in a rock bed in the insulated crawl space beneath the house. The migrating warm air exits the boxes and transfers its heat to the rock. Underneath the greenhouse, two variable-speed, 800-cfm fans blow the air back into the greenhouse for reheating. In summer, the same blowers force cool forest air up into the house. On cloudy days, pipes carry heated water from a fireplace coil to a heat exchanger in the crawl space (see detailed diagram).

CEILING VENTS

GREENHOUSE

FLOOR VENTS

FAN

Stuart Hall

COOL SUMMER AIR

DOMESTIC- HOT WATER TANK

PREHEATING WATER TANK

EXPANSION TANK

Water-heating system

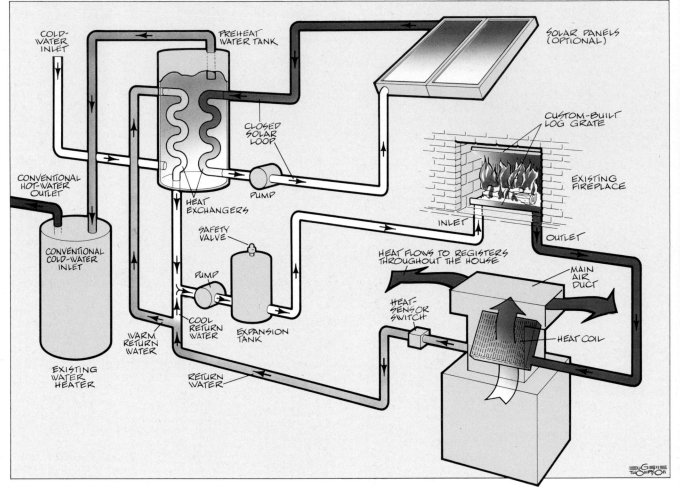

Linking wood and solar, the SWHIFT system heats house air and hot water in the Idaho house. The fireplace has sealed glass doors and a floor vent for outside combustion air. Water flows in a loop through the fireplace grate to a heat exchanger in the furnace ducting, then to the preheating water tank (also heated via solar panels) and through a safety-valve expansion tank back to the fireplace grate.

a heat-transfer system in two adjoining fireplaces.

Called SWHIFT (Solar and Wood Heat Inventions for Today), the system was developed by Lou Baribault (SWHIFT Fireplace Systems, 3170 Western Ave., Idaho Falls, Idaho 83401). The system differs from other fireplace heat exchangers in its versatility and built-in safety features (see diagram).

The system's basic component—a hollow, tubular grate filled with circulating water—is custom-built and so can be inserted into any existing fireplace or wood stove. In my house, the heated water is pumped to a heat coil that resembles an automobile radiator and fits into the main forced-air duct next to the furnace. But the hot water could just as easily be pumped directly into an existing hot-water baseboard heating system—or to a large, insulated storage tank.

When the thermostat calls for heat, the furnace fan switches on and blows cold air through the heat coil, extracting the heat and distributing it around the house through the existing heat registers. When the house is warm enough, a switching valve directs the hot water to a preheating tank coupled to the main domestic-hot-water tank.

In either case, the cooled water is pumped through an expansion tank equipped with a relief valve before returning to the log grate in the fireplace for reheating. The expansion tank ensures that if pressure builds up in the system, it will be released harmlessly through the valve instead of rupturing a pipe.

This versatile system is designed to use solar energy as well as wood heat. I chose one of the simpler options and connected two solar collectors to the preheating hot-water tank. As the tank was in place anyway, this allows

me to heat the hot-water supply during sunny days without building a fire.

Controlling the elements

With solar energy heating the house air on sunny days, solar collectors heating the hot-water supply, and the fireplaces heating both the house and the hot-water supply on cloudy days and at night, I needed an efficient way to control and distribute the energy. Because the house is large, approximately 5,000 square feet, getting maximum control was essential and not merely a case of fine-tuning the system.

I found the solution at a small local electronics firm. JBJ Controls, Inc. (P.O. Box 1256, Idaho Falls, Idaho 83402), had only recently developed the Thermatrol 6180, a unique, relatively inexpensive programmable controller. The modular unit can control almost any type of heating system.

The foundation for an energy-efficient house features a rock heat-storage chamber, shown here under construction. Foilfaced foam board insulates the plenum. The vertical concrete pipe transmits cool air to the greenhouse in summer.

diameter concrete pipe. The pipe goes five feet down into the ground, where it turns 90 degrees and runs under house footings and 60 feet into the woods. Where it resurfaces, the air is relatively cool due to transpiration of the trees. Thus, the house is naturally air-conditioned during summer.

Comparing system components

The modified-envelope theory employed in this house is a particularly effective means of using warm air from a greenhouse, air that can reach temperatures as high as the mid-80s on a sunny winter's day. But the envelope is not easily retrofitted to an existing home.

The SWHIFT wood-heat and solar-panel system, however, can be integrated into new construction or installed in an existing home that uses either a hot-water baseboard heating system or an electric or gas forced-air furnace. This flexibility allowed me to install the system after I had already occupied the house and at a time when I was financially ready to make the purchase.

The Trol-A-Temp motorized dampers can also be retrofitted. Some type of heat-zone control, such as that provided by these dampers, is vital in a large house such as mine in which some rooms lose their warmth more rapidly than others. And when more-expensive electric heat must be used, the dampers prevent the furnace from heating areas of the house that are already adequately warm.

However, none of the above components, alone or in combination, would be quite as effective in my house if the JBJ programmable controller or some comparable unit were not used to monitor the house and control the system as required.

Before I installed the fireplace heat exchanger, when the house was heated by a combination of solar energy and electricity, my winter electric bills ran as high as $425 per month. Last winter, with the JBJ controller operating the heat exchanger and the other system components at maximum efficiency, the average bill was about $125—and the comfort level was higher. And that is the bottom line.
—*By Ronald A. Cordes. Illustration by Stuart Hall. Drawing by Eugene Thompson.*

It has six sensor inputs and up to six thermostat inputs. Temperature set points can be set at the factory or at the site, and changes in factory calibrations can be made at the site. There are 12 output connectors (either 115 or 24 VAC) for components such as fans, pumps, and dampers. The Thermatrol 6180 has one more advantage—because it's modular, you pay only for the complexity needed. You can add plug-in modules later if you want to expand your system. I paid about $300 for a high-end model.

For further control, I installed Trol-A-Temp (Trolex Corp., 740 Federal Ave., Kenilworth, N.J. 07033) automatic motorized dampers in the air ducts for each house zone. They ensure that whatever heat is available through the ducting is delivered only to that part of the house calling for heat.

How does the control system work? The 6180 controller monitors temperatures in five separate areas: the greenhouse, the rock storage area, and the east wing, center, and west wing of the house. If the greenhouse temperature rises above 70 degrees F on a winter day, the 6180 turns on three attic blowers and two floor blowers. The blowers move the envelope of warm air through the central portion of the house and through the rock storage chamber. When the greenhouse temperature drops to 67½ degrees F, the 6180 turns off the fans.

If the temperature in any of the house zones (but not in the rock storage area) drops below 68 degrees F, the 6180 controller opens the damper to that zone and checks for a source of heat.

First it checks the automatic spill damper in the main air duct near the furnace (see illustration). When the fireplace-heat-exchange system is operating, this damper "spills" excess warm air into the rock storage area. The controller shuts the spill damper and directs heat from the fireplace to the house zone where it's needed. When the temperature in that zone reaches 70 degrees F, the 6180 closes that zone's damper. If no other zone needs heat and the preheating hot-water tank is at the correct temperature, the controller reopens the spill damper so excess heat can once again be dumped into the rock bed for storage.

If the fireplace system isn't operating, however, the 6180 searches for a backup source. It first checks the rock heat-storage chamber. If there's heat available, the controller simply turns on the furnace fan, which draws its air from the chamber. If there's not enough heat stored in the rocks, the 6180 turns on the backup electric furnace.

In summer, when heat is not required during the day, the 6180 turns on a cupola fan to vent any excess heat in the greenhouse. Another fan sucks replacement cool air into the rock storage chamber through a one-foot-

foam home

The large shell of what was rapidly becoming a house stood strangely white at the top of a gentle knoll. When we got to the construction site, it was apparent that the walls of the house were made of large white blocks, each labeled with a letter and number. Similar blocks formed the roof of the house, and a stack of them stood nearby, each with identical indentations in their edges. They were blocks of expanded-polystyrene (EPS) foam insulation. But in this house they were not *added* to the walls and roof; they *were* the walls and roof.

The house, on the outskirts of Madison, Wis., will soon be home to Don Peterson and his wife, Bonita. Peterson invented its unusual system of construction and is president of Cubic Structures, Inc., the company that he estab-

Chunky blocks of expanded-polystyrene foam (opposite page) are light enough for one worker to hoist two. Foam can be easily carved to form arches or other architectural features (top). Because the foam roof gives an R-value of 54, Cubic Structures houses usually do not have an attic; inside, cathedral ceilings soar to the 12-foot peak at the center. Cuts in foam blocks (left) are made at the factory. Note the slender slits where the PVC air stops will go. Cubic Structures model (above) near Madison, Wis., looks conventional.

lished to develop and market it.

Peterson's system is fundamentally this: The 12-inch-thick blocks of EPS-foam insulation board that form the walls of the house have channels in the edges to hold a special polymer-modified concrete called Insul/Crete and steel reinforcing bars, thus forming a post-and-beam skeleton. The roof is made of 14-inch-thick foam blocks laid between standard wood rafters. The foam is covered inside and out with a coating of Insul/Crete to give it strength, durability, and fire resistance. The result: a superinsulated house that is simpler to build than most and as energy efficient as anything available, says Peterson.

The customary way to build a superinsulated house is to erect, on site, double 2×4 stud walls, put eight to 12 inches of cellulose or fiberglass insulation between them, and perhaps add a sheathing of rigid insulation board. Then you wrap the house in a vapor barrier to keep moisture away from the insulation and to stop air infiltration. Finally, you finish the inside with wallboard and the outside with wood siding or the like.

Anatomy of a foam house

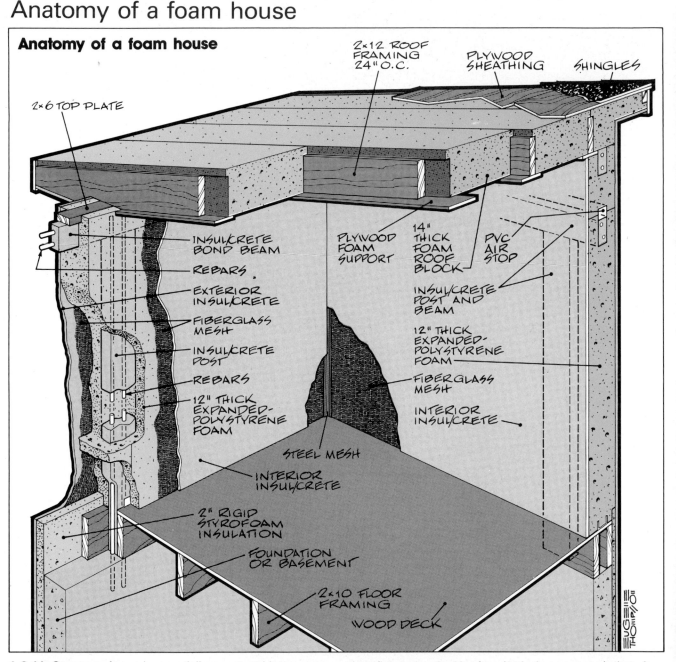

Anatomy of a foam house

2×6 TOP PLATE

2×12 ROOF FRAMING 24" O.C.

PLYWOOD SHEATHING

SHINGLES

INSUL/CRETE BOND BEAM

REBARS

EXTERIOR INSUL/CRETE

FIBERGLASS MESH

INSUL/CRETE POST

REBARS

12" THICK EXPANDED-POLYSTYRENE FOAM

PLYWOOD FOAM SUPPORT

14" THICK FOAM ROOF BLOCK

PVC AIR STOP

INSUL/CRETE POST AND BEAM

12" THICK EXPANDED-POLYSTYRENE FOAM

FIBERGLASS MESH

INTERIOR INSUL/CRETE

STEEL MESH

INTERIOR INSUL/CRETE

2" RIGID STYROFOAM INSULATION

FOUNDATION OR BASEMENT

2×10 FLOOR FRAMING

WOOD DECK

EUGENE THOMPSON

A Cubic Structures house is essentially a post-and-beam structure. But the normal role of wood posts and beams instead is played by steel rebars and a specially modified concrete called Insul/Crete. Here's how it's done.

Twelve-inch-thick blocks of expanded-polystyrene foam have channels for the posts and beams. Rebars for the posts are tied conventionally into the foundation, slab, or basement, and the foam blocks are stacked around them to form the walls. Then Insul/Crete is poured into the channels to form the posts. Around the tops of the foam walls is a continuous horizontal channel. It, too, is fitted with rebars, and Insul/Crete is poured into the cavity to form the supporting beam. The Insul/Crete beam is topped with a 2×6, to which the rafters are attached.

The roof of the house is made of 14-inch-thick foam blocks, cut to fit between 2×12 rafters (24 inches on center); the rafters are supported at the ridge by a steel I-beam, laminated wood beam, or interior bearing wall. The blocks rest on thin plywood strips below each rafter and overlap the rafters at the top.

Walls and roof, inside and out, are covered with Insul/Crete— a ¾-inch coating inside, and a ⅜- to ½-inch coating outside. First a fiberglass mesh is laid over the foam (wire mesh is employed as reinforcement around corners and openings). Inside, a base coat of Insul/Crete is troweled on, and this is followed by a top coat that looks like plaster. Outside, the Insul/Crete can be troweled over the mesh on the walls to look like stucco, aggregate can be laid in it, or other siding can be applied over it. Plywood sheathing goes on top of the roof, and shingles (or other roofing materials) are installed over the ply.

The result is a wall with an R-value (resistance to heat flow) between 32 and 46. (A conventional wall with 3½ inches of fiberglass insulation has a rating of R-11.) But for the house to perform up to specs, there must not be any gaps in the insulation or any holes in the vapor barrier. That means the house must be built with considerable care.

The Cubic Structures approach to superinsulation simplifies both the sandwich and the site work. The EPS-foam blocks are custom-formed at the foam factory following patterns supplied by Cubic Structures. The blocks are coded to indicate which goes where, then shipped to the building site. A standard four-by-eight-foot, 12-inch-thick block weighs about 32 pounds, so it's easy to carry. The wall blocks are joined by thin PVC air stops to block air infiltration. The EPS foam is not compromised by moisture, so no vapor barrier is required.

The week before I visited the Peterson house, the foam walls were propped in place and the rebars for the posts tied to the foundation reinforcement. Then the Insul/Crete team raised buckets of the stuff with a crane, and directed it into the cavities in the walls with a special funnel on the bottom of the bucket. "The spacing of the posts depends on the design of the house," said Peterson. "The maximum span is eight feet, but we often stand the blocks on end and place them every four feet."

At the tops of the walls, the builders used the same materials to form a continuous bond beam. Then they constructed the roof. Later, Insul/Crete will be troweled on inside and out to complete the walls and roof. "What we have," explained Peterson, "is a simple, unified system with R-46 walls, R-54 roof, minimum air infiltration, and no thermal bridging." The diagram (opposite page) illustrates the scheme.

Interior walls are standard stud walls; windows, too, are standard. The house will have double-glazed windows throughout. "No sense building a superinsulated house and putting in single windows," Peterson remarked.

A Cubic Structures house can use any type of heating system. Peterson's will have a sun room to collect solar heat, an energy-efficient fireplace, and a wood stove in the basement. Chopping wood is recreation to Peterson: "One of the few things I can do to forget business pressures is to run a chain saw."

The final backup heat source will be a heat pump. It could also provide air conditioning in summer, but Peterson does not expect to need it. A whole-house fan in the kitchen's dropped ceiling will help cool and ventilate the house. An air-to-air heat exchanger will keep the inside air fresh and the humidity comfortable.

Trial by fire

The idea for a foam home evolved, step by step, over many years. Peterson was working with the McFarland-based Insul/Crete Co., Inc., whose prime business was retrofitting commercial buildings by adding polystyrene board to the outside. Insul/Crete, a combination of portland cement, acrylic, and chopped fiberglass, was developed to coat the foam. It looks like stucco, but it's stronger, more resilient, and bonds better to polystyrene. Originally these retrofits were for looks, but since the 1973 oil embargo they've been done mostly for energy efficiency.

Noting how strong the foam boards became after Insul/Crete was applied, Peterson began to wonder if, with thicker foam, these panels could be used as the walls of a house. Paper studies and tests indicated that it would work, so in June and July 1982 he built a small (500-square-foot) structure and launched a blitz to prove the concept.

On July 29, Peterson had 13,000 pounds of stone evenly distributed across the center line of the structure's roof. Observers detected no deflection of the roof, no cracking of the Insul/Crete—indeed, no sign of stress. On August 2, he replaced the stone with a 15,000-pound Mack truck. Still the little house showed no structural damage.

Then came the fire test. "We outfitted the house with kitchen cabinets, carpeting, and draperies," said John Lehman, spokesman for Cubic Structures. "We even bought furniture from Good Will. Then we called in local fire departments to supervise the torching."

The scheme was to start a fire simultaneously in the kitchen, living room, and bedroom. But in that tight house the fire wouldn't burn. Finally they left the doors and windows open to get the fire going. They let it rage 45 minutes before firefighters doused the flames.

All the furnishings were reduced to a char, and the foam did melt a bit in two spots—but there was no substantial damage. A fire marshal said that a conventional house would have burned to the ground in such a test. One reason the foam house didn't, Peterson maintains, is that the walls are solid, whereas stud walls have hollow cavities that act as a flue during a fire. "We went in a couple of days later with a pressure-washer and hosed everything down," said Peterson, "and patched the places where the foam had melted." Since then, the building has been used as a showroom and office.

These melodramatic tests got Peterson a great deal of publicity (as intended) and netted some 10,000 inquiries from around the world. Seven firms subsequently became distributors for Cubic Structures houses, and 15 houses have been built. Five are in the Madison area; others are in Texas, Minnesota, Georgia, and Florida. And the city of Milwaukee is building two to use for low-income housing.

The Wisconsin Electric Power Co. plans to monitor the energy use of the Milwaukee houses. But for now, no rigorous data are available to verify a foam home's heating and cooling efficiency. Based on blower-door tests for air infiltration and on computer simulations, Cubic Structures calculates that the houses use about 1.5 Btu per degree-day per square foot of floor space—right in the ballpark with other superinsulated houses. A conventional house with R-11 walls and an R-19 ceiling would require about 12 Btu/degree-day/sq. ft. A 1,500-square-foot foam house in Madison with electric baseboard heat was heated with $116 worth of electricity (at five cents per kilowatt-hour) last winter. Heating the same-size conventional house would have cost about $800, according to Peterson.

How much does a foam home cost? "We're competitive with other superinsulation systems that give equal R-values and equal airtightness," Peterson told me. Though these houses can be built faster than the double-stud-wall type, foam insulation is more expensive than fiberglass or cellulose, so the costs about balance out: in the $48-to-$60-per-square-foot range, according to Peterson. "That's about 12 percent higher than 2×6 stud walls with six-inch fiberglass batts, and about 15 percent higher than 2×4 stud walls with 3½-inch batts," he noted. Considering the savings on heating and cooling, the additional first-cost of a foam house should be a good investment in many cases. But the payback depends on the climate, the cost of heating and cooling fuel, and the interest you have to pay on the additional money.

Cubic Structures (4307 Triangle St., McFarland, Wis. 53558) offers several stock house plans or will adapt your own. A Homeowner's Portfolio, which includes floor plans, cost information, test data, and background on the company, is available for $10—*By V. Elaine Smay. Illustration by Eugene Thompson.*

truss-framed construction

They may call it a revolution in home building, but it hails from a most unrevolutionary organization—the U.S. Forest Service. It's a new technique called truss-framed construction for building light-frame houses.

Unlike "stick-built" homes, the main structural elements of a truss-framed house are prefabricated. The truss frames, consisting of interconnected floor trusses, rafters, and wall studs, are tipped into position on site, much as you'd stand a deck of cards on end one at a time. The frames are then tied together with blocking at top and bottom.

Truss-framed construction could be a boon to a housing industry that is hard-pressed to keep costs down; the technique saves time and money by cutting down on the labor and material necessary to build a house.

The Forest Service's Forest Products Laboratory originally developed the technology to build rugged homes in disaster-prone areas. Engineers took a normal plate-frame roof truss, which is used in about 90 percent of new homes, and tied it directly to wall studs. The wall studs were in turn tied to a flat-floor truss. They found that the resulting house had, in effect, a strong, unitized frame.

The average house requires no more than 26 trusses, so an entire set of frames can be transported on a single truck. A do-it-yourselfer can easily handle construction—except for building the truss frames, which need the attention of a design engineer and the quality control of a truss fabricator. The job is too tedious and demanding for people without the proper equipment. Besides, by the time you pay retail prices for the materials, you'd save little, if anything, over

purchasing the completed trusses from a professional supplier.

What about the price of the house? Because there are no floor beams, headers, or interior columns, the cost

for lumber is significantly reduced. Construction costs (material and labor) average about 10 percent less than costs for a comparable house built conventionally. The saving can

Truss frame tips into position easily. Instead of trussed rafters, this end frame has vertical nailers for attaching gable sheathing. Frames go on 24-inch centers.

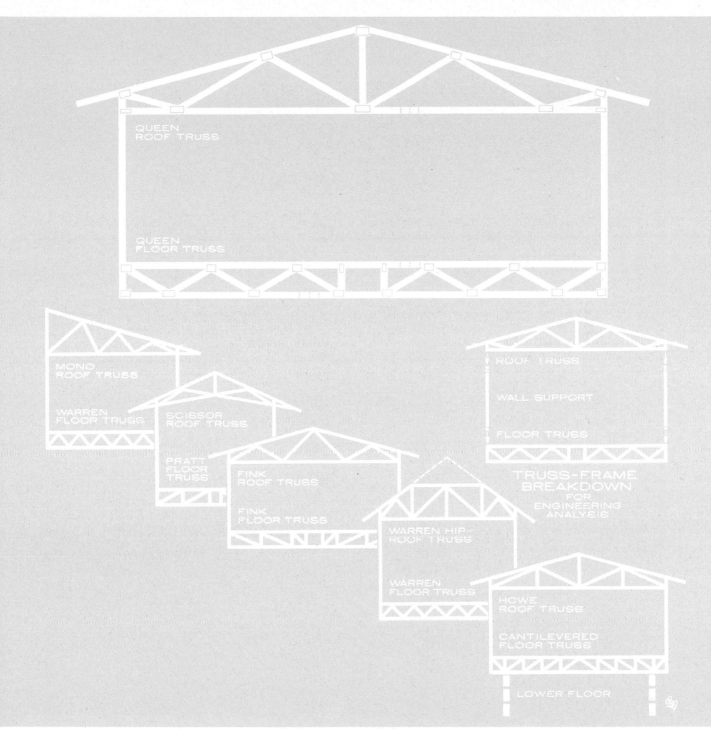

Truss frames can be made in a variety of designs, depending on size and shape of structure. In every design, upper end of each outside stud becomes part of roof truss to which it's attached. The bottom end of stud runs all the way to the lower edge of floor truss. The most important stipulation in designing trusses is that they must conform to standard design specifications, such as those outlined by the Truss Plate Institute. The guidelines give required lumber size and grade and identify the truss-plate requirements at joints. The frame members are typically 2×4s, but larger stock could be used—in fact, 2×6 frames *must* be used for long spans (greater than 30 feet). The 2×6 frames should be used, too, in earthquake zones or in areas where strong winds or heavy snow loads are prevalent.

go as high as 25 percent, however. Part of the saving comes from the open space left by the floor trusses, which makes for easy installation and lowered labor costs for heating and cooling ducts, electrical lines, and plumbing.

Putting the trusses up involves three main operations: getting the frames into the correct position, aligning them properly, and bracing them. The frames can be carried by hand, or a light crane or forklift can do the work.

First the end wall goes up: You square and anchor it to the foundation. Because it serves as the guide for the rest of the truss frames, it must be exactly vertical. The subsequent frames, remember, are spaced with blocks at the top and bottom of each stud. Check

Frames can be erected and braced in two hours. With standard methods, same-size house might take two days to frame.

each member for alignment with a level, and plumb every fourth one at the center and both walls to be sure alignment is maintained. If one frame member is out of alignment, the following ones will be, too; the cumulative effect can put the whole building out of whack.

Once the frames are up, brace them temporarily so that the house doesn't collapse like a row of dominoes. Ideally, you would install permanent wall

sheathing, which provides the real bracing strength, as soon as the first end wall and truss frame are aligned. You'd nail on the remaining sheathing as succeeding frames go up.

Windows, doors, fireplaces, and other wide openings can be a problem. However, you can put up the truss frames and then cut them, framing out the openings in a conventional way.

More than 1,200 homes have been built using truss-framed construction.

Many more are likely to be seen soon—*By Charles A. Miller. Drawings by Carl De Groote.*

NOTES ON FURTHER INFORMATION
To ensure that this new technique is made available to all, the Forest Service has patented the system in the name of the American people. For detailed brochures on the system, write Forest Products Laboratory, Box 5130, Madison WI 53705. The National Assn. of Home Builders Research Foundation, Box 1627, Rockville MD 20850, has prepared a detailed 48-page manual titled "Truss-Framed Construction," available for $5.

Don't need a whole-house truss? Just truss-frame the floor

Trussed floors can by themselves be money savers. Trussed floor joists generally consist of parallel 2 × 4s (top and bottom) with lightweight galvanized-metal supports—called space joist webs—between. The metal webs attach directly to the top and bottom plates without nails; they range from 12 to 28 inches, depending on the strength required. Trussed joists can also be constructed using 2 × 4s between top and bottom plates with the sides covered by plywood, but this is usually a more expensive method.

What are the advantages of a trussed floor? Trussed joists are light and easy to install, reducing labor. They're anchored in place by nailing to the sill plate—no sawing required.

Trussed joists are also strong. The allowable spans are much greater than for conventional framing systems: For most homes, trussed joists can span the entire width of the house. This eliminates the need for supporting beams, bearing walls, and additional concrete footings in the foundation, saving both material and labor. And when used between floors in a two-story home, the clear span beneath allows flexibility in room design.

The open spaces within trussed joists can be used to pass air ducts, plumbing pipes, and wiring without having to saw or drill holes. This, too, not only saves time but eliminates the possible weakening of the floor structure.

Trussed joists save time and labor, too. They can be easily installed by the do-it-yourselfer and can be purchased from most truss fabricators. They should, however, be designed by an expert to ensure proper floor strength.

A truss-joist fabricator will need, at the very least, your foundation or floor plan. A full set of plans is preferable, however. The span of the truss is the critical factor in design—*Herb Hughes.*

prefab home with foam-core walls

"Building a dream house shouldn't be a nightmare," shout the advertisements for manufactured homes. But it's never an easy job to erect the house of your dreams. And another problem is that many prefab homes are not energy efficient.

A new kit home from Pre-Cut International Homes, however, is claimed to be both easy to build and energy efficient. It features an exterior wall—called a Thermo-Lam wall—with two inches of insulating foam glued between laminated 1×8 cedar boards.

The R-value of the wall is 17.9, though the company claims it performs as well as an R-23 wall because the insulation is continuous—there are no interruptions from studs as there are in conventionally insulated walls. Even if you discount that claim, the wall is likely to be a good performer, thanks to its solid profile: There's no way condensation can build up inside a stud cavity, and there are no interior air currents.

The lamination glue lines serve as moisture barriers, and because beads of adhesive are used in the constrution process (along interlocking seams), there's no infiltration.

Prices range from about $11,000 for a small leisure home to more than $84,000 for a big three-bedroom lodge—more if you want a larger custom house. The house is available in cedar only.

All the material necessary to make a weathertight shell comes with the kit: floor, roof, windows, doors—even nails and caulking. The price doesn't include foundation, finish, floor covering, cabinets, plumbing, heating, or wiring. Pre-Cut Intl. Homes, Inc., Box 886, Woodinville, Wash. 98072—*By Charles A. Miller.*

Foam core runs throughout exterior walls (right). Beads of adhesive are placed along shoulders of cedar laminations.

Cedar-and-foam home has interlocking walls made of laminated boards glued to two inches of expanded polystyrene.

little big house

It's just a little house in the woods in western Massachusetts. In fact, the house measures a mere 24 feet square. Inside, however, a sense of spaciousness belies its compact outside dimensions. The key is a soaring cathedral ceiling that opens up the ground floor.

"The idea," says architect John Fulop, "was to design a simple house that wasn't just a box, but one with an expansive use of space—a house that didn't give you the claustrophobic feeling you can get in 24-by-42-foot builder houses, for example, which would cost at least as much."

In fact, perhaps the most remarkable fact about Fulop's little house is that it was built two years ago for just $35,000. I'll describe Fulop's cost-cutting techniques later.

Aside from the cathedral ceiling, the house has several other space-expanding features:

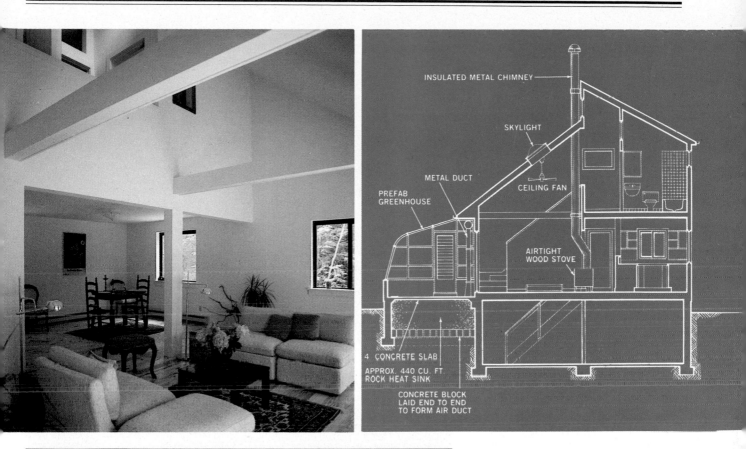

INSULATED METAL CHIMNEY

SKYLIGHT

METAL DUCT

CEILING FAN

PREFAB
GREENHOUSE

AIRTIGHT
WOOD STOVE

4 CONCRETE SLAB
APPROX. 440 CU. FT.
ROCK HEAT SINK

CONCRETE BLOCK
LAID END TO END
TO FORM AIR DUCT

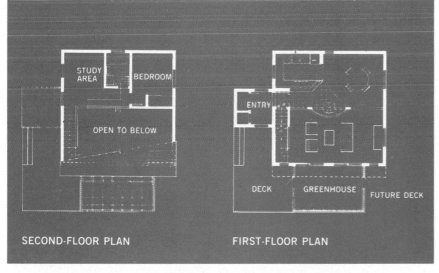

STUDY
AREA | BEDROOM

OPEN TO BELOW

SECOND-FLOOR PLAN

ENTRY

DECK | GREENHOUSE | FUTURE DECK

FIRST-FLOOR PLAN

● Double sliding glass doors give onto the deck, opening the interior to the outdoors.

● A clerestory admits light and solar heat to the upper-level bedrooms and bath.

● Small windows in the north wall provide a view and balance the light.

● An air-lock entry with storage closets shields the living area from blasts of wintry air.

As built for Fulop's client, the house is a direct-gain solar type: Sunlight enters the living space through south-facing windows.

Fulop's plans call for a greenhouse where the present deck is located. The greenhouse, with its integral rock-bed heat storage (see cross section), is sized to provide a substantial amount of the home's space-heating needs. A thermostatically controlled fan blows hot air from the greenhouse peak onto the rocks under the floor slab. Concrete blocks laid on their sides form the air plenums in the rock bed. At night, the process is reversed to maintain greenhouse temperatures. In this case, the home is an indirect-gain solar type.

An airtight wood stove in the living room handles most auxiliary-heat needs. Electric baseboard heaters are installed as backups but are rarely used. In fact, the owner reports that electric bills average $29 a month.

How did Fulop design the house to keep building costs so low?
● Dimensions are based on multiples of standard building materials to minimize waste and cut labor costs.
● Kitchen and bath are stacked to minimize plumbing runs.
● The home's 24-by-24 foot size permits use of less-expensive 2×8 floor joists. (Going to 28 feet would have required 2×10s or 2×12s.)
● In side walls, 2×6s on two-foot centers cost less than 2×4s on 16-inch centers and permit extra insulation.

Unfortunately, one of Fulop's cost-saving features wasn't included. Because a local building inspector insisted on a masonry chimney, the double-wall prefab metal chimney specified in the plans had to be dropped—*By Richard Stepler. Architect: John Fulop.*

WHERE TO SEND FOR PLANS
Complete sets of working plans with dimensions and construction details, including those for the greenhouse, have been prepared by the architect. Send $75 for one set of plans, $25 for each additional set (needed for construction, financing, and filing) to John Fulop Assoc., 561 Broadway, New York, N.Y. 10012.

you can transform a tract house

Seldom has a remodeling job accomplished this much. When I first saw this house—and its before-and-after floor plans (right)—I knew it was a story POPULAR SCIENCE should tell. The transformation is far more than cosmetic: The entire character of the house has been changed from drably functional to excitingly spacious. As an important bonus,

window-siting errors were corrected and additions made that greatly improve the home's energy efficiency.

Even if your present home isn't as uninspired as this one was, you can probably adapt many of the ideas detailed here. Some of them may look familiar: I first saw this project on the PBS television series "This Old House," hosted by Boston renovator

Bob Vila. Normally, the show deals with the restoration of antique houses. But when I learned last year that Vila was tackling a 1950s ranch-style house familiar to thousands of our readers, I felt his many improvements were too shrewd to leave to the limited exposure of educational television.

First of all, note that the floor-plan orientation switches from *layered*

Most dramatic face lift is along north walls. "Decorative" shutter slats were scrapped and surfaces re-sided with same natural-finish vertical boards used as siding on breezeway. Garage-door entry was sealed into energy-saving solid wall. Home's canopied front door moved from dead center of wall to center of new breezeway, with privacy screen added.

zoning (with privacy areas—bedrooms and bath—at top, and public space—living, dining, kitchen—below) to *vertical* zoning (with private rooms to the left, public to the right). In a house this size, vertical floor-plan zoning is more practical for simultaneous dual function: Family members or house guests can retire for the evening while group activity continues in the other area.

As with so many quickly built, cheap mass-market houses of the postwar era, access to this home was through ill-planned doors that swung directly into living space. Not only was that awkward; it was energy-wasting since heated or cooled air was vented directly outside each time either the main entry or side door was opened. In the revised floor plan, that dead-center main entry was sealed (the top part of its opening became the bath-room window) and the main entry was moved to the new breezeway. The side door into the kitchen was retained, but since the kitchen was doubled in size (by absorbing an adjacent, undistinguished dining area), it was practical to tack on a mud room-pantry that serves as a kind of entry air lock. This side entry is totally restyled, with its stoop compressed and its stairs turned 90 degrees to climb along the wall. A new screen wall provides privacy from the street for both entries and deflects gusty winds from this entry patio.

One of Vila's shrewdest alterations was shifting that picture window from

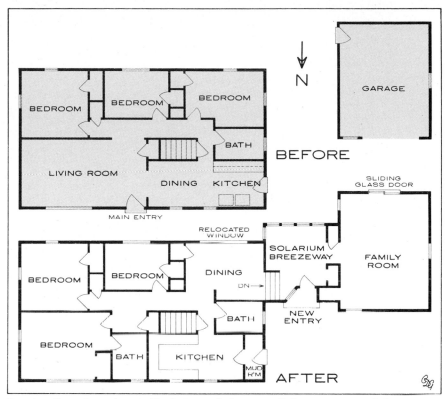

Compare floor plans above with photos on facing page. Only new structure is breezeway to connect house with unused garage. Converting garage to family room then creates new wing that wholly alters zoning of private and public areas.

Connecting structure changes character of entire house. Foundation of new solarium is concrete slab laid on grade, so it's at same level as garage floor. Old corner bedroom becomes dining area, with arched opening cut in outer wall through which stairs descend from original floor level. Note relocated picture window behind dining table. Solarium (right) has quarry-tile floor. This is now home's main entry—and first impression.

Old garage walls are finished off with drywall, pierced with new windows; rafters and tie beams are closed with wood strips.

Spacious new kitchen has room for breakfast table and improved triangular placement of the sink, range, and refrigerator.

Out goes the picture window from the front of the house. Simply removed as a unit and carried around to the opposite

corner, at back, it was installed in rough opening framed to take it (photo above; note corner of garage at left).

Concrete is dumped between new block footings connecting garage to house. Once slab cures, breezeway structure is

erected on it (right). Breezeway's ridge beam is tied into garage roof at far end and into cutaway wall in foreground.

The bridging breezeway is two-faced, providing new entry for front of house (left) and heat-capturing solarium for

south-facing back (above). New windows in former garage at left are same as seen in color interior at top of facing page.

the north wall—the street facade—where it not only got no sun but also compromised the privacy of the living room. As the top-right photos show, it was simply carted around back where

it contributed to the solar gain—and gave the new dining room a view of the wooded area out back. Its old opening was partially closed up (and, of course, insulated) for the installa-

tion of a new wide but shallow double-glazed window, to provide better privacy for the master bedroom that replaces the living room at the front corner. (A second window was added around the corner.)

The prize of Vila's remodeling, however, is the recreational suite added on the home's right end. By insulating and finishing off the detached garage and joining it to the house by means of a tile-floored solarium, he created not only a gracious entry but an activity area larger and more inviting than the discarded living room. The house is no longer a cramped box, and its architectural interest is greatly enhanced, both inside and out. To bridge the distance between existing structures without adding support posts, Vila created a massive ridge beam of four 2×12s. He also beefed up the vertical framing in the existing walls to handle the transfer of load from the new roof.

The alterations also increased the home's efficiency through better sitting of the windows for solar gain. The solarium, facing south, is an especially good passive collector. Its quarry-tile floor is laid over an eight-inch concrete slab atop a foot-deep bed of crushed stone. Rigid two-inch foam insulates the footings to a depth of two feet. This heat sink soaks up and later radiates heat from solar exposure. If insulating drapes were drawn across the panels of glass at night, the heat stored in the slab should keep the area cozy on all but the most severe winter evenings. For those, it might be best to close this area off from the family room—and draw an insulated drape across the sliding-glass door there, as well.

The entire remodeling project was budgeted at $25,000—including all new appliances for the kitchen and a wood-burning stove for the family room. The remodeling took longer than the original construction: This house was just one of 400 tract homes thrown up by a Boston developer in the mid-1950s. On average, he finished two a day, each house taking seven weeks from start to finish. What a contrast with today's homebuilding pace!

With new-housing starts continuing at such a low ebb that over 75 percent of all homes purchased by first-time buyers are now *existing* houses, projects like the one we've shown here offer just the type of inspiration people need to transform those less-than-ideal cookie-cutter houses into homes worthy of pride and devotion—*By Al Lees.*

extra living space within your walls

It started out simple, as home-improvement projects often do. We wanted to divide a studio/work area from our dining area with a partition. But we soon realized that, unless we created additional rooms, we'd soon outgrow our home. We commissioned architect Jeff Milstein to develop a complete interior redesign. Our requirements were:
- A master bedroom with closets and dressing area.
- A guest or child's bedroom.

- Two work areas, one for a graphic designer, a second for a writer-editor.
- Built-in shelves for a large collection of books.
- A walk-in storage closet.

In addition, since most of the space we were working with had no direct access to windows, daylighting and ventilation had to be carefully considered.

Along with his preliminary drawings, Jeff prepared a scale model of the project. This helped us visualize the new rooms and make changes before we actually started building. As you can see from the final floor plans, Jeff created a multi-level set of interlocking rooms, all contained in an interior area that measures about 12½ by 24 feet.

While our project was designed for

When you're carving a new room out of an existing one, a curved wall lessens the impact of the intrusion. Hallway with entrance to dressing room is at left, walk-in closet is at right. Master bedroom (inset) is on upper level, behind curve. Half walls are topped with cherry wood.

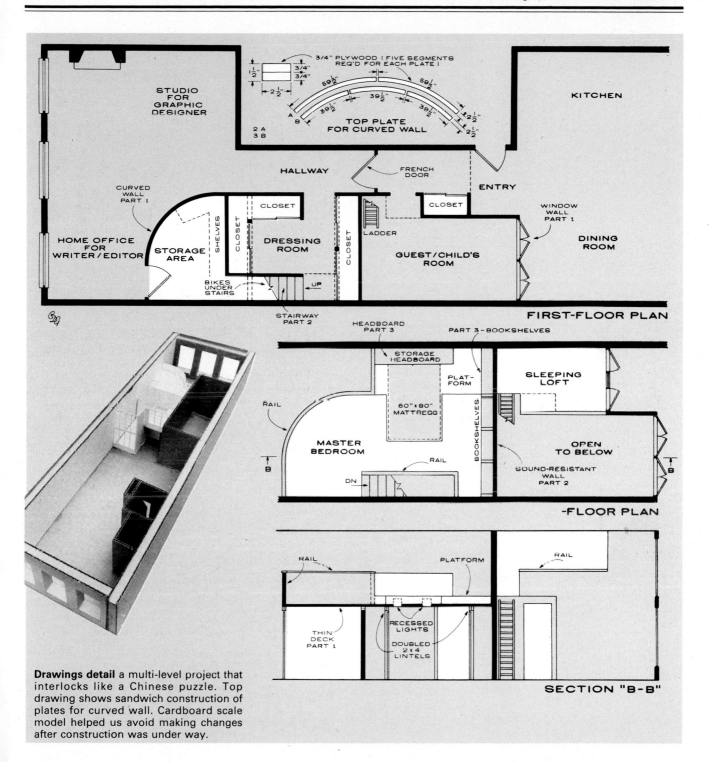

Drawings detail a multi-level project that interlocks like a Chinese puzzle. Top drawing shows sandwich construction of plates for curved wall. Cardboard scale model helped us avoid making changes after construction was under way.

a full floor with 12½-foot ceilings in a 100-year-old cast-iron loft building-turned-residential-condominium, many of the ideas and construction techniques we used could be adapted to your own home-remodeling projects. This article shows you tricks for faster framing; how to construct a curved wall; and how to install an ultrathin deck that might just make a second level practical—for storage or as a sleep loft—in a room with a lower ceiling than ours. There are ways to

build stairways and sound-resistant walls, lighting tips for low ceilings, and detailed plans of built-ins for the master bedroom.

We began by drawing chalk lines to mark the location of first-floor walls. A fast way to frame partitions is to use metal channels as bottom plates. Screw the channel to the floor and then pop studs in one at a time, fastening each with two screws, one driven from each lip of the channel. (A screw gun is an essential tool.) We

used wood studs and top plates—doubled in most walls—for the strength needed to support the deck. To save space, we used 2 × 3 studs throughout most of the project.

We used a six-foot-long string to mark the location of the curved wall's bottom plate. Then we temporarily tacked strips of ¾-in. plywood to the floor and scribed the same curve on them. These were removed, cut, and assembled for top plates (see drawing and photo for details). We cut the

Curved plates are sandwiches of five segments cut from ¾-in. plywood (see drawing, page 21). Skil's Sand Cat belt sander smooths edges once segments have been glued and screwed.

(see drawing, page 21)

Framing for the curve: 2×3 studs are oriented radially. Decking is nailed to curved top plate. Note higher hallway headroom with conventional 2×6 joists to support the ceiling.

Studs were screwed to metal channel plates. Skil's cordless Boar Gun makes working on a large project easier (no snaking extension cords). Note doubled top plate and t&g decking.

How to build stairways

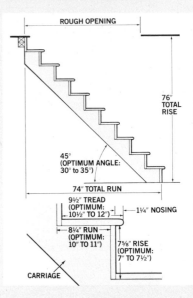

The most comfortable angle for a stairway is 30 to 35 degrees, but any angle between 20 and 50 degrees is possible. Minimum width for a stair is 24 in.; for two-way traffic, width should be at least 36 in. If you follow these rules, the stairway will be safe and comfortable to use: 1 run + 1 riser = 17 to 18 in.; 1 run + 2 risers = 24 to 25 in.; 1 run × 1 riser = 70 to 75 in. Generally 30- to 35-degree stairs are designed with a rise of 7 to 7½ in. and a run of 10 to 11 in. The run plus the nosing give the tread width. It's essential that all risers be equal and all treads be equal, or you'll trip on uneven steps.

One of the industrial shielded light fixtures we used inside closets (see text).

How to build sound-resistant walls

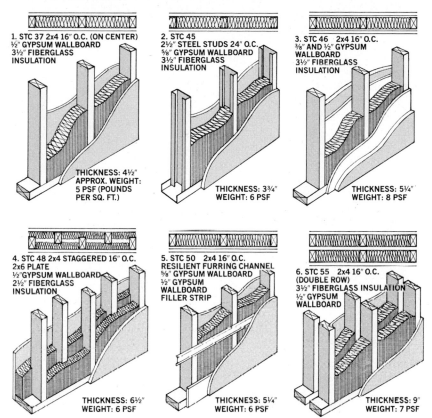

1. STC 37 2x4 16" O.C. (ON CENTER)
½" GYPSUM WALLBOARD
3½" FIBERGLASS
INSULATION

THICKNESS: 4½"
APPROX. WEIGHT:
5 PSF (POUNDS
PER SQ. FT.)

2. STC 45
2½" STEEL STUDS 24" O.C.
⅝" GYPSUM WALLBOARD
3½" FIBERGLASS
INSULATION

THICKNESS: 3¾"
WEIGHT: 6 PSF

3. STC 46   2x4 16" O.C.
⅜" AND ½" GYPSUM
WALLBOARD
3½" FIBERGLASS
INSULATION

THICKNESS: 5¼"
WEIGHT: 8 PSF

4. STC 48 2x4 STAGGERED 16" O.C.
2x6 PLATE
½" GYPSUM WALLBOARD
2½" FIBERGLASS
INSULATION

THICKNESS: 6½"
WEIGHT: 6 PSF

5. STC 50   2x4 16" O.C.
RESILIENT FURRING CHANNEL
⅝" GYPSUM WALLBOARD
½" GYPSUM
WALLBOARD
FILLER STRIP

THICKNESS: 5¼"
WEIGHT: 6 PSF

6. STC 55   2x4 16" O.C.
(DOUBLE ROW)
3½" FIBERGLASS INSULATION
½" GYPSUM
WALLBOARD

THICKNESS: 9"
WEIGHT: 7 PSF

For typical sound walls shown, STC ratings indicate how well a wall stops noise. Here's what they mean in terms of blocking loud speech, according to Certainteed: STC 30—loud speech audible and understandable; STC 35—loud speech audible but not understandable; STC 40—loud speech barely audible; STC 45—you must strain to hear loud speech; STC 50-loud speech not audible. There are three ways to reduce sound transmission; added mass, with extra layers of gypsum board; discontinuous construction to minimize direct connection of wall materials; and fiberglass batts to absorb sound in the wall.

channel almost through with a carbide saw blade every five inches and then screwed it to the floor along the chalk line. Studs for the curve are 12 inches on center; we determined where gypsum-board joints would fall and used doubled studs at those points. Finally, we nailed on the top plate.

We used ⅜-in. gypsum board horizontally, and applied it dry—without first wetting or dampening it. We first nailed one end firmly to the starting stud. Then we *slowly* bent the sheet around the curve, nailing it at each stud as we went. We lapped two ⅜-in. layers on the outside of the curve for strength. Tips: You'll need two people—one to bend, the other to nail. Be sure to use lots of nails. And finally, when it comes to spackling and finishing the joints, use lots of compound.

To preserve headroom, Jeff devised a tongue-and-groove deck that takes up only 1½ inches of space. For a 12-foot-six-inch ceiling, that leaves six feet two inches-plus for each level.

"The 2 × 6 t&g decking will just support the loads if no span exceeds seven feet," Jeff advised. Besides the doubled top plates of first-floor walls, two doubled 2 × 4 lintels support the decking. The lintels keep maximum spans within specs.

We installed the decking one piece at a time, snugging each joint as tightly as possible. Hammering blocks of scrap decking are essential to avoid damaging the t&g joints. We facenailed the boards with two 16-penny nails at each support. The "finish" side of the decking faces down; it's the ceiling for the first floor. Gray industrial carpeting covers the top.

When the deck was finished, the project began to look as though we were building a small house inside our home.

The architect's plans called for a stairway for access to the master bedroom. (For the guest bedroom's smaller and higher sleeping loft, we opted for a simple ladder.) Because of our

tight space limitations, the stairway is only 24 inches wide, just adequate for one-way traffic. It also rises at a 45-degree angle. That's about as steep a stair as you'd want to use in residential construction, according to Humanscale, a design guide published by MIT Press. Humanscale specifies a 45-degree stair with eight-inch risers and nine-inch treads, including the nosing (see "How to Build Stairways," above.) In our case we had a total rise of 76 inches and a total run of 74 inches. That allowed 10 risers at 7⅝ inches and nine treads at 9½ inches, including a 1¼-inch nosing. While it's not intended for continuous use, the stairway is more than adequate for access to a single room. It's also reasonably comfortable to climb and descend, keeping in mind that it is a short flight of stairs. For most general-purpose stairs, however, follow the guidelines outlined in the box above.

For privacy between the adjoining bedrooms, plans called for a sound-resistant wall. We decided on a wall that provides an STC (sound-transmission class) rating of 50. At 5¼ inches thick (see example 5), the wall takes up almost no more space than a normal partition. It uses metal channels applied horizontally on 24-inch centers to studs to minimize the direct connection of drywall on one side. Fiberglass batts fill stud cavities to further reduce sound transmission. In sound-wall construction, it's important to seal all joints carefully; we caulked around all edges—and all electrical outlets, as well.

When framing is complete, electrical work can be done. While electricians installed the wiring (required by code in my locality), we started the drywall, taking care not to enclose *both* sides of any one wall before it had been wired.

Low-ceiling lighting

Lighting our new rooms presented special problems. In closets the low (six ft. two in.) ceiling precluded, for obvious safety reasons, the bare bulbs normally used. We chose industrial-type steel-and-glass safety lamps, commonly called "vaportights," (see photo). Vaportight fixtures are available from electrical-supply houses, or the manufacturer listed at the end of this article can provide a list of local dealers.

The dressing room demanded adequate lighting, yet it, too, had only a six-ft.-two-in. ceiling. We used two recessed lights—Progress P 7's—equipped with Fresnel-lens trims that are flush with the finished ceiling. The

7¾-in.-deep recessed fixtures are housed inside the platform bed in the master bedroom above.

The hallway also has a relatively low (seven foot) ceiling, which prevented us from using track lights or hanging fixtures. This ceiling is framed with 2×6s that provide a cavity adequate for three Progress P 6 recessed lights. These shallow housings are only five inches deep. They're fitted with step baffle trims and reflector floods to light artwork on the hallway walls.

The master bedroom occupies the new second story we added above the dressing room and closets, and is reached via its own staircase (at lower right in the photo below). It's a generous room, measuring 12½ by 18 feet at its longest point (see floor plan). The built-ins contribute to the efficient use of space in the master bedroom:

● The peninsula position of the carpeted platform bed eats less floor space.

● The bed's storage headboard gets maximum use from normally wasted space.

● The wall of bookshelves holds a 750-volume library and cuts only 9¼ inches from the room.

Carpet bed

The platform bed, made for a queen-size mattress, takes up less space than a conventional bed. And since it's covered with the same carpet as the floor, it also looks smaller than it really is. Construction is simple:

Atop the bedroom's tongue-and-groove 2×6 floor, we built a 12-inch-high box of ¾-inch-thick plywood. (Inside the box: recessed lights for the first-floor dressing room.) The box is

Wall of shelves holds a sizable book collection with ease. A pair of clip-on spotlights on headboard illuminates artwork gives reading light, too.

Dressing room has walls of closets. Birch-veneer sliding doors hang on Stanley's extruded-aluminum tracks and adjustable nylon rollers.

Shaker-style pegboard mounted on one wall of dressing room is handy for hanging clothes. Behind wall: stair to master bedroom.

DETAIL OF FLOOR-TO-CEILING BOOKSHELVING

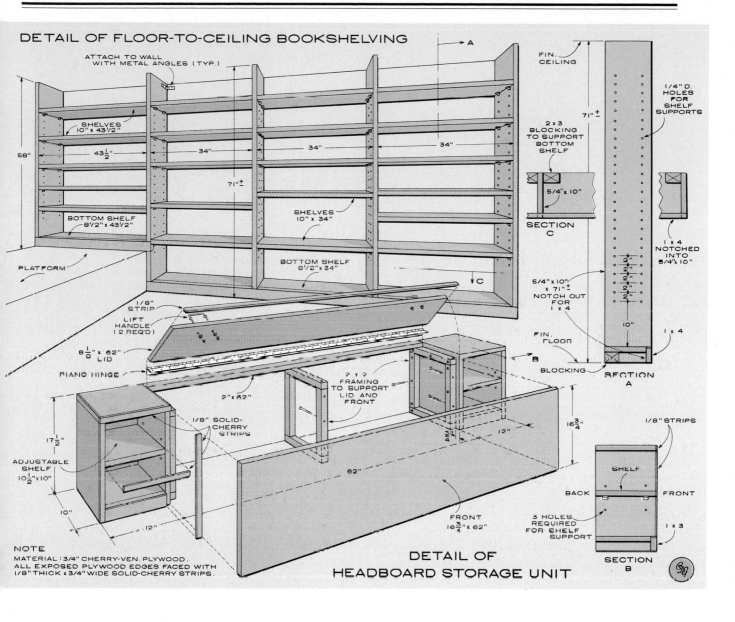

ATTACH TO WALL WITH METAL ANGLES (TYP.)

SHELVES 10" x 43½"

43½"

58"

71"±

BOTTOM SHELF 8½" x 43½"

SHELVES 10" x 34"

34"

34"

34"

BOTTOM SHELF 8½" x 34"

PLATFORM

1/8" STRIP

LIFT HANDLE (2 REQ'D)

8½" x 62" LID

PIANO HINGE

2" x 62"

1/8" SOLID-CHERRY STRIPS

2 x 2 FRAMING TO SUPPORT LID AND FRONT

17½"

ADJUSTABLE SHELF 10½" x 10"

10"

12"

62"

FRONT 16¾" x 62"

16¾"

12"

FIN. CEILING

1/4" D. HOLES FOR SHELF SUPPORTS

71"±

2 x 3 BLOCKING TO SUPPORT BOTTOM SHELF

5/4" x 10"

SECTION C

1 x 4 NOTCHED INTO 5/4" x 10"

5/4" x 10" x 71"± NOTCH OUT FOR 1 x 4

2"
2"
2"
2"
2"

10"

FIN. FLOOR

BLOCKING

SECTION A

1 x 4

1/8" STRIPS

SHELF

BACK

FRONT

1 x 3

3 HOLES REQUIRED FOR SHELF SUPPORT

SECTION B

NOTE
MATERIAL : 3/4" CHERRY-VEN. PLYWOOD. ALL EXPOSED PLYWOOD EDGES FACED WITH 1/8" THICK x 3/4" WIDE SOLID-CHERRY STRIPS.

DETAIL OF HEADBOARD STORAGE UNIT

reinforced by a 2 × 3 knee wall in the middle. The entire platform and bedroom floor are covered with well-padded carpeting.

The headboard has handy shelves for reading material, and a generous storage bin for bedding. This 62-inch-long-by-17-inch-deep-by-9½-inch-wide compartment is accessible through the hinged lid on top.

Using a table saw, I first cut out all pieces needed for the unit, as shown in the drawing above. All parts came easily out of a four-by-eight-foot sheet of ¾-inch-thick cherry-veneer plywood. Next I assembled the two mini bookcase units for each end of the headboard. They're glued and screwed together. I countersank all exposed screws and filled the holes with plugs cut from solid cherrywood. All exposed plywood edges are faced with ¾-inch-

wide-by-⅛-inch-thick strips, ripped from solid cherry.

The center bin's components—the headboard and top—are screwed from the inside to 2 × 2 bracing. The bracing is screwed to the end units and to the plywood platform. A piano hinge and brushed-aluminum-wire pulls complete the sleek, high-tech look of the unit. As finish for the cherry, I rubbed on tung oil.

What better location for a wall of books than against a sound-resistant wall? The bookshelves line the entire sound wall from floor to ceiling. For a unified look, I used ⁵/₄-by-10-inch lumber for both uprights and shelves. This stock is a full 1¼ inches thick, which allows the shelves in the left-hand bay to span its 43½-inch width unsupported.

All shelves except the bottom-most

are adjustable, resting on steel pins inserted into ¼-inch holes in the uprights. Four pins support each shelf. I bored the rows of ¼-inch holes on a drill press, clamping several uprights together and drilling them simultaneously. The center uprights have holes bored through them; I set the drill-press depth adjustment so that the bit stopped halfway through the end uprights.

The uprights are attached to the floor with 2 × 3 blocking (see drawing). Steel angles secure them to the wall. A coat of clear sealer helps preserve the wood's light tone—*Richard Stepler. Design by Jeff Milstein. Drawings by Carl De Groote.*

MATERIAL SOURCES
Recessed lights: **Progress Lighting**, Erie Ave. & G St., Philadelphia PA 19134. Sliding-door hardware: **Stanley**, New Britain CT 06050. Vaportight fixtures: **Rab Electric Mfg. Co.**, 321 Rider Ave., Bronx NY 10451.

weary old house gets a room with a view

The front of my 100-year old house was falling down. The two-tiered porch pillars that were built of staves, like barrels, were coming apart. An overly dark attic and a glassed-in upper sleeping porch under an overhang were virtual breezeways. The roof was in an advanced stage of disrepair. It had got to the point where the town had given me an ultimatum: Remove the violations or face the consequences.

I already had given some thought to remodeling and, prodded by the incentive supplied by the town, now launched into the project. Unfortunately, I quickly discovered that I lacked the skills of a professional, someone adept at designing and piecing together the details that would work with the existing structure. Help, as luck would have it, was not far away—I found the man for the job in my own town: John Hartwell Bennett, an architect and skilled building mechanic.

Our choices were pretty clear: We could build upward,

Two little-used dormers and a sleeping porch were eliminated on this house and replaced with a handsome shed dormer-studio.

expanding and finishing the attic to make a bright new room that conserved energy, or we could build out, enlarging the front rooms by eight feet (the depth of the porches). The latter, however, would mean expensive reconstruction, a new heating source, bigger fuel bills, and greater taxes. We could, of course, just restore what I had, but I would gain little and would have to live with the old discomforts and too-high fuel bills.

We raised the roof. Expanding the attic by adding an 18-foot-long shed dormer gave me a dramatic new studio room at the top of the house that measures 17 by 27 feet. Andersen casement windows in the dormer offer a spectacular view of the waterfront at the end of the street and vent the house effectively in summer (a big chimney effect) yet keep it snug in winter.

The old attic stairs had come up from a bedroom closet and allowed only a crouching entrance under the eaves. We gave this space back to the closet and brought new stairs, centrally located, through the ample-size, old-house bathroom. Entrance is now from the second-floor hall, and you come into the studio (standing erect) at the north end of the room. The new stair location gives the whole house better air circulation in both summer and winter.

By removing the glassed-in sleeping porch, we got rid of a white elephant—its sole function had become dark-ening all the front rooms. The old diamond panes on the porch had charm, but the frames were not reparable. The glazing caused my family to bake in summer and shiver from winter drafts.

After taking down the porch and pillars, we further improved the view by adding two windows on the facade upstairs. We also replaced the existing windows at the front with Andersen Perma-Shield Narroline double-hung units. Partly because they're carefully caulked, they closed dozens of heat leaks. All the new windows (both casements and double-hung) have Andersen's Perma-Clad vinyl cladding outside, relieving me of having to repaint the window trim in the years ahead. I bought the maker's storm-screen combinations, which give me triple glazing when necessary. It feels comfortable inside the house now.

The general renovation

We replaced the wood front door and aluminum storm door with a modern insulated steel door. The Pease Ever-Strait door we chose, with a 7.22 R-value and factory weatherstripping, effectively keeps all heat and cold away from the area of the entryway, which is located on the severe-weather side of the house. A thermometer tells me it's about six times more effective than the old double doors. The embossed door, with a Schlage drive-in latch and bolt

DETAIL OF ROOF AND DORMER FRAMING

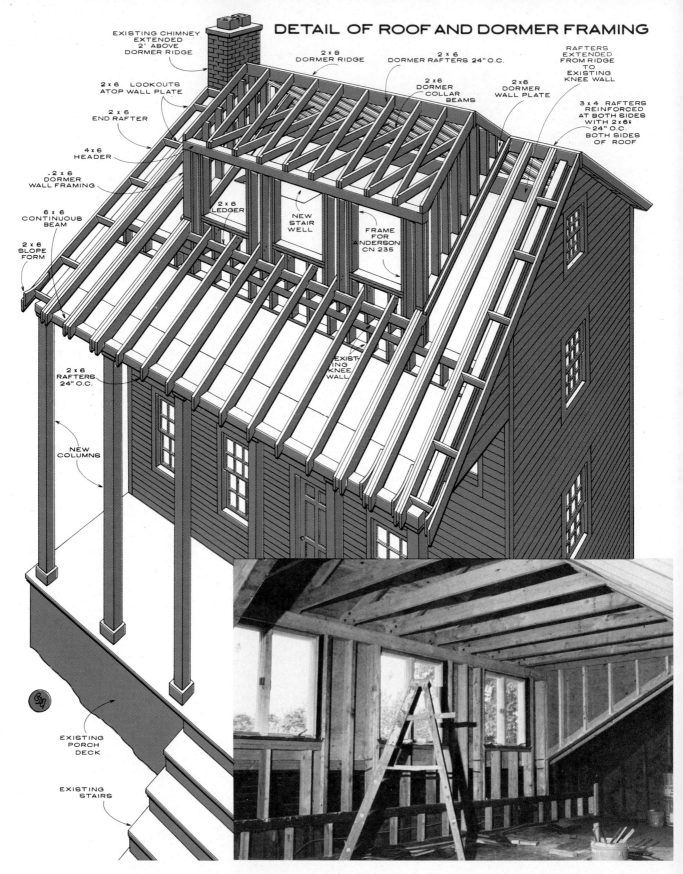

EXISTING CHIMNEY EXTENDED 2' ABOVE DORMER RIDGE

2 x 6 LOOKOUTS ATOP WALL PLATE

2 x 6 END RAFTER

4 x 6 HEADER

2 x 6 DORMER WALL FRAMING

6 x 6 CONTINUOUS BEAM

2 x 6 SLOPE FORM

2 x 6 RAFTERS 24" O.C.

NEW COLUMNS

EXISTING PORCH DECK

EXISTING STAIRS

2 x 8 DORMER RIDGE

2 x 6 DORMER RAFTERS 24" O.C.

2 x 6 DORMER COLLAR BEAMS

2 x 6 DORMER WALL PLATE

RAFTERS EXTENDED FROM RIDGE TO EXISTING KNEE WALL

3 x 4 RAFTERS REINFORCED AT BOTH SIDES WITH 2 x 6's 24" O.C. BOTH SIDES OF ROOF

2 x 6 LEDGER

NEW STAIR WELL

FRAME FOR ANDERSON CN 235

EXISTING KNEE WALL

The new upper room was part of a general renovation of the house. The house's roof was raised by sandwiching each affected 3 × 4 rear rafter with a pair of 2 × 6 rafters. That elevated the roof ridge four feet to create a cantilevered framework over the 18-foot middle section, which provides sufficient clearance overhead. The pitch of the rear of the new shed dormer matches that of the existing roof, and the front slope is parallel to the front roof. There is a series of 2 × 6 collar beams, which are through-bolted to the existing and new rafters to add strength. The taller front wall of the dormer, which resulted from the extension of the rafters, made space for larger casements. The height of the wall added space to the attic area, too. When it was built, the entire house had been framed with full-dimension long-grain fir. The original studs and rafters are 24 inches on center, and this spacing was maintained in the new construction. The new windows fit so that there are no heat leaks or tight pinches; they can be fitted with storm glazing.

28

The chimney had to be extended to accommodate the raised ridge. Johns-Manville shingles cover old roof contours. Bright and airy studio was formed by the renovation of the attic. Andersen casement windows seal room from weather.

lock and simple burnished-metal colonial-style plate, provides a handsome focus for the new facade.

All this work required re-siding the front, and I was lucky to find enough cedar drop siding to match the house.

I had previously tried to insulate the exterior walls with foam, but when I stripped the inside of the exterior walls, I found the foam had shrunk away from the studs and in some areas was nonexistent. These areas were packed with fiberglass insulation.

In the bath we added a linen cupboard under the new stair just inside the door and installed a five-foot Owens-Corning Fiberglas bath-shower unit. Because I no longer needed the long hallway leading to the sleeping porch, we turned the space it occupied into a walk-in closet for one of the front bedrooms.

For the new roof we selected Johns-Manville Woodlands Seal-O-Matic fiberglass shingles in Seadrift Grey to go with the stained cedar shingles on the dormer. This roofing casts an edge shadow that makes it look like wood shingles and handsomely masks irregularities in an old roof. Johns-Manville's Seal-O-Matic shingle stripe works with the sun's

heat to bond shingles together, and the new roof lies much tighter than did my previous asphalt roof. My house stands on the side of a hill just 300 feet from the water and takes punishment in winter storms. It's good to know that the new roof is warranted for 25 years and has a Class A fire-resistance rating (the highest) from Underwriters' Laboratory. The shingles also have a UL wind-resistance label, which means they should withstand the beating they take, even over an extended period.

When the building was done, I repainted the entire house with Olympic Stain paint (two coats), using Navajo red and Interlux semi-gloss white trim for the pillars and soffits. So far, the paint has weathered beautifully and shown no faults. Bennett, the architect, says it should be good for more than six years—*By David D. Vigren.*

SUPPLIERS OF MATERIALS

Andersen Corp., Bayport MN 55003; **Manville Corp.**, P.O. Box 5108, Denver CO 80217; **Olympic Stain** (Clorox, Inc.), 2233 112th Ave. N.E., Bellevue WA 98004; **Owens-Corning Fiberglas Corp.**, NMX Meeks, Fiberglas Tower, Toledo OH 43659; **Please Co.**, 900 Forest Ave., Hamilton OH 45023; **Schlage Lock Co.**, P.O. Drawer 3324, San Francisco CA 94119.

skinny skylights speed sun-room conversion

It was charming; it was unique; it was useless. The very details that made the fieldstone porch picturesque also made it unsuitable for summer relaxation. On three sides, elegant columned arches framed the view—and let in the bugs. And the steep roof, with its exposed-beam ceiling, created a dark and gloomy interior.

The owner's solution? Enclose the porch with glass to preserve the view, and insert skylights in the roof to bring in light. The result? A cozy, inviting sun room.

Such a conversion need not be a major construction job. By choosing materials that are relatively easy to install, a weekend carpenter can create a similar sunspace from a porch, breezeway, even a garage.

Here, the homeowner removed the arched trim, framed the openings with 2×4s, then inserted stock, double-glazed Caradco picture windows and doors between the columns.

To open up the roof without destroying the exposed beams, he used Dayliter Long-Lites skylights, made by the APC Corp. (Hawthorne, N.J.), to fit between rafters. No structural members needed to be cut, nor did the roof openings have to be framed to accept the 69½-inch skylights (see drawing). The skylights come in three other lengths and fit beams spaced either 16 or 24 inches on center—*By Susan Renner-Smith.*

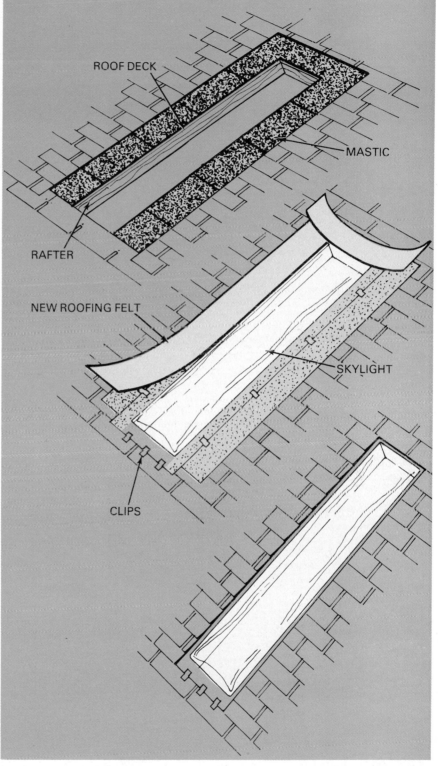

Diagram labels: ROOF DECK, MASTIC, RAFTER, NEW ROOFING FELT, SKYLIGHT, CLIPS

Rustic, open fieldstone porch (below) was dark and uninviting. Slim skylights slotted into the roof of the now glassed-in porch (main photo, left) help transform it into an airy, year-round sun room. Double-glazed, bronze-tone skylights fit between roof rafters, allowing the 50-year-old exposed beams in the ceiling (top) to remain intact. Stock double-glazed windows and doors fill in the wall openings. Homeowner stripped roofing down to the decking (above) before installing skylight, but old roofing paper can be left on (see illustration at right).

To install skinny skylights, first measure the opening from inside and drive nails through to the outside at each corner. Remove the shingles from around the marked area, but leave the bottom course intact as shown (top). To avoid gumming up the saw, strip away roofing paper inside the cutout area. To ensure straight cuts, snap chalk lines between nails. Now cut through the roof deck with a circular or saber saw. Next, apply a bed of mastic over the existing roofing paper bordering the cutout. Set the skylight in place, snap on the special clips, then nail them to the roof. To prevent leaks, lay strips of roofing felt in a bed of mastic, arranging the strips to overlap the top and sides of skylight flange (see middle sketch). Replace the shingles, lapping them over the skylight flange then trimming them to fit against the dome. Note that bottom edge of skylight is left uncovered to promote drainage.

four add-on sunspaces

1   **Sunny breezeway** forms a stylish connection between house and garage. All Pella glazing units have natural wood frames on the inside, ready for stain or paint. Vertical glazing units can be double or triple glazed, with fixed exterior glass and removable interior panels. Joint details B and C, labeled here, are constructed like those of the same letters in the dormer diagram (next page).

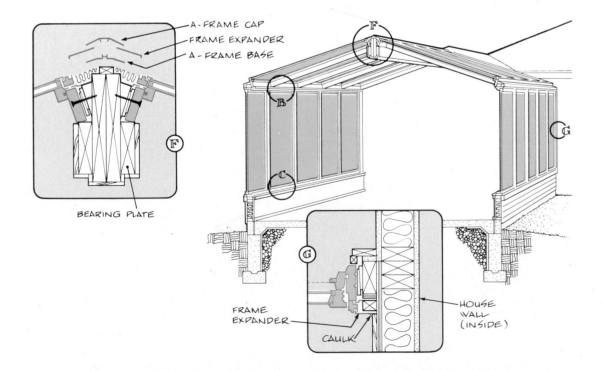

A-FRAME CAP
FRAME EXPANDER
A-FRAME BASE

BEARING PLATE

FRAME EXPANDER

CAULK

HOUSE WALL (INSIDE)

It's called the Sloped Glazing System, and it's new from Pella: an integrated line of overhead, 7/8-inch tempered, insulated-glass units that you can combine in various ways and numbers with standard vertical windows and doors. Placement, size, and design of each sunspace is determined by your needs.

All glazing is framed in wood and clad on the outside with aluminum in a white or brown enamel finish. Aluminum flashing strips, in various configurations and finished to match the exterior of the glazing units, attach to the wood structure you build to give the whole sunspace a custom look and low-maintenance exterior. Anyone who'd tackle a standard room addition can easily build a sunspace with this system.

The four add-ons shown here—dormer, breezeway, air-lock entry, and daylight basement—are all from Pella Windows and Doors, 100 Main St., Pella, Iowa 50219—*By Al Lees and V. Elaine Smay. Drawings by Eugene Thompson.*

2

Dormer sun room can add warmth, light, ventilation, and headroom to an attic space. Pella's sloped and vertical glazing units fit together (with caulk and mullion covers) to form the dormer in the size and shape you want. Vertical glazing units can be fixed or operable. Pella also makes triangular (and trapezoidal) glazing units for the dormer sides. Or you can build and finish opaque sides to match the house.

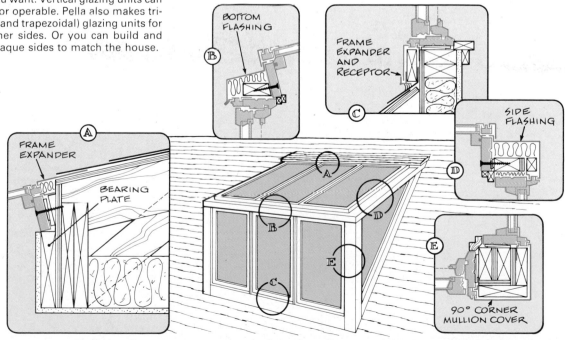

3

Basic Pella sun room, shown in exploded diagram, is similar to air-lock entry and illustrates typical framing and construction methods of all such structures. Pella offers detailed plans for this sun room only. Where techniques vary for other structures, a Pella distributor can give guidance. Other Pella instructions tell how to assemble multiple-glazing units.

4

Sun-room walk-out can transform a dreary basement with both light and solar warmth. To preserve privacy and to control solar gain, Pella offers vertical glazing units with narrow-slat blinds between the panes and similar blinds that can be attached under the glass of the sloped glazing units. (Joint detail D here is illustrated in the dormer diagram, page 33.)

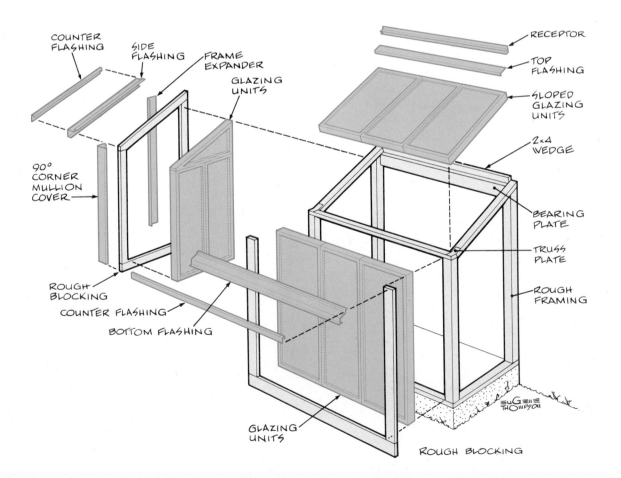

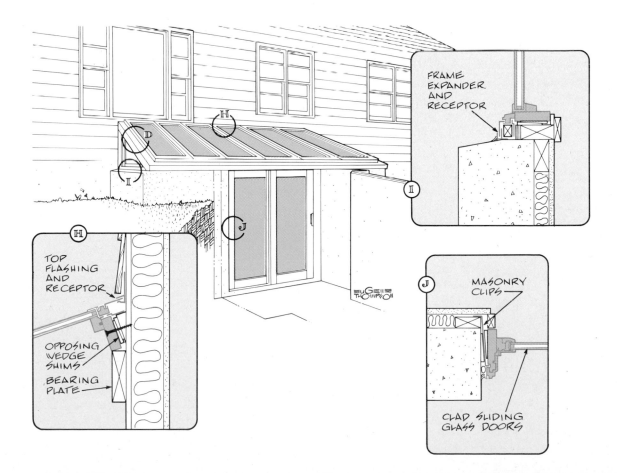

FRAME EXPANDER AND RECEPTOR

TOP FLASHING AND RECEPTOR

OPPOSING WEDGE SHIMS

BEARING PLATE

MASONRY CLIPS

CLAD SLIDING GLASS DOORS

EUGENE THOMPSON

cutting a roof truss

You expect to see waves at the seashore, not on a living-room ceiling. But incredibly, they were there. I was standing in a house in New Jersey, and the ceiling above my head dipped up and down like a roller coaster. It was not a new decorating effect, but a small disaster.

A contractor had cut several of the ceiling joists to make a stair opening to the attic. But those weren't merely ceiling joists that he'd cut; they were the bottom chords of roof trusses. When the chords were cut, the ends pulled apart and sagged.

The strength and balance of a truss are dependent on each structural member. Most of us know not to violate the framing of a truss. Yet almost all tract-built homes are now constructed with trussed roofs, and many of these houses—like the one I just described—are built on slab-on-grade foundations. So people often turn to their attics to find extra storage or living space. Installing a skylight window in a trussed roof involves the same problem of altering trusses (see drawings, opposite page).

Does truss construction mean that the attic is unusable, entirely off limits? The answer is no—not if the truss is redesigned in the right way and carefully reconstructed. The secret to cutting a truss successfully is to build a box around the cutout piece. The box will bridge around the gap, rejoining the cut member. But the box must be designed so it reacts to roof forces in the same way as the missing truss piece. The box must transfer the forces to keep the truss in balance.

Basically the top chords of trusses are in compression from roof loads (roof weight, snow, and wind), and they push out on the bottom chord, putting it in tension (see drawing). Most trusses in new homes are complex in design, and have short internal members. Plywood or metal gussets secure the joints between truss members.

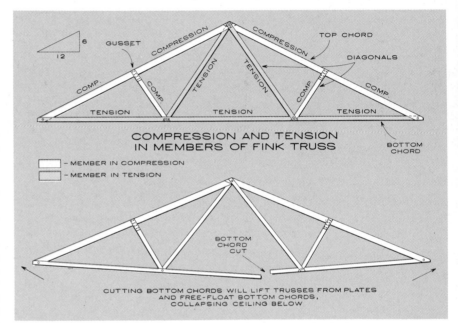

COMPRESSION AND TENSION IN MEMBERS OF FINK TRUSS

☐ – MEMBER IN COMPRESSION
▢ – MEMBER IN TENSION

CUTTING BOTTOM CHORDS WILL LIFT TRUSSES FROM PLATES AND FREE-FLOAT BOTTOM CHORDS, COLLAPSING CEILING BELOW

Forces on trusses from the roof compress top chords, which push out on the bottom chord, holding it in tension (top drawing). If bottom chord is cut, it will sag or drop, depending on interior partitioning and extension of the truss over outside walls. Most trusses today are 2 × 4s in complex designs, such as Fink trusses shown here. Short internal members of these trusses are in compression or tension themselves, so should not be cut either.

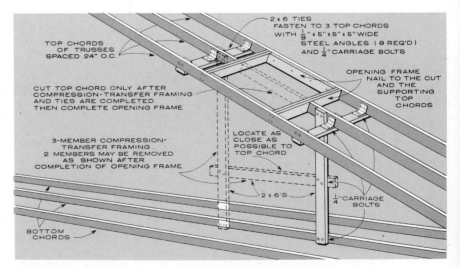

Skylight installation often requires cutting a top chord. Short vertical member can be used in a knee wall. Additional braces increase strength.

There is an appropriate box design for cutting either a top chord, bottom chord, or both (see drawings). Before any truss is cut, the truss members and gussets should be inspected. If they are sound, the truss must be thoroughly braced—both internally as well as to several adjacent trusses on both sides of the cutout.

After bracing and cutting the truss, the box can be built. Particular care must be taken at joints on a bottom chord, because that chord (in tension) will be pulling away from the box. Lumber and truss members are double-bolted, not just nailed, at all box joints. The braces can be removed only after the box is completed.

Complex-shaped lightweight trusses divide attic space awkwardly, and they can bear only limited amounts of weight. If you have some usable area between truss members, it doesn't mean that the 2×4s or 2×6s of the bottom chord will permit heavy storage or use as a living area. How much weight a bottom chord can bear depends on the dimensions of the lumber, spacing of trusses, and many other factors. Before starting a truss project, check with an architect or engineer to determine the limits of attic use, and work from professionally approved, detailed drawings—*By Paul Bolon. Concepts and sketches by Carl De Groote.*

Bottom chords of several trusses can be cut to install a staircase (photo above). Vertical and horizontal box members (drawing, left) were used to continue tension across the bottom chord of Fink trusses. Only Douglas fir or other dense, select structural lumber should be used as framing for any of the box configurations.

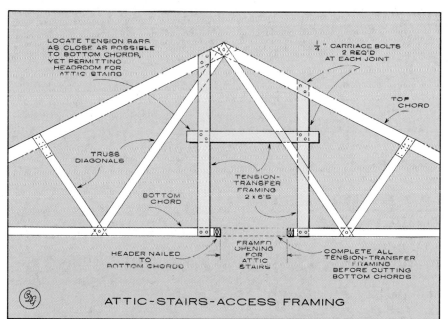

LOCATE TENSION BARS AS CLOSE AS POSSIBLE TO BOTTOM CHORDS, YET PERMITTING HEADROOM FOR ATTIC STAIRS

¼" CARRIAGE BOLTS 2 REQ'D AT EACH JOINT

TOP CHORD

TRUSS DIAGONALS

TENSION-TRANSFER FRAMING 2×6'S

BOTTOM CHORD

HEADER NAILED TO BOTTOM CHORDS

FRAMED OPENING FOR ATTIC STAIRS

COMPLETE ALL TENSION-TRANSFER FRAMING BEFORE CUTTING BOTTOM CHORDS

ATTIC-STAIRS-ACCESS FRAMING

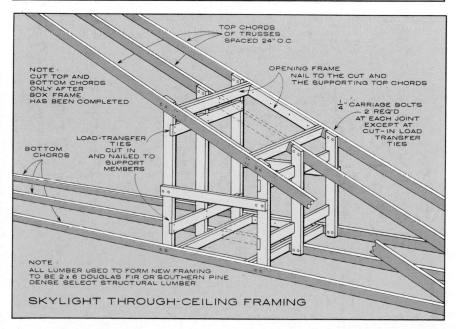

TOP CHORDS OF TRUSSES SPACED 24" O.C.

NOTE: CUT TOP AND BOTTOM CHORDS ONLY AFTER BOX FRAME HAS BEEN COMPLETED

OPENING FRAME NAIL TO THE CUT AND THE SUPPORTING TOP CHORDS

¼" CARRIAGE BOLTS 2 REQ'D AT EACH JOINT EXCEPT AT CUT-IN LOAD TRANSFER TIES

LOAD-TRANSFER TIES CUT IN AND NAILED TO SUPPORT MEMBERS

BOTTOM CHORDS

NOTE: ALL LUMBER USED TO FORM NEW FRAMING TO BE 2×6 DOUGLAS FIR OR SOUTHERN PINE DENSE SELECT STRUCTURAL LUMBER

SKYLIGHT THROUGH-CEILING FRAMING

Cutting both top and bottom chords requires building the most complicated type of box (drawing at left). Such a box would serve when adding a through-the-attic skylight in a shallow-sloped roof. In new construction, it would be simpler just to double the adjacent trusses. Lining the box walls with plywood will strengthen it.

solar water heaters

I n the early days of the automobile, you didn't just have to choose between makes and models. You had to start by choosing a steam car, an electric car, or one with an internal-combustion engine. Shopping for a solar water heater is something like that today. First you have to choose between a passive (breadbox or thermosiphon) and an active (direct or indirect) system. About the time you learn what a drain-down system is, someone mentions a drain-back—both of which use water in the collectors.

Others use air—or antifreeze. If antifreeze is what you want, you'll have to choose among a half-dozen different solutions. Furthermore, solar water heaters use different types of collectors—made of different materials.

If you are considering buying a solar water heater, learn all you can about what's available. This article can only outline some choices and a few pros and cons. (Consult sources at the end for further details.) There are also more-fundamental questions:
● Would a solar water heater be a good investment for you?
● Can you get a quality system that will perform well—and last?
● How can you get the best performance for your dollar?

The answer to the first question must be conjured from a caldron of variables. I'll get back to it later.

The answer to the others: Your chances of getting a quality system are pretty good, it seems. And now there are standardized ratings that let you compare the performance of all kinds of solar water heaters.

Solar water heaters have been around, in quantity, for a good many years, and numerous researchers (mostly in pre-1982, DOE-sponsored projects) have compiled mountains of data about them. The general conclusions: Most systems, though not all, work pretty well—some, very well.

Today's equipment is likely to be even better. The manufacturers that have survived have learned from those tests and from experience. "From my viewpoint, and from what I hear from the testing laboratories," says Arlen Reimnitz, executive vice-president of the Solar Rating and Certification Corp. (SRCC), "a lot of manufacturers are doing their own tests to ensure an excellent product."

The SRCC is an independent organization formed by the Solar Energy Industry Assn. and the Interstate Solar Coordination Council (a confederation of state solar-energy offices). It has been certifying, testing, rating, and labeling solar collectors since 1980, and now lists 450.

In December 1982 SRCC started a similar program for solar water heaters, which should make choosing a quality system easier. To be certified, a system must meet standards established by the Interstate Solar Coordination Council. "When you buy a solar water heater with our label," says Reimnitz, "you can be sure it has met minimum standards for durability, reliability, and safety."

It also has been put through performance tests and labeled with efficiency ratings (see the sample label and explanation). The ratings are based on test methods developed by the American Society of Heating, Refrigerating, and Air-Conditioning Engineers. Tests are done in independent laboratories. Only 12 systems

SOLAR RATING & CERTIFICATON CORPORATION	SOLAR WATER HEATING SYSTEM RATING			
	RATING CATEGORY	TERM	RATING	UNIT
	SOLAR ENERGY DELIVERED	Q_{NET}	24,500	**BTU/DAY**
	RESERVE ENERGY CAPACITY	Q_{RES}	12,100	BTU
	HEAT LOSS COEFFICIENT	L	26.85	BTU/HR°F
	AUXILIARY ENERGY CAPACITY	Q_{CAP}	NA	BTU
	AUXILIARY ENERGY CONSUMPTION	Q_{AUX}	NA	BTU/DAY
	PARASITIC ENERGY CONSUMPTION	Q_{PAR}	NA	BTU/DAY
	STANDARD TEST LOAD	Q_{DL}	40,199	BTU/DAY

Test System Type: __Integral Collector Storage__
Test System Classification: __Solar Preheat__

Manufacturer: _____
Address: _____
Model No.: _____ Trade Name: _____
No. of Collectors: __Two Units__ Gross Collector Area: __20 Ft.^{2}/Unit__
Storage Tank Capacity: __39 Gallons__ Transfer Fluid: __Water__
SRCC System Certification License Number: _____

SOLAR WATER HEATING SYSTEM STANDARD

200-82

The SRCC label gives manufacturer, model, type, and classification (see text) of the solar water heater. Efficiency ratings are based on tests performed in a test chamber under standard conditions that approximate a mild (71.6 degrees F), partly sunny day (1,500 Btu). Researchers withdraw water from the system three times a day (usually for four days) and calculate the amount of solar energy collected. From that they arrive at a net Btu/day collected—the Q_{NET} rating. That is the most important rating to consider when comparing solar water heaters.

The reserve-energy capacity (Q_{RES} indicates how much solar heat is left in the system at the end of the last Q_{NET}-test sequence. These ratings apply to all systems. Heat-loss coefficient applies only to integral collector-storage and thermosiphon systems. It indicates the rate of heat loss when no heat is being added. Auxiliary energy capacity and consumption (Q_{CAP}, Q_{AUX}) apply only to solar-plus-supplemental systems (see text) and measure performance on the auxiliary heating device. Parasitic energy consumption (Q_{PAR}) measures the electricity used by forced-circulation systems. The standard test load is constant: 40,199 Btu/day.

have completed the tests (see table at end of article). But more are in the labs, and the first public listing is due in July. Any packaged solar water heater (one in which all important components are furnished by the manufacturer) is eligible for testing.

The SRCC groups solar water heaters by classification and by type. The classifications: solar preheat—meaning the system preheats the water before it goes to a conventional water heater, which is not part of the system; solar only—water from the solar heater is piped directly to household taps; and solar plus supplemental—the packaged system includes both a solar heater and an auxiliary heat source. The types: integral collector-storage, thermosiphon, and forced-circulation systems. Any classification can come in any type.

Sorting out the lingo

So what about direct and indirect systems? What are drain-downs and drain-backs? And how about closed-loop and antifreeze solar water heaters? The diagrams accompanying this article explain those terms.

In the SRCC types, all solar water heaters except integral collector-storage (often called batch or breadbox) heaters and thermosiphon systems fall into the forced-circulation category. That includes drain-down, drain-back, and antifreeze systems. It also includes air-type systems. These use air in the collector, a fan to circulate the air, and an air-to-water heat exchanger. We don't show a diagram, but the flow paths are similar to those of antifreeze systems. Forced-circulation systems are, by definition, active systems: They use pumps or fans. Integral collector-storage heaters and thermosiphon systems are passive.

As you can surmise from the diagrams, the design of a solar water heater is largely influenced by the fluid you circulate through the collectors. The ideal fluid would remain stable over a wide temperature range, have a high specific-heat index (that determines its efficiency) and a low viscosity (so that it doesn't take a lot of energy to pump it), and be nontoxic and noncorrosive. No fluid meets all the requirements. Water has the highest specific heat, for example, and air the lowest, and the antifreeze solutions range (widely) in between.

One antifreeze, ethylene glycol, is stable at low temperatures (as long as no one dilutes the concentration) but can't stand too much heat. "When you've got gobs of solar energy and not much hot water being used—such as when you take a summer vacation—your system is going to reach very high temperatures," explains Bruce Baccei, formerly of the Solar Energy Research Institute in Golden, Colo. "Collectors are designed to withstand that—they have to be. But the ethylene glycol will break down and form acids." Baccei knows from experience. It happened in his own solar water heater. "You have to check the acidity," he advises. "If it's bad, you have to exchange the antifreeze." If you

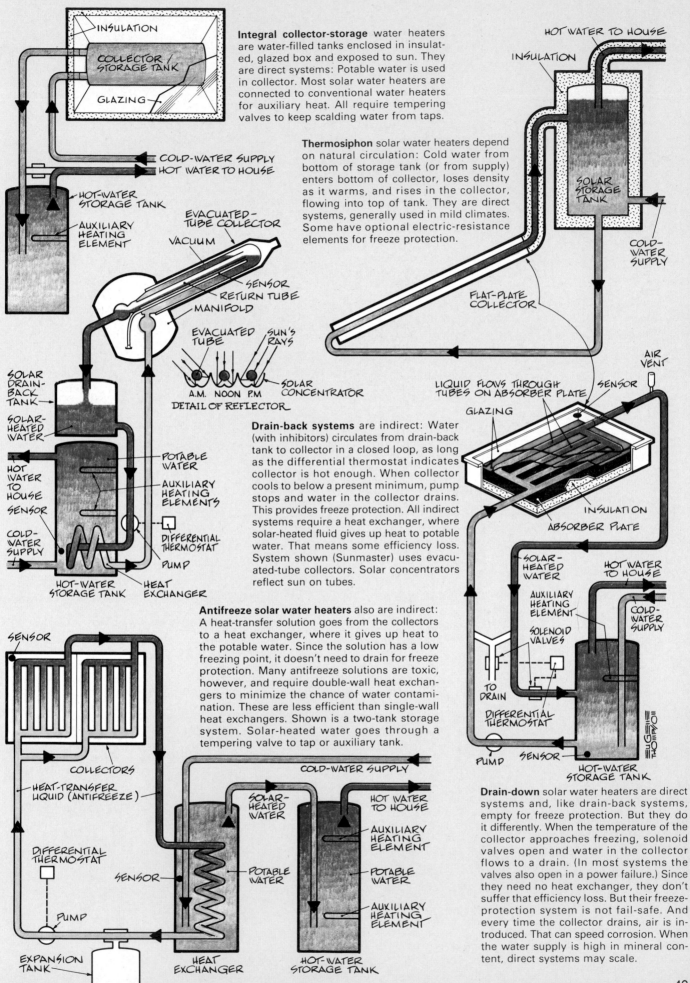

Integral collector-storage water heaters are water-filled tanks enclosed in insulated, glazed box and exposed to sun. They are direct systems: Potable water is used in collector. Most solar water heaters are connected to conventional water heaters for auxiliary heat. All require tempering valves to keep scalding water from taps.

INSULATION
COLLECTOR / STORAGE TANK
GLAZING
COLD-WATER SUPPLY
HOT WATER TO HOUSE
HOT-WATER STORAGE TANK
AUXILIARY HEATING ELEMENT

Thermosiphon solar water heaters depend on natural circulation: Cold water from bottom of storage tank (or from supply) enters bottom of collector, loses density as it warms, and rises in the collector, flowing into top of tank. They are direct systems, generally used in mild climates. Some have optional electric-resistance elements for freeze protection.

HOT WATER TO HOUSE
INSULATION
SOLAR STORAGE TANK
COLD-WATER SUPPLY
FLAT-PLATE COLLECTOR

EVACUATED-TUBE COLLECTOR
VACUUM
SENSOR
RETURN TUBE
MANIFOLD
EVACUATED TUBE
SUN'S RAYS
A.M. NOON P.M.
SOLAR CONCENTRATOR
DETAIL OF REFLECTOR

SOLAR DRAIN-BACK TANK
SOLAR-HEATED WATER
HOT WATER TO HOUSE
SENSOR
COLD-WATER SUPPLY
POTABLE WATER
AUXILIARY HEATING ELEMENTS
DIFFERENTIAL THERMOSTAT
PUMP
HOT-WATER STORAGE TANK
HEAT EXCHANGER

Drain-back systems are indirect: Water (with inhibitors) circulates from drain-back tank to collector in a closed loop, as long as the differential thermostat indicates collector is hot enough. When collector cools to below a present minimum, pump stops and water in the collector drains. This provides freeze protection. All indirect systems require a heat exchanger, where solar-heated fluid gives up heat to potable water. That means some efficiency loss. System shown (Sunmaster) uses evacuated-tube collectors. Solar concentrators reflect sun on tubes.

LIQUID FLOWS THROUGH TUBES ON ABSORBER PLATE
SENSOR
AIR VENT
GLAZING
INSULATION
ABSORBER PLATE

SOLAR-HEATED WATER
HOT WATER TO HOUSE
AUXILIARY HEATING ELEMENT
COLD-WATER SUPPLY
SOLENOID VALVES
TO DRAIN
DIFFERENTIAL THERMOSTAT
PUMP
SENSOR
HOT-WATER STORAGE TANK

Antifreeze solar water heaters also are indirect: A heat-transfer solution goes from the collectors to a heat exchanger, where it gives up heat to the potable water. Since the solution has a low freezing point, it doesn't need to drain for freeze protection. Many antifreeze solutions are toxic, however, and require double-wall heat exchangers to minimize the chance of water contamination. These are less efficient than single-wall heat exchangers. Shown is a two-tank storage system. Solar-heated water goes through a tempering valve to tap or auxiliary tank.

SENSOR
COLLECTORS
HEAT-TRANSFER LIQUID (ANTIFREEZE)
DIFFERENTIAL THERMOSTAT
PUMP
EXPANSION TANK
HEAT EXCHANGER
SENSOR
POTABLE WATER
SOLAR-HEATED WATER
COLD-WATER SUPPLY
HOT WATER TO HOUSE
AUXILIARY HEATING ELEMENT
POTABLE WATER
AUXILIARY HEATING ELEMENT
HOT-WATER STORAGE TANK

Drain-down solar water heaters are direct systems and, like drain-back systems, empty for freeze protection. But they do it differently. When the temperature of the collector approaches freezing, solenoid valves open and water in the collector flows to a drain. (In most systems the valves also open in a power failure.) Since they need no heat exchanger, they don't suffer that efficiency loss. But their freeze-protection system is not fail-safe. And every time the collector drains, air is introduced. That can speed corrosion. When the water supply is high in mineral content, direct systems may scale.

don't, your collector may corrode.

Propylene glycol, another commonly used antifreeze, also forms organic acids if it gets too hot. It has one advantage over ethylene, however: It is generally considered nontoxic. Other companies use silicone, glycerine, mineral oils, or synthetic hydrocarbons. Each has some desirable characteristics, some undesirable.

The beauty of the SRCC's solar-water-heater tests is that they consider the whole system. Thus you have a valid performance comparison between systems that use different heat-transfer fluids. They also let you compare a system that uses a standard flat-plate collector with one that uses an evacuated-tube collector or a solar concentrator (see diagrams). But the performance ratings, while excellent for comparing systems, can't tell you exactly how a solar water heater will perform in your house. "The performance you get will depend on your weather conditions and geographic location," cautions Reimnitz.

Is a solar water heater a good buy for you? To answer, you must study prices, tax credits, future fuel costs, and paybacks. Prices for packaged solar water heaters start at perhaps $400 for an integral collector-storage system you buy as a kit to assemble and install yourself. On the other end of the scale are forced-circulation systems you have a contractor install. Sears, which sells solar water heaters made by Ametek, quotes prices of $2,000 to $5,000 for contractor-installed, forced-circulation systems.

As you know, Uncle Sam will give you a 40 percent income-tax credit up to $4,000. (Unless extended, this will end December 31, 1985.) Many states also offer substantial tax benefits.

How much could you save with a solar water heater? A standard rule of thumb is to allow 15 to 20 gallons of hot water per person per day. How much hot water a solar heater would provide depends on your climate and how big a system you buy. Lennox gives these examples for its Solarmate water heaters: A family in Los Angeles using 60 gallons of hot water a day would get 60 to 70 percent of its hot water with a one-collector system ($2,100—$2,700 installed, before tax credits) or 80 to 90 percent with a two-collector system ($2,700-$3,500 installed, before credits). In Massachusetts, however, the one-collector system would provide 40 to 50 percent of that family's hot water; the two-collector system, 60 to 70 percent, according to Lennox.

How long would it take for a solar water heater to pay back its original cost in energy savings? The now-demised Northeast Solar Energy Center in Boston figured these paybacks (assuming a family of four, a solar heater that provides 50 percent of the hot water, and an electric heater providing the rest): With electricity at 6.5 cents per kWh and increasing by 10 percent each year, the family would save $1,565 within five years, $4,081 within 10, and $8,136 in 15 years. These calculations do not consider interest paid or lost. And, of course, they will be overly optimistic if the cost of conventional energy increases more slowly than predicted.

Consider, too, that a solar water heater requires space for the collector and storage tank and will need routine maintenance. You may want to investigate alternative ways to reduce hot-water costs: Turn down the thermostat on your water heater, insulate the tank, and install water-saving devices in your house. Or consider a heat-pump water heater or the tankless kind. Economically, you may do better with another approach, even if, philosophically, you prefer a hot shower furnished by the sun—*By V. Elaine Smay. Drawings by Eugene Thompson.*

Solar water heaters: certified and rated

Company	Model	Type	Class	Q_{NET} (Btu)
Amcor Group Ltd. 7946 Alabama Ave. Canoga Park CA 91304	Solon 120 (1 unit)	Thermosiphon	Solar pre-heat	20,100
Cornell Energy, Inc. 245 S. Pulmer Ave. Tucson AZ 85719	360-32 (2 units)	Integral collector-storage	Solar pre-heat	19,900
Entech Marketing, Inc. Box 549 Tualatin OR 97062	SF 240-001 (2 units)	Integral collector storage	Solar pre-heat	26,400
Gulf Thermal Corp. 1645 12th St. Sarasota FL 33577	PT-40 (2 units)	Integral collector-storage	Solar pre-heat	24,600
Raypak, Inc. 31111 Agoura Rd. Westlake Village CA 91361	DHWS-66PMC SW-82-AD-1 (2 units)	Forced cir. (drain-down)	Solar pre-heat	36,700
	DHWS-84 PMC SW-120-AD-1 (2 units)	Forced cir. (drain-down)	Solar pre-heat	39,300
Servamatic Solar Systems 1641 Challenge Dr. Concord CA 94520	600 RD (2 units)	Integral collector-storage	Solar pre-heat	20,041
Solar Edwards, Inc. 7636 Miramar Rd. Suite 400 San Diego CA 92126	L305 (2 or 3 units*)	Thermosiphon	Solar pre-heat	25,000
	L440 (3, 4, or 5 units*)	Thermosiphon	Solar pre-heat	25,000
	L600 (4, 5, or 6 units*)	Thermosiphon	Solar pre-heat	25,000
Solahart California 3560 Dunhill St. San Diego CA 92121	80GE (3 units)	Thermosiphon	Solar plus supp.	35,400
Sunwizard, Inc. 1424 W. 259th St. Harbor City CA 90710	120 (1 unit)	Integral collector-storage	Solar pre-heat	11,500

*Only the system with the least number of collectors was performance-tested to determine Q_{NET} ratings. Larger systems meet certification standards but were not put through performance tests (which are very costly).

Preliminary listing of certified solar water heaters was obtained from a state energy office and includes only systems tested and approved at our publication date. You can get a more up-to-date list from your state energy office. Only the models with the stated number of units (collectors or collector-storage units) are certified and performance rated. A solar water heater's absence from the list doesn't mean it wouldn't meet certification standards. Most haven't been submitted for approval.

FOR FURTHER INFORMATION

The Solar Rating and Certification Corp. (1001 Connecticut Ave., N.W., Suite 800, Washington DC 20036-5584) offers single copies of the directory that lists certified solar water heaters. Standards and test methods are available.

Design and Installation of Solar Heating and Hot Water Systems, by J. Richard Williams, Ann Arbor Science (Ann Arbor MI), 1983.

Handbook of Experiences in the Design and Installation of Solar Heating and Cooling Systems, by Dan S. Ward and Harjinder S. Oberoi, American Society of Heating, Refrigerating, and Air-Conditioning Engineers, Inc., and the Solar Energy Applications Laboratory (Colorado State University, Fort Collins CO), July 1980.

Installation Guidelines for Solar DWH Systems in One- and Two-Family Dwellings, by Franklin Research Center (Philadelphia PA) for the U.S. Dept. of Housing and Urban Development, April 1979.

Passive Solar Water Heaters, by Daniel K. Reif, Brick House Publishing Co. (Andover MA), 1983.

Domestic Hot Water Installations: the Great, the Good, and the Unacceptable," *Solar Age* (official magazine of the American Section of the International Solar Energy Society, Inc.), October 1981.

"Solar Water Heaters," *Consumer Reports,* May 1982.

25 heat leaks and how to plug them

At his front door, Dr. Charlie Wing looked me squarely in the eye and said, "I cut my heating bill in this house from $1,970 to $389 a year."

If it weren't for the look on his face, I'd have considered what he said a cue to laugh. The house he was talking about looked like a classic heat sieve—at least that was my first impression as Wing and I walked around the outside. From the inside it didn't look much better. I certainly wouldn't expect the kind of performance he was describing from an 80-year-old, two-story, six-room structure with an unfinished basement and attic.

I was in for a surprise as Wing took me through, pointing out the hidden updated features of the house, I could not find so much as a pinhole through which heating dollars—or even dimes—could be lost.

As we poked into nooks and crannies, I didn't immediately see how Wing had lopped more than 80 percent from his energy bill. "It couldn't just be from plugging holes, could it?" I asked.

"No. I also insulated, installed new windows and doors, and replaced appliances with energy-saving models," he explained. "But plugging holes in this house—holes I call hidden leakers—saves me about 25 percent in heating costs."

Wing is the author of the book *House Warming* (Atlantic/Little, Brown) which describes how he renovated the house I was in. This book (and others he's written on home energy conservation) have brought him national attention: He is now featured in a 13-part television series on saving energy dollars being shown on PBS stations throughout the country.

Back in 1976, Wing founded an outfit called the Cornerstones Energy Group. Cornerstones is an educational center that instructs architects and builders on how to design and construct buildings, including homes, that save energy. All this from a physicist who has a doctorate in phys-

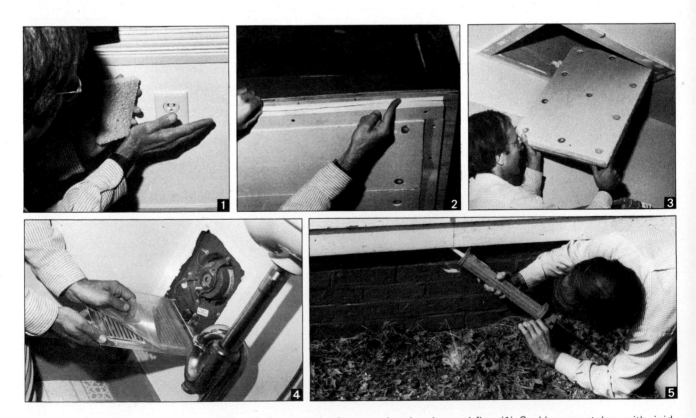

Heat loss can be detected by de-pressurizing the house and using a wet hand to detect airflow (1). Seal basement door with rigid-foam and tension strip (2). Weatherstrip and insulate attic-access panel (3). Seal unused fan outlets with plastic film (4); remove in the spring. Caulk seam between foundation and lower edge of siding (5).

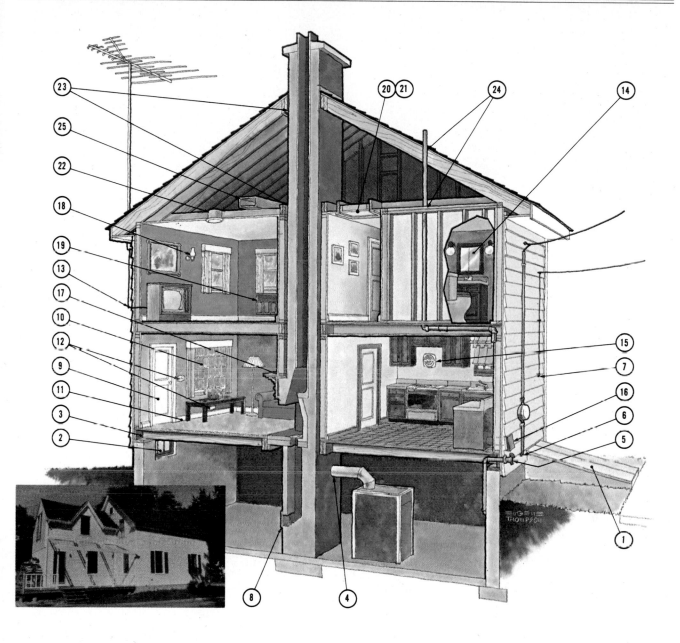

A day spent going from room to room plugging holes can save a lot of money. This drawing, keyed to the table on the next page, tells you where to look for heat leaks, what to do when you find one, and what to use to seal it.

How to find a leak

Some leaks are extremely difficult to detect. To find them, you could hire an energy auditor, who might use a blower door—a calibrated high-speed fan that is placed in a door frame—and an infrared scanner. The blower door pressurizes and de-pressurizes the house while the auditor makes a survey with the scanner. This service costs from $200 to $400.

However, you can make a fairly thorough inspection yourself without the high price, using only a wet sponge. Wing recommends that you wait for a day when the outside temperature is 32 degrees F or lower. See that all windows and outside doors, as well as the fireplace dampers, are closed. Then de-pressurize the house by turning on all equipment that exhausts air—kitchen and bathroom ventilating fans, clothes dryer (use the "air only" setting), and an oil burner, if you have one. This increases the amount of cold air that enters the house, especially through areas that leak.

Wet a sponge and, with the sponge, your hand. Now, room by room and in the basement and attic, draw your hand around possible air-leak areas: windows and outside doors, ceiling fixtures, electrical outlets and switches, baseboards, and wall-ceiling butt joints. Keep in mind that where two dissimilar materials meet—wood and masonry, for example, or wood and wallboard—you're most likely to find a leak. As you make the inspection, use the wet sponge to keep your hand damp.

When you feel a draft, you've found a leak. Mark the spot with chalk.

How to plug a leak

What should you use to seal leaks? Wing's inventory of heat-leak stoppers

The text begins: ical oceanography from the Massachusetts Institute of Technology.

New heat-saving products

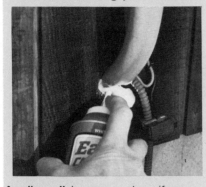

Acrylic caulk in an aerosol can (from a variety of manufacturers) is used like conventional caulk to plug heat leaks (top photo). The flow of caulk is regulated by varying the amount of pressure to the nozzle.

New heat-shrink window covering stops cold air. To install, you outline a window with double-sided tape, then cut the insulating sheet to size and press it to the tape. With a hair dryer, you blow warm air over the sheet until the material is taut.

Flexo-Therm (Columbia Energy Systems, Somerville, Mass.), promises a 12-percent saving in homes that have baseboard heating systems. Placed behind convection fins, Flexo-Therm prevents heat loss caused by heat being conducted away from the room—especially on outside walls (not recommended for cast-iron baseboards).

Where you can plug heat leaks

Leak areas[1]	Sealing materials[2]	Special instructions
1. Basement door	Caulk, closed-cell and rigid-foam weatherstrip, tension strip	Caulk frame-to-siding joint—stuff closed-cell foam into gap if it's wide enough; nail rigid foam to outside face of door if panels are leaking; adhere tension strip to doorstop
2. Basement windows	Caulk	
3. Sill plate	Unfaced fiberglass insulation, caulk[3]	Push oversize piece of insulation against inside of plate from basement or crawl space
4. Furnace flue	Unfaced fiberglass insulation, furnace cement	If crack between flue and chimney is wide enough, stuff with insulation; if not, seal with cement
5. Outside faucet	Closed-cell foam, caulk[3]	
6. Electric service cable	Unfaced fiberglass insulation, caulk[3]	Stuff entry hole with insulation, working from inside if accessible
7. Telephone cable	Caulk	Seal where cable passes through wall on outside of house
8. Fireplace clean-out door	Furnace cement	Cement around frame; make sure door closes tightly
9. Outside doors	Caulk, weatherstrip, flexible threshold	If there's a mail slot in the door, consider installing an outside mailbox and stuffing existing slot with insulation
10. Windows[4]	Caulk, duct tape, weatherstrip	
11. Baseboards	Unfaced fiberglass insulation	Remove baseboards and stuff gaps with fiberglass; replace baseboards
12. Outlets and switches	Foam gaskets	Remove plate, install gasket, replace plate; also insert plugs that come with gaskets into receptacles when not in use
13. TV-antenna or -cable entrance	Caulk	
14. Medicine cabinet	Foil-faced fiberglass insulation, polyethylene	Remove cabinet, install insulation in wall, apply polyethylene vapor barrier to back and side of cabinet, reinstall cabinet.
15. Ventilating fan	Polyethylene	Remove grille, cut polyethylene to size, place sheet on back of grille, reinstall grille[5]
16. Clothes-dryer vent		Make sure lint isn't keeping vent damper open
17. Fireplace[6]	Closed-cell foam insulation, caulk	Stuff insulation into gap where fireplace meets wall; caulk
18. Wall-mounted fixture	Unfaced fiberglass insulation	Turn off electricity, remove fixture, stuff gaps with fiberglass, reinstall fixture
19. Room air conditioner	Duct tape, polyethylene, caulk	For in-wall unit, cover with polyethylene and caulk perimeter; for window unit, cover with polyethylene and tape perimeter
20. Attic door	Caulk, weatherstrip, flexible threshold	Treat this door the same as an outside door
21. Attic scuttle	Closed-cell and rigid foam	Apply closed-cell foam to perimeter; nail rigid foam to back of scuttle
22. Recessed light fixture	Plywood, unfaced fiberglass insulation	Build box around appliance that projects above ceiling; insulate up to and over box[7]
23. Chimney	Unfaced fiberglass insulation	Apply where chimney passes through attic floor and roof
24. Plumbing vent	Unfaced fiberglass insulation	Apply where vent passes through attic floor and roof
25. Ducts	Caulk, duct tape, foil-faced fiberglass insulation	Where ducts are in unheated areas, seal joints with caulk or duct tape; wrap duct with insulation[8]

[1]This table begins with the basement foundation, proceeds to the living quarters, and ends in the attic. The numbers next to each potential heat-leak problem coincide with the numbers in the drawing on the opposite page.
[2]The term "caulk" describes a variety of different compounds in tubes and cans that are used to seal joints and seams. You may not need all the materials listed; use whatever works in your situation.
[3]Where you can seal a leak from both the inside and outside, do so.
[4]If windows have sash cords, consider removing them and sealing holes with caulk or duct tape—then install tension strip.
[5]Remember to remove the polyethylene covering in the spring so you can use the fan.
[6]If the fireplace damper does not close tightly, seal the damper and don't use the fireplace, or install a glass fireplace door to prevent cold air from entering the room and warm air from escaping.
[7]Caution: The National Fire Code specifies a clearance of three in. around recessed lighting fixtures.
[8]In one job, Dr. Wing cut a heating bill in half by doing this. However, there's no sense in treating ducts if the area is heated because heat radiating from ducts contributes to the overall warmth of the space.

consists of caulk, closed-cell-foam weatherstripping, rigid weatherstripping, foil-faced and unfaced insulation, polyethylene sheeting, duct tape, foam gaskets, and tension weatherstripping.

One kind of tension strip, made by 3M Co., is a half-inch-wide plastic strip that folds into a "V" and is called, aptly, V-Seal Weather Strip. One side of the "V" is adhesive-coated, so you can attach it to window frames and doors. The material is flexible, so windows and doors can be opened and closed many times before the strip loses its sealing ability. On double-hung windows with sash cords, install tension strip and remove the cord. The strip is enough to keep the window open.

Where are the most common leaks? According to Wing, there are 25 of them, and they're listed in the table above. The table also lists materials you can use to seal leaks and special instructions Wing offers for doing the job. Remember, however, that because of the unique characteristics of each house, there may be leaks in your house at places not listed in the table, so don't rely on it alone—*By George Sears. Drawing by Eugene Thompson.*

invisible insulation you put on your windows

A faint whoosh of air retreated out the door as I went in, for this was a clean room, pressurized to minimize infiltration. At the far side stood a massive machine, bellowing loudly as its rollers spun in synchrony. It looked like a printing press, but it wasn't putting ink on paper. Instead, it was laminating layers of thin-film plastics. At the end of the line, rolling up at a rate of about 130 feet per minute, was the final product: a Dagwood sandwich whose center is a polyester film with a thin metal coating on one side. On top of the metal is a polypropylene film, which protects it and prevents oxidation. On the other side of the polyester is a water-activated adhesive, and finally, a peel-off plastic backing. But for all its complexity, the slinky laminate looked like ordinary plastic film.

If you apply this film to your windows, however, you will find that it is not ordinary. Though you can barely see it, this plastic film will reduce heat loss through the glass by at least a third. That means it can make single glass perform almost as well as double glazing. And it can make a standard double-glazed window approach the performance of a premium triple-glazed unit. "All without the expense or inconvenience of putting in new windows," says Calvin Hill.

Hill is vice-president for marketing and sales at Gila River Products, where I saw this film being made. The company has been making window films in this Phoenix suburb for most of its 10-year history; a half-dozen other companies make them, too. But these older films are solar-control films; they reduce solar gain and cut air-conditioning costs. You see them on commercial buildings and on some homes, primarily in the South. Other windows films, called winter films, not only reduce solar gain but also reduce heat loss by reflecting infrared radiation. From the inside, though, they darken windows. From the outside (and from inside at night), they give windows a mirrored look.

The new film—called Advanced Energy Technology, or AET, film—is different. In fact, it bears more resemblance to Heat Mirror film than it does to solar-control films. Heat Mirror is the film that was developed at the Massachusetts Institute of Technology and finally brought to market by the Southwall Corp. Like Heat Mirror, AET film's metallic coating is wavelength-selective: It reacts differently to different wavelengths of electromagnetic radiation. Specifically, it transmits 72 percent of the visible light, so it looks nearly clear. But it reflects 72 percent of the long-wave infrared energy emitted by room-temperature objects, so it reduces heat flow through the glass. (Those specs are for the clear version of the film; there is also a bronze-tinted version.) Heat Mirror does the same thing— even more effectively—but its metallic coating is unprotected, so the film can be used only as the center pane in a triple-glazed window. AET film can be applied to existing windows.

If *what* AET film does piques the imagination, *how* it does it could boggle the mind. The secret is in that metallic coating, which, though only a few hundred atoms thick, is not one layer but three. Dr. Stephen Meyer, a

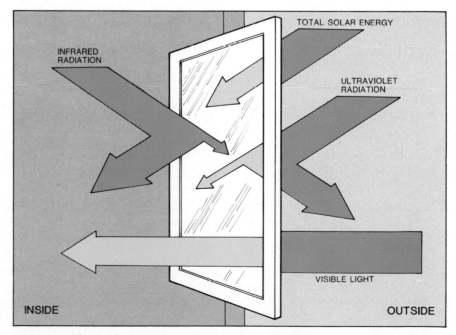

AET window film is wavelength-selective: Clear version transmits 72 percent of the visible light and 50 percent of the total solar energy. Yet it reflects 72 percent of the longwave infrared energy emitted by room-temperature objects. Also, it rejects 70 percent of the ultraviolet radiation, the prime cause of fabric fading.

young physicist who has been working on selective-metallic coatings since 1980, explains it this way: "A metal reflects light because it has free electrons—unattached to an atom and thus capable of moving around. When a propagating wave of electromagnetic radiation (infrared, for example) goes from air, which does not have free electrons, to a metal, which does, the electric field of the wave accelerates the free electrons in the metal. But they're always 90 degrees out of phase with the wave itself." That's what causes the reflection we see off a metal.

"Reflectivity is a function of the wave's frequency," Meyer continues, "because the free electrons have a maximum velocity at which they can move (it's different in different metals). As you increase the frequency of the waves—say, from long-wave infrared up to visible light—the free electrons tend to lag behind the alternative electric field of the wave. Result: You get less reflection and more transmission of the higher-frequency waves. Thus, while most of the relatively long-wave infrared would be reflected by a very thin metal coating, a good bit of the shorter-wave visible light would get through.

"The next thing we asked," says Meyer, "was, Is there anything we can do to improve the transmission of the higher-frequency wavelengths without reducing the reflection at the lower frequencies?" It turns out there was. They sandwiched the metal layer between two layers of a dielectric—a transparent, nonconductive metal oxide. The dielectric layers act as a halfway house between the air and the metal. Or, as Meyer explains it, they serve to eliminate that 90-degree phase shift.

Just how that's done gets tricky, though. To a scientist, Meyer would explain what happens by writing equations that involve complex numbers (numbers with both real and so-called imaginary components). "It turns out that a whole bunch of physical properties [including the refractive indices of metals] can be analyzed with complex numbers," says Meyer, "but the only thing you can observe or measure is the real component. It's just a mathematical trick," he adds, "but if you follow the mathematics through, son of a gun, that's exactly what happens.

"It boils down to this," Meyer explains: "The only way you can get around the 90-degree phase shift is to introduce an additional 90-degree shift on each side of the metal." That's

what the dielectric layers do. The dielectric must have the right refractive index, and the thickness of the layers must be precisely controlled.

To apply these atoms-thick metal and dielectric layers, they use a process called sputtering. The glossy-white cylinder where it's done looks like something that should be orbiting Earth or crawling on the bottom of the ocean. It's a high-vacuum chamber that can be pumped down to one-millionth of a thousandth of an atmosphere. The metal and dielectric to be sputtered are in different cathodes in the machine, and a gas or mixture of gases is admitted to the evacuated chamber. "We ionize the gas, and it's shot like a bullet at the metal in the cathode," says Bob Miliano, a chemist recently hired by Gila River. "And

To install AET window film, you need a clean spray bottle filled with warm water and detergent (¼ teaspoon to eight oz.), a single-edge razor blade, sponge, squeegee, and soft cloth. When you've cut the film to size (see text), you separate film from backing by putting a piece of masking tape on each side and pulling (top). The "good" side will have a slight tint to it. Film and backing are easier to separate if you spray with the water solution as you pull them apart. You also spray the cleaned window thoroughly. Both film and window should be wet when you apply the film. Let the film overlap the window edge on three sides, using a factory-cut edge on the fourth. Put it on carefully, and avoid wrinkles. Next, spray the film with the water solution to lubricate. Then start squeegeeing about two in. from the top of the window, working toward the sides with short strokes. Work from top to bottom but not all the way to any side, and keep the film moist. Next, trim the film using a straightedge and single-edge razor. Leave about a ¹⁄₁₆-in. gap on all sides so you can get out all the water. Firm pressure on the squeegee is required. If bubbles remain near the edges, wrap a soft cloth around a putty knife and use it to squeeze them out. Use the cloth to dry the edges. To clean, use soap and water; squeegee dry. Never use ammonia, vinegar, or paper towels.

How typical window films compare

Type of film*	% solar reflected	% solar transmitted	% solar absorbed	% visible light transmitted	% ultraviolet rejected	Design U-value	Median U-value	Shading coefficient	Emissivity
AET clear	30	50	20	72	70	0.85	0.77	0.61	0.28
AET bronze	38	36	26	56	85	0.83	0.75	0.46	0.25
Silver winter	50	19	31	24	84	0.84	0.76	0.28	0.27
Bronze reflective	26	20	54	22	99	1.10	1.03	0.38	0.68
Light-gray nonreflective	9	54	37	51	99	1.21	1.16	0.73	0.88
⅛-in. window glass	8	90	2	90	33	1.16	1.10	1.00	0.81

*Specifications given are for films made by Gila River Products; other companies make similar solar-control films and may soon introduce films similar to Gila River's AET

Numbers tell best how window films differ. Values given assume all films are applied to standard ⅛-inch window glass. Comparable values are given for the glass alone. The second, third, and fourth columns refer to the total solar energy falling on the glazing: It is either reflected, transmitted, or absorbed. The fifth column tells how much visible light gets through the glazing, and the sixth column indicates how much of the ultraviolet *does not* get through the glazing. U-values given are both winter U-values, calculated under standard conditions: Design U-values assume 68 deg. F indoors, 18 deg. outdoors, and 15-mph wind. Median U-values assume 68 deg. indoors, 45 deg. outdoors, and 15-mph wind. The shading coefficient compares the sun-control capability of other glazings with that of ordinary window glass (1.00). The lower the number, the more sun is rejected. Emissivity indicates what percentage of long-wave infrared radiation is absorbed (and then emitted—mostly toward the outside). The lower the emissivity, the less IR the glazing absorbs. What isn't absorbed is reflected. Thus indirectly, emissivity indicates how much IR the glazing reflects (and so AET film is called a low-emissivity glazing).

some of its energy is transferred to the metal. The metal's atoms get knocked off, hit the polyester film, and condense there." The control of the gases is critical. "Too much and you end up with Reynolds Wrap," says Miliano, "too little and you have a film that is essentially worthless."

On the market

From the sputtering chamber, the coated film is delivered to the laminating machine at the Gila River plant. The first shipment of AET films created there reached hardware stores and home centers in early summer, 1983.

How much heat would you save with AET film? That depends on many factors. The median winter U-value (a measure of heat flow through a material) of standard ⅛-inch window glass is 1.10 (see table). Apply the clear AET film to that window, and its U-value drops to 0.77. (The lower the U-value, the slower the heat tranfer.) Standard double-glazed windows with a ¼-inch air space have a median winter U-value of 0.71—not a lot better than single glass with AET film. Applied to a standard double-glazed window, clear AET film reduces the U-value to 0.46. That approaches the

0.37 rating of premium triple-glazed windows with two ½-inch air spaces.

The film will likely reduce heat loss more than these U-values suggest. "When people think of heat loss they usually look at air temperature only," says Meyer, "but what they should look at is heat loss from their skin. If you could have a room that reflected all of your body heat, the air could be at absolute zero and you'd still feel comfortable." In the real world that's impossible. But materials that reflect most of the infrared will make you feel warmer than those that absorb it. That means you can perhaps tweak you thermostat back a few degrees. In turn, the lower air temperature may raise the humidity a bit, again increasing your comfort level at a lower setting.

One caution about humidity: Plain glass absorbs most infrared radiation, and that warms it up. When you apply AET film to a window and reflect the IR, the glass itself stays colder. That could cause a condensation problem. In practice, such problems haven't occurred, Calvin Hill reports.

If you are considering AET film for your windows, you should note that it does block about half of the solar gain (see table). (Though glass varies, a

single pane typically blocks 10 percent; double and triple panes more than double and triple the loss.) Although that can reduce your air-conditioning load in summer, in winter you may pay a price. In general, AET film should be most cost-effective on east and west windows, because that should reduce both your heating and cooling loads. North windows should be the next choice. "Outfitting your south windows might be the least cost-effective," Hill continues, "but in many northern climates, especially where cloudy skies prevail, it should still pay off."

How to apply invisible insulation

I put the clear AET film on my glass terrace door. And although installing it wasn't what I consider recreation, it was not difficult either. You begin by vacuuming the area and shutting off all fans to minimize dust. Next, wash the window with water and detergent. While it's wet, scrape it with a single-edge razor blade. "Glass is fairly rough," says Calvin Hill, "and that also gets off things the soap may not remove.

Next, you cut the film an inch bigger than the window panel on all sides. You'll trim it to fit later. The film is as slippery as silk, so I used a clothespin on each end of the roll to keep it from unrolling. Then you remove the backing (see photo and caption) and apply the film. The job would be easier with a helper.

I am impressed with the transparency of the clear film. Though the glass door I covered is adjacent to an uncovered window, the slight tint the film gives the glass is hardly perceptible by day; at night (and from outside) it has a slight bronze-mirror look. The effect would probably be less noticeable if the adjacent glass were covered also. Furthermore, a slight change in the coating has eliminated the effect in later production runs, Hill tells me. My film also has some imperfections in it (or contaminants under it), and they show from close up.

AET film is sold in home centers and large hardware stores from bulk rolls and in kits, precut to lengths of 48, 78, and 96 inches. All rolls are 35 inches wide. The clear film sells for $1.75 to $2.50 a square foot, the bronze for $1.50 to $2. Professional installers also handle the film; look under "Glass Coating and Tinting" in the Yellow Pages, and expect to pay $1 to $1.50 more a square foot—*By V. Elaine Smay.*

cut heat loss: insulate foundation walls

Once you've insulated your attic, installed storm windows, and weatherstripped or caulked every opening in the skin of your home, the next step is to insulate your foundation.

Heat loss through foundations, which may be relatively insignificant in uninsulated houses (usually under 10 percent of the total), becomes a major factor in well-insulated structures, where 15 to 35 percent of the heat still lost escapes through concrete foundations. That's not surprising when you consider that eight inches of concrete rates an R-value of just over one, little higher than that of glass. Worse yet, concrete acts as a wick, collecting heat from lower portions of the house and passing it to exposed, above-grade areas of the foundation.

Is foundation insulation worth it? Based on calculations with ASHRAE formulas, a four-foot depth of four-inch-thick polystyrene (with two feet of the foundation exposed and the boards rated at R-4 per inch) would save $302 per year in Boston, assuming a basement temperature of 65 degrees F and oil heat at a low $1.20 a gallon. If a home's perimeter is 150 feet and we assume an insulation cost of $1.50 per square foot (a high estimate), the cost of the insulation job is $900, giving a three-year payback period. In other climates, the payback period may range from as little as a year and a half to about six years, depending on your type of heat.

Before starting the project, you must decide whether to use extruded polystyrene, such as Dow's Styrofoam (U.S. Gypsum makes a similar product called Formular), or one of the expanded-polystyrene (EPS) product, manufactured by perhaps 150 different companies. Although Styrofoam has a higher R-value (R-5 per inch of thickness compared with R-3.5 per inch of expanded polystyrene), it's twice as expensive (about 30¢ per board foot compared with 15¢ for EPS).

Both kinds of rigid board must be protected from impact and UV radiation. Both also expand and contract significantly due to temperature changes, so any covering must be either flexible enough to tolerate these changes or tough enough to provide restraint.

Typically, a mixture of a portland-cement matrix reinforced with chopped fiberglass, plus an acrylic or acrylic-latex bonding agent, makes a covering hard enough to withstand hammer blows and limit board movement. But since the panels still move under any covering, expansion joints should go every 12 feet or so.

You could, of course, cover the exposed insulation with cement board, exterior plywood, or other weatherproof panel, as shown in our sketch, but an applied coating is still cheaper. You can buy pre-coated insulating panels—practical if much of your foundation is above ground. These are made by Conproco, W. R. Bonsal, and Thermboard. They save time and work, but the coating may not be as

thick as one you'd apply yourself, and the overall cost could be nearly double. You don't have to coat the part of the board below grade, so it may be worth it to buy unfinished panels and trowel on a coating only where needed.

Once you've decided which material and technique to use, you'll have to determine how much insulating board you need (it's usually sold in panels that measure two by four feet or two by eight feet). This decision depends on how far below grade you want to go. Two feet of insulation below grade greatly reduces heat loss by preventing the concrete from wicking heat up above ground level and out

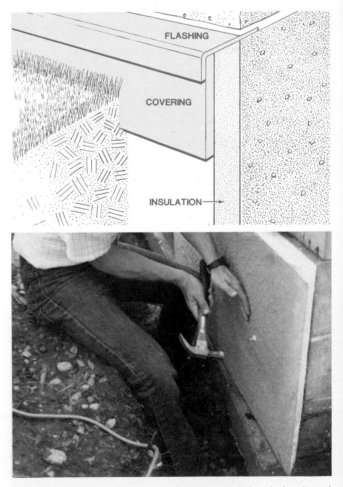

Sketch at top shows facing panel that protects insulating board from sun exposure and impact. Covering panel should project two inches below grade; buried part of insulation needs no facing. Metal flashing, inserted into grout line, caps top. Photo shows pre-coated board attached with nylon anchors.

into the air. Insulating all the way to the footing increases energy saving another 10 percent or so, but you may not feel that's worth it, especially if you have to dig an additional six to eight feet.

After digging the trench you must measure, cut to size, and miter panels (where necessary). Cut the pre-coated panels with a circular saw equipped with a masonry blade; cut uncoated board with a utility knife, hacksaw blade, or fine-toothed crosscut saw.

The panels may be installed either by mechanical means or with a mastic. Expandable nylon anchors work well, but drilling four to six holes per panel into masonry can get tedious.

Choose a mastic that's compatible with your insulation—such as Dow #11 for Styrofoam. You can apply it in walnut-size dots (avoid the tendency to use too little), with a serrated trowel (a lot of work), or in ribbons (a good compromise). Tacking time is generally about two minutes. Prop the panels in place while the mastic sets.

Once set, the boards are ready to be coated. The compound used in the job pictured was supplied by Conproco, and is made by mixing a bag of its Structural Skin (cement-fiberglass mix), a gallon of its K-88 (latex acrylic), and about a quart of water (the compound doesn't come pre-mixed). The final consistency resembles that of soft ice cream. The coating should be applied with a trowel to a thickness of ⅛ to ¼ inch. It should cover all the exposed board, down to about two inches below grade.

You make expansion joints by installing—before troweling—pre-manufactured thin-coat stucco control joints (available from Plastic Components of Miami), or by simply scoring the still-wet surface coat with a trowel.

You can leave the protective layer with its natural stucco finish; it's a visual improvement over most unfinished foundations. But, if you prefer, you can choose from a variety of finishes, including factory-blended finish stucco or any breathable latex paint suitable for masonry—*By Mark Bittman.*

Trial-fit the elements of the system (top) before doing final lay-up and installation. At center: Trowel coating onto unfinished panels to thickness of ⅛ to ¼ inch after mastic has set (or after fastening boards in place mechanically). Above, finished job, with gravel backfill and flashing in place.

MANUFACTURERS OF INSULATING PRODUCTS
Coating products: W. R. Bonsal, 8201 Arrowridge Blvd., Charlotte NC 28224; **Conproco Corp.,** Box 368, Hookset NH 03106, **Expanded polystyrene: Amotex Plastics of Maryland,** 1127 S. Howard St., Baltimore MD 21230; **Insulair, Inc.,** Rte. 6, Box 228, Gainesville GA 30501; **Plymouth Foam Products,** 1800 Sunset Dr., Plymouth WI 53073; **Texcon Products, Inc.,** Box 4154, Houston TX 77210; **Vertex, Inc.,** 4200 Charter St., Vernon CA 90058; others. **Expansion joints: Plastic Components of Miami,** 7570 NW 79 St., Miami FL 33166. **Extruded polystyrene: Dow Chemical Co.,** Styrofoam Products Dept., Midland MI 48640; **U.S. Gypsum,** 101 S. Wacker Dr., Chicago IL 60606. **Mastic: Dow Chemical Co.** (address above); **H.B. Fuller Co.** (Maxbond), 315 S. Hicks Rd., Palatine IL 60067. **Pre-coated boards: W. R. Bonsal** (address above); **Conproco Corp.** (address above); **Thermboard Mfg. Co.,** 1909 Lomes Blvd. NW, Albuquerque NM 87104.

tiling for passive solar

The floors of passive-solar buildings are frequently used for thermal mass. An add-on greenhouse built on a poured or concrete-block slab thus avoids the need for water drums, rock beds, or internal masonry walls. However, it is important that the floor be finished with material that readily absorbs heat and conducts it to the underlying mass. The common-sense choice is ceramic tile.

Depending on the color and density (but not the finish or glaze) of the tile, performance will vary considerably. Major tile manufacturers specify the following thermal characteristics for their products: absorptance (the percentage of incident solar energy absorbed); specific heat (the quantity of heat needed to raise tile temperature by one degree F); emittance (percentage of absorbed energy reradiated as heat); diffusivity (rate at which a temperature wave progresses through the tile); thermal conductivity (quantity of heat transmitted through tile per unit of time); and thermal expansion (change in size of tile with change in temperature). Suitable tiles for passive solar have absorptance and emittance of around 80 percent.

Not all sunspaces can be built over concrete. The drawings on the facing page show the comparative performance of three common tile-floor constructions.

For more information, write to American Olean (Publicity Dept., 1000 Cannon Ave., Lansdale, Pa. 19446) for booklet 1960—*By Daniel Ruby. Illustration by Gerhard Richter.*

Dark colors are best, but medium shades of tile (like these blue-brown Primitive Encore tiles from American Olean) can be sufficiently absorptive for solar applications. Shuffling boxes of tiles before laying (1) ensured a scattered color scheme. Slightly larger-than-usual joint was left (2) to allow for thermal expansion. Random tiles were checked for evenness of bond (3) because air pockets hamper heat conduction. Floor was laid so that cut tiles abutted rear stone wall (4), which provides greenhouse with additional thermal mass.

Sunspace for fieldstone house was added over existing patio after reinforcing and leveling. Tile readily conducts heat between slab and room air.

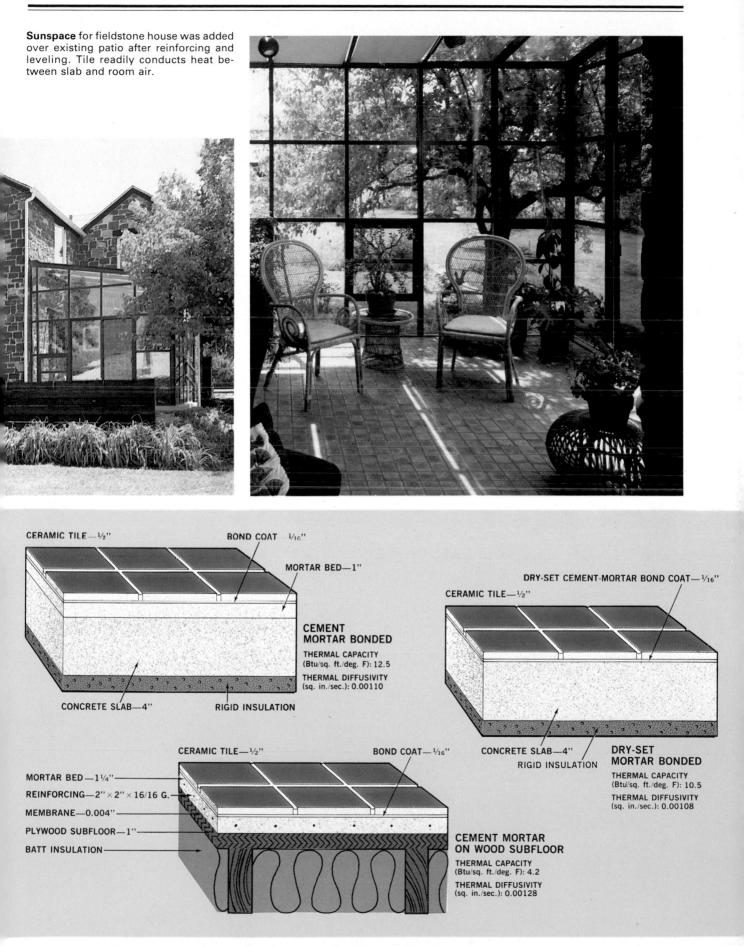

CERAMIC TILE—½" BOND COAT ¹⁄₁₆"

MORTAR BED—1"

CEMENT MORTAR BONDED

THERMAL CAPACITY
(Btu/sq. ft./deg. F): 12.5

THERMAL DIFFUSIVITY
(sq. in./sec.): 0.00110

CONCRETE SLAB—4" RIGID INSULATION

DRY-SET CEMENT-MORTAR BOND COAT—¹⁄₁₆"

CERAMIC TILE—½"

CONCRETE SLAB—4" **DRY-SET**
RIGID INSULATION **MORTAR BONDED**

THERMAL CAPACITY
(Btu/sq. ft./deg. F): 10.5

THERMAL DIFFUSIVITY
(sq. in./sec.): 0.00108

CERAMIC TILE—½" BOND COAT—¹⁄₁₆"

MORTAR BED—1¼"

REINFORCING—2" × 2" × 16/16 G.

MEMBRANE—0.004"

PLYWOOD SUBFLOOR—1"

BATT INSULATION

**CEMENT MORTAR
ON WOOD SUBFLOOR**

THERMAL CAPACITY
(Btu/sq. ft./deg. F): 4.2

THERMAL DIFFUSIVITY
(sq. in./sec.): 0.00128

two kitchen dividers

Want the airy feel of a large, open kitchen in limited floor space? Room dividers are a good way to define separate areas while maintaining overall spaciousness. They can also provide useful storage and display space.

Both kitchens shown here feature dividers that offer a wine rack as the centerpiece of their designs. The country kitchen uses a floor-to-ceiling divider whose open-grid wine rack, shelving, and rough-texture wood lend a rustic tone

to the home. The modern kitchen (below) has a floor island whose counter height permits access and conversation between dining and working areas while providing elegant storage for an ample collection of wines.

Both dividers are easy to build with pine and plywood (see captions). Sheet-vinyl flooring from Congoleum completes the decorating schemes of the two kitchens—*By Daniel Ruby. Designs From Congoleum Corp.*

Floor-island divider features storage for standard-size wine bottles and cabinets for pots and dishes (not shown in drawing) on both sides. Build wine rack to desired size by cutting ½-by-6¾-in. slots at four-in. intervals in ½-in. boards with bevel-cut ends. After painting, slip pieces together in eggcrate fashion. Now assemble storage unit with four-in. base, vertical divider, and shelving. Slip rack into place, then add moldings, doors, and counter top. Fill all nail holes, and paint as desired.

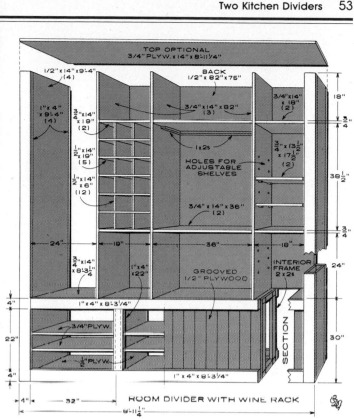

ROOM DIVIDER WITH WINE RACK

Labels on diagram: TOP OPTIONAL 3/4" PLYW. x 14" x 8'-11 1/4"; 1/2" x 14" x 9'-4" (4); 1" x 4" x 9'-4" (4); 3/4" x 14" x 19" (2); 1/2" x 14" x 19" (5); 1/2" x 14" x 6" (12); 3/4" x 14" x 8'-3/4"; BACK 1/2" x 82" x 75"; 3/4" x 14" x 82" (3); 1 x 25; HOLES FOR ADJUSTABLE SHELVES; 3/4" x 14" x 36" (2); GROOVED 1/2" PLYWOOD; 1" x 4" x 22"; 3/4" x 14" x 18" (2); 3/4" x 3 1/2" x 17 1/2" (2); INTERIOR FRAME 2 x 2 1/2; 18"; 5 3/4"; 38 1/2"; 3/4"; 24"; 30"; SECTION; 1" x 4" x 8'-3/4"; 3/4" PLYW.; 1/2" PLYW; 4"; 22"; 4"; 4"; 32"; 8'-11 1/4"; 24"; 19"; 36"; 18"

Floor-to-ceiling divider provides open shelving for laundry room in base section and storage and display space for dining-room side above the counter. Build interior frame of counter first, then add bottom board, shelving, and face paneling. Add a plastic-laminate counter top, then erect the upper divider frame. On left side, a vertical box beam bulks up the design. Wine rack is made by nailing two six-in. vertical pieces to each horizontal board, then stacking and toe-nailing. Finish with satin polyurethane.

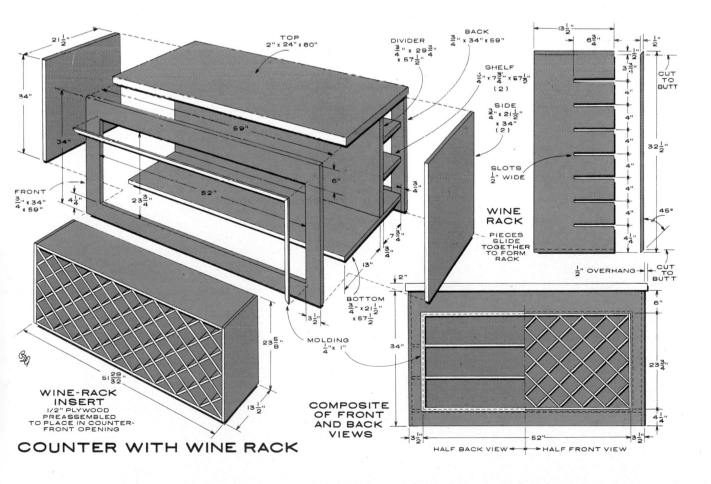

COUNTER WITH WINE RACK

WINE-RACK INSERT 1/2" PLYWOOD PREASSEMBLED TO PLACE IN COUNTER-FRONT OPENING

WINE RACK — PIECES SLIDE TOGETHER TO FORM RACK

COMPOSITE OF FRONT AND BACK VIEWS

Labels: TOP 2" x 24" x 60"; DIVIDER 3/4" x 29 3/4" x 57 1/2"; BACK 3/4" x 34" x 59"; SHELF 3/4" x 7 3/4" x 57 1/2" (2); SIDE 3/4" x 21 1/2" x 34" (2); SLOTS 1/2" WIDE; FRONT 3/4" x 34" x 59"; BOTTOM 3/4" x 21 1/2" x 57 1/2"; MOLDING 1/4" x 1"; 21 1/2"; 34"; 34"; 59"; 6"; 23 3/4"; 52"; 4 1/4"; 3/4"; 7 3/4"; 13"; 2"; 3 1/2"; 23 5/8"; 51 29/32"; 13 1/2"; 13 1/2"; 6 3/4"; 1/2"; 3 1/2"; 4"; 32 1/2"; 45°; 1/2" OVERHANG; CUT TO BUTT; 6"; 34"; 23 3/4"; 4 1/4"; 3 1/2"; 52"; 3 1/2"; HALF BACK VIEW; HALF FRONT VIEW

wraparound counter for attic built-ins

A room of one's own is a prize for any teen-ager—even if the "room" is little more than a broad landing at the top of the attic stairs. But converting a pocket of attic space into the welcoming aerie shown at right required both creative design and careful selection of materials. By combining the classic simplicity of natural pine with the clean lines of multi-level built-ins, the architect created a room that looks—and is—more spacious than seems possible in such a small area.

The bed, a simple platform of ¾-inch plywood, is sized to accept the teen-ager's existing box spring and mattress. But a more conventional foam mattress could also rest on the platform.

The built-ins establish the open look of the room while providing essential work and storage space. The desk, for example, is tucked into a corner where the ceiling slants low. But the desk-top position allows the student to be far enough away from the knee wall so there's ample headroom when rising. The storage cabinet at the end of the wall unit also puts an otherwise awkward space to good use.

Extending the desk-counter around the wall not only adds extra shelf space: It also carries the eye around the room, making the space seem larger. The counter's mate, on the other side of the bed, can serve as a conventional bedside table or as a stand for whatever artifacts the teen-ager wants to display.

Even the 1×6 pine trim that finishes the plank headboard has several functions. Extended to sweep around the wall, the board not only repeats the room-expanding lines of the counter below but also serves as a mounting surface for pegs and lights. In this installation, the trim conceals the track-light wiring. Light fixtures could, of course, be clipped directly to the board, and it could be studded with as many peg hangers as needed.

A bookshelf suspended between the eaves expands the natural-pine motif beyond the built-ins. Both the eave window and the skylight are trimmed in polyurethane-finished pine, and the stairwell is framed in it. Even a support column has been clad in the wood. These finishing touches erase any look of attic rawness about the room.

Congoleum's Contempora sheet-vinyl flooring (in the "Royal Court" design) does more than add pattern to the room. The flexible, tear-resistant flooring cuts easily with scissors and can be fitted around obstacles with minimal difficulty. In a room such as this, where it may be impractical to construct the furniture elsewhere, the Contempora flooring can be neatly laid after the built-ins are in place—*By Susan Renner-Smith. Drawing by Eugene Thompson.*

The multilevel shelf looks like a continuous unit; however, the units are mounted separately on cleats nailed to wall studs (usually 16 in. on center). First assemble the bed platform and mount the headboard; then construct the flanking shelf and table. Next, assemble and install the cabinet and counter top. Finally, install the natural-pine headrail.

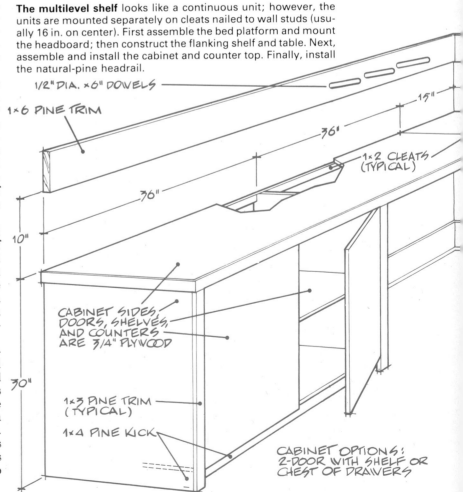

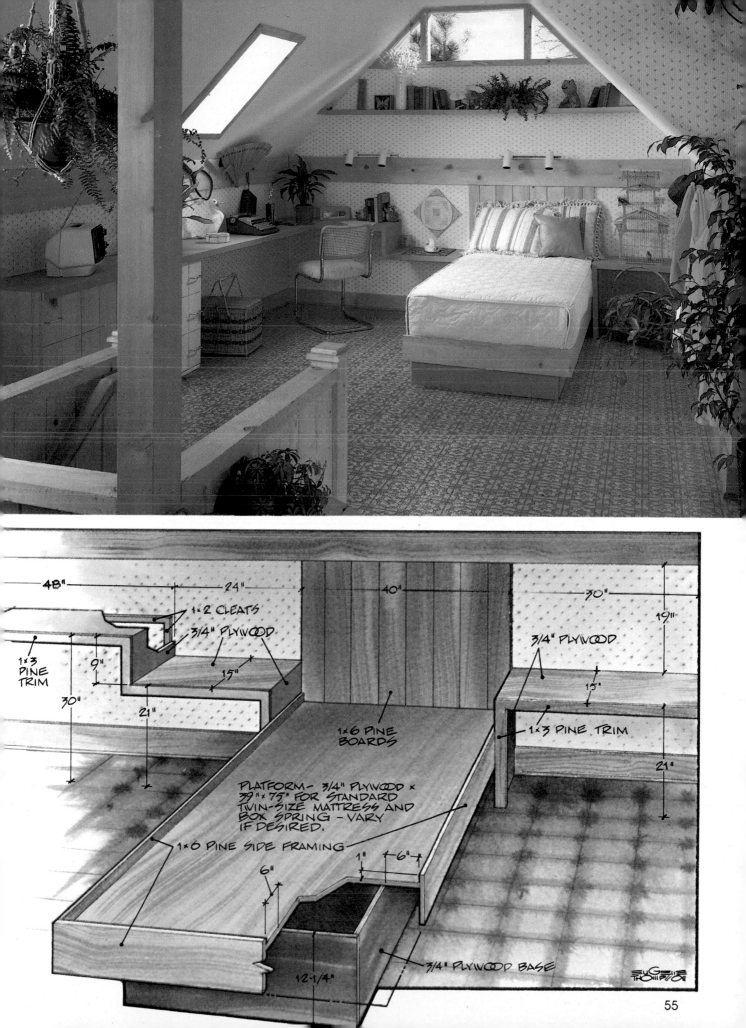

48"

1×2 CLEATS

3/4" PLYWOOD

24"

40"

30"

19"

1×3 PINE TRIM

9"

15"

3/4" PLYWOOD

30"

21"

1×6 PINE BOARDS

3/4" PLYWOOD

15"

1×3 PINE TRIM

21"

PLATFORM- 3/4" PLYWOOD × 39"×75" FOR STANDARD TWIN-SIZE MATTRESS AND BOX SPRING - VARY IF DESIRED.

1×6 PINE SIDE FRAMING

1"

6"

6"

3/4" PLYWOOD BASE

12-1/4"

built-ins for a window bay

Hidden beneath the cracked plaster, rotted moldings, and layer upon layer of paint in the old San Francisco townhouse were some charming features. In Marshall Roath's all-redwood renovation, the three-foot-deep window bay became the living room's visual centerpiece with the addition of a built-in bench and adjacent cabinet. And they provide what almost every living room, new or old, lacks: concealed storage space.

While the entire room is surfaced in redwood, a wide range of grades, textures, and board sizes are used for variety. The windows themselves are framed with smooth redwood 1 × 4s to contrast with the rough-textured resawed paneling that covers the walls and front faces of the cabinets. Simi-

larly, top-quality clear-all-heart boards are varied with sapwood-streaked clear-grade for greater interest. (For complete information on the types and uses of redwood, write to the California Redwood Assn., 591 Redwood Hwy., Mill Valley, Calif. 94941, for a literature list.)

The seat and cabinet are framed with lumber as shown, then faced with tongue-and-groove paneling applied directly over the framing in some places and glued to plywood sheathing in others. Both storage units have a hinged center panel for access (a lid or a door) featuring unobtrusive hardware. Three long 2×12 shelves over the cabinet give space for display—*By Daniel Ruby*.

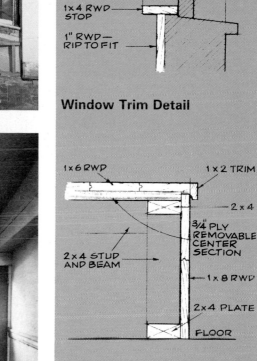

Remove existing trim and stops

Window Trim Detail

1x4 RWD STOP
1" RWD RIP TO FIT

Section—Window Seat

1x6 RWD
1x2 TRIM
2x4
3/4" PLY REMOVABLE CENTER SECTION
2x4 STUD AND BEAM
1x8 RWD
2x4 PLATE
FLOOR

Section—Cabinet

1x8 RWD PANELING
2x6 RWD COUNTER
3/4"
SEMI-CONCEALED HINGE
1x2
3/8" PLY
3/8" x 8" RWD OVER 3/8" PLY DOOR
3/4" PLY
1x4 RWD
FLOOR
3"

Run-down interior offered several niches for built-in storage—notably a window bay.

Window seat's lid lifts to give access to 15 cu. ft. of easy-to-reach storage. T&G planks are used for all cabinet surfaces.

Windows get the redwood treatment after existing casings are stripped. Original curved top sashes were retained.

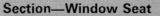

build an add-on kitchen-island rack

I was running out of space. I urgently needed some sort of space-saving unit in which to store my growing collection of cookware—something that wouldn't get in the way. Happily, I solved the problem with a combination kitchen rack and wine-glass hanger. With it, I store my cooking utensils (including lids, thanks to shelving at the top of the rack) and safely stow long- and short-stem wine glasses.

I used custom-milled oak for the project, cut to full dimensions. There is no reason why nominal lumber wouldn't work, though it should be a quality hardwood. A radial-arm saw is best for all the cuts and dadoes, but

Kitchen island didn't have enough space for heavy, bulky pans. Rather than cutting into island top, author notched uprights with a dado blade on a radial-arm saw.

Holes for carriage bolts and nuts are countersunk with a ⅞-in. Forstener bit then drilled on center with a ⅜-in. bit. On the inside of the cabinet are large washers (1½ in.) against the cabinet wall, then a lock washer and nut. The carriage bolts at the top use standard washers. The detail at top right shows the profile of the top rack. The shelf holds lids, and the molding provides a rest for the long-stem wine glasses. J-hook attaches to oak slider with round-head wood screws.

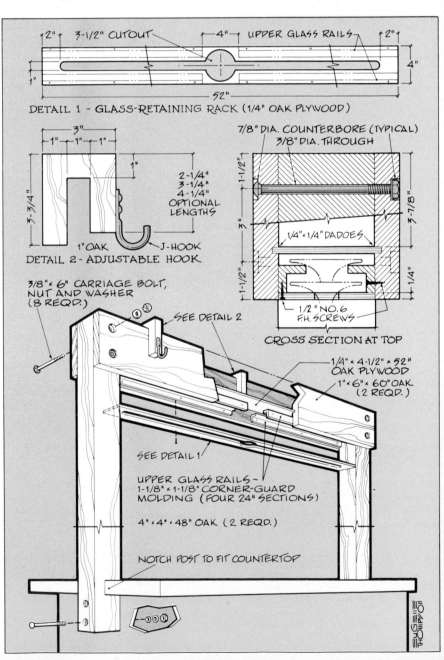

a table saw (with dado blades) would do just as well. The uprights are 48 inches long, which provides ample counter space below the rack; the rack causes no interference at the counter level, even when fully loaded.

To build the rack: Before assembling the pieces, drill and countersink the bolt holes, then dado the grooves on the inner face of each horizontal 1 × 6 to accept the ¼-inch-plywood upper shelf. After that, fasten 1¼-inch corner molding on the inner face of both 1 × 6s. Use flathead wood screws. The molding runs from the faces of the 4 × 4 uprights to within two inches of the center cutout. If you're using glue, apply it to the shelf edges and clamp the assembly together.

To make the cutout in the hanger for the wine glasses, first mount a ¼-inch piece of oak plywood (cut to width and length) on a length of 1 × 6 pine, making sure it's square; this is a backup piece to add working stability. Rip parallel cuts as shown. Now, with a coping saw, fashion the two semi-circular finish cuts on either end and the large insertion cutout in the center. Fit the finished piece onto the bottom of the rack, and (with the lid shelf in place) attach it with ½-inch brass screws to the corner molding.

Finish to suit, assemble the rack and uprights, then fasten the uprights to the island. The utensils hang from chrome hooks on sliding wooden hangers, which are finished to match—*By W. David Houser. Photos by the author.*

How far should glasses extend? You can choose by placing them in the rack—the long-stem glasses go on the inner molding, and the short-stem glasses hang from the cutout at the bottom of the horizontal assembly. The hooks fit on either side of the rack. Each hook is a different length to accommodate different-size pots and pans.

easy-to-build home design center

Design center holds matte boards and architectural-style drawings conveniently. Supplies go on shelves and in drawers.

If you or someone in your family constantly clutters the house with large matte boards and rolls of working drawings, this home design center can help eliminate the mess. It provides ample work space along with a place to store art supplies of all sizes conveniently.

The project was designed by Clell Boyce for Louisiana-Pacific Corp. (111 S.W. Fifth Ave., Portland, Ore. 97201) to show the versatility of Waferwood, L-P's brand of waferboard.

The design center consists of three basic cubes—small, medium, and large. Its base is made of waferboard, which is braced to support the weight of the drawers and cabinetry. Included are rolled-paper holders and a board holder tucked out of the way below the counter top. For this project, the counter top is covered with plastic laminate for a smooth writing surface, but the rest of the unit is coated with clear polyurethane.

Waferboard sands to a clean edge with fine-grain sandpaper, but where an especially smooth edge is desired, apply wood-filler paste, sand lightly, and finish. For variety, you can use standard wood molding nailed and glued in place; corner-guard molding wraps around an edge and half-round molding covers it, adding a softer look.

Most of the joints in the design center are butt joints held with small nails or screws and glue. There should be no problem with these simple joints, as long as they are not overly stressed.

Cut out the pieces carefully. Glue and nail together with 4d finishing nails to form the basic boxes. When assembling the boxes, match diagonal measurements (measure from corner to corner) to be sure each box is square. Attach backs with glue and ¾-inch brads.

The rolled-paper storage rack is made of a series of mailing tubes glued together. The door below is made of waferboard with a piece of plastic laminate cemented to it—*By Charles A. Miller.*

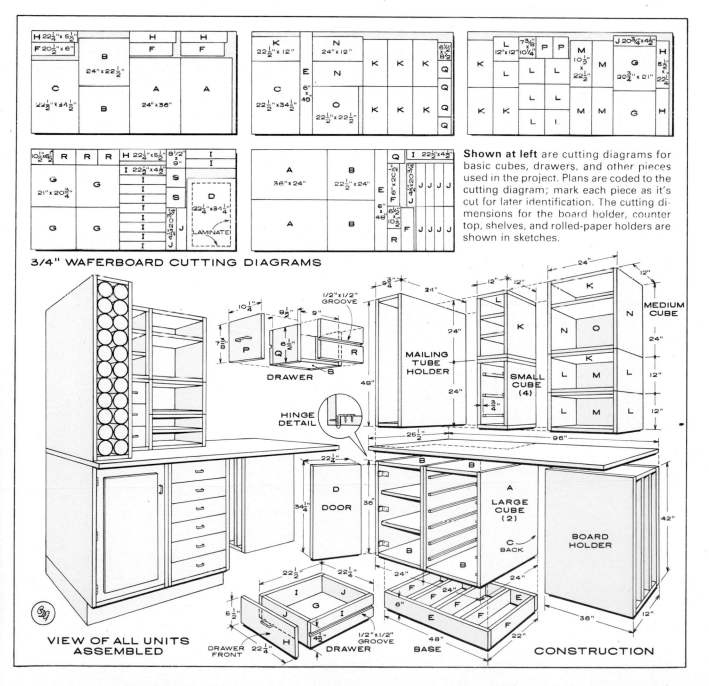

3/4" WAFERBOARD CUTTING DIAGRAMS

Shown at left are cutting diagrams for basic cubes, drawers, and other pieces used in the project. Plans are coded to the cutting diagram; mark each piece as it's cut for later identification. The cutting dimensions for the board holder, counter top, shelves, and rolled-paper holders are shown in sketches.

VIEW OF ALL UNITS ASSEMBLED

DRAWER

BASE

CONSTRUCTION

colonial dollhouse

The Stanley Colonial Dollhouse is based on an actual house built in the "1776" period in New England. This house is still in use today and is an excellent example of a most attractive, sturdy, functional and lasting form of domestic architecture.

Families were big, so there were many bedrooms. People didn't have many clothes, so there were no bedroom closets. And of course, there were no bathrooms since indoor plumbing did not come into general use until late in the nineteenth century.

There were fireplaces in almost every room since there was no such thing as central heating. All cooking was done over the open fire in the kitchen-keeping room. It became the most important room in the house, the place where the entire family would gather for meals, warmth, and companionship.

On the third floor or attic there was often a smoke oven for smoking hams, sides of bacon, and game. Hickory bark or corncobs were burned in the oven to provide the smoke.

We have adapted the room arrangements of the original house so the plan functions well as a dollhouse. We have also changed certain materials so the dollhouse can be built with supplies that are readily available. For example, door hinges in Colonial houses were generally wrought iron strap, H, or H-L hinges made by a local blacksmith. But because miniature versions of these are not commonly available, we have used butt hinges instead.

These plans provide detailed instructions for making an authentic replica, like the realistic model in the photograph. You can also make a simpler version. Just build the basic structure out of plywood, paint it, and add shadows to give the appearance of real shingles and siding. For an easy window substitute, use clear plastic with painted white divider strips stapled to the inside of the window opening.

General Construction:

Exploded view shows method of construction. First, build base and then add the two end panels. Next, install the first floor partition, then add the second floor along with its partitions and stairs from first to second floor. Install third floor and partitions and stairs. Add front and rear panels. Add fixed section of roof, then movable sections of roof and, finally, the chim-

MATERIALS FOR BASIC HOUSE:

3 sheets—4′ × 8′ × ⅜″ plywood—two sides good
18′—1 × 2 for base and blocking
7′—1 × 1 for corner posts, front and back steps
6 flathead screws—1¼″ No. 10 for end panels
1 box No. 18 brads 1″ long
1 box No. 18 brads ¾″ long
1 box No. 18 brads ½″ long—for trim
Carpenter's white wood glue
Hinges*: 6—¾″ × ⅝″ for roof
　　　　4—¾″ × ⅝″ for front and back door
　　　　8—1½″ × ⅞″ for front and rear panels

Note: Balsa and basswood required if you install trim, paneling,
stairs, windows, etc., are available at hobby shops.
*Stanley Classic Brassware solid brass hinges.

Please note that the overall dimensions of the Colonial Dollhouse are 38″ long, 30″ wide and 30″ high. If you plan to move the dollhouse from the area in which it is built, measure doorways, etc., to make sure the dollhouse can be moved through easily.

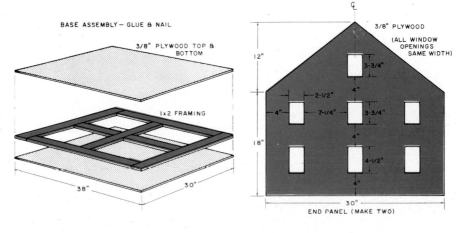

ney. Siding and roofing go on last.

To insure a perfect match of identical elements—base panels, floor panels, end panels, front and rear panels and movable section of roof—clamp the pieces together and cut both at the same time. If you are going to install the wood windows, openings for them must be cut very accurately to insure a perfect fit.

Because of restricted access, complete each floor—painting, staining, paneling, trim, wallpaper, etc., before proceeding with next floor. Apply wallpaper before installing interior trim, chair rails, and corner posts. Paint all interior and exterior trim and elements for windows before cutting to size. Use glue and ½-inch brads to apply all trim.

Detailed dimensions on drawings show measurements to fractional parts of an inch, but variations are bound to occur as the work progresses, so measure for each element and make necessary adjustments as needed—*Courtesy of The Stanley Works.*

Build base

1. Use glue and one-in. brads to assemble 1 × 2 frame and plywood panels. Stain or paint top of upper panel that serves as first floor. Make up the two end panels, and cut openings for windows with brace and bit and keyhole saw. Note the first-floor windows are taller than those on second and third floors. Secure panels to base with glue and three 1¼-in. screws per panel.

Install first floor partitions

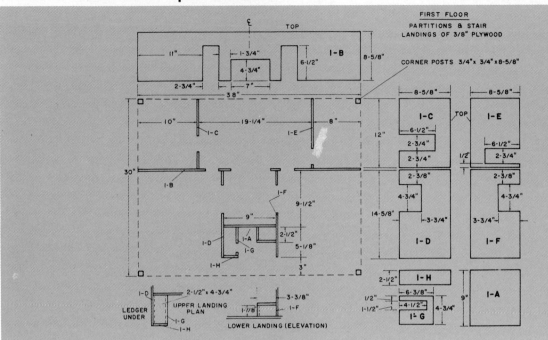

2. Start with center partition B. Temporarily tack this into place and then C and E. Add panel A—the chimney enclosure. Add partitions D, F, H, and G. Note height of G is only 6⅜ in. The upper landing of stairs will rest on top of G. You can indicate the understairs closet door on G with trim rather than installing a hinged door.

Remove partitions and install paneling if desired. Details of paneling are given in Fig. 11.

Before final installation of partitions, apply wallpaper, if desired, to exterior walls in dining room and parlor. Seal the plywood first with latex paint. Coat back of paper with wallpaper paste or dilute white glue and allow to remain until paper is damp before applying paper. Install trim around windows, corner posts and chair rails (Fig. 12). On all non-paneled walls ³⁄₃₂-by-⅛-in. chair rails can be set 2½ in. above floor. Install partitions with glue and ¾-in. brads toe-nailed into floor.

You'll need nine pieces of ³⁄₃₂-by-⅜-in.-by-36-in. long balsa for all the interior trim and paneling for a room. You will also need four pieces of ⅛-by-4-in. basswood 22 in. long for panels for all the paneled walls. For fireplace details, see Fig. 13.

Add second floor

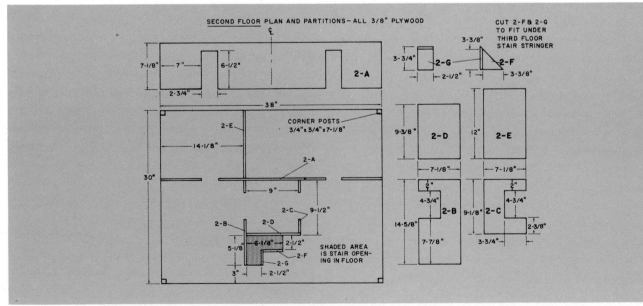

3. Cut L-shaped opening in floor panel for stairs. Paint underside of floor panel that serves as first-floor ceiling. Secure floor panel to end panels with glue and one-in. brads. Add support to first floor partitions by driving ¾-in. brads through second floor into top edge of first floor partitions. Make up second floor partitions, and install in same manner as first floor partitions. You'll need five pieces of 36-in. long ³⁄₃₂-by-⅜-in. balsa for trim around second-floor windows and door and for chair rails.

Install first floor stairs

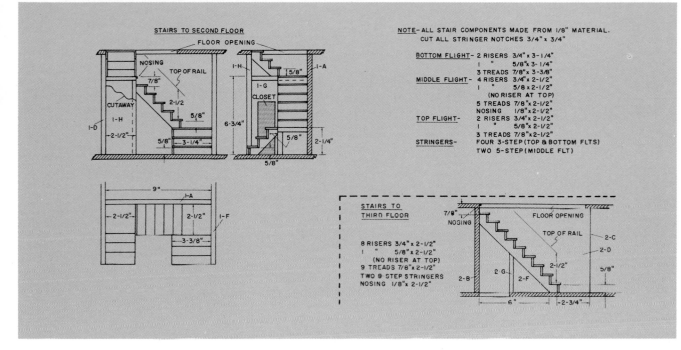

4. Make stringers out of ⅛-in. basswood. Glue inside stringers to wall. Outside stringers are glued at top and bottom to floor and landing. Install lower short stringer to wall. Construct lower landing with L-shaped support to hold it in place (Fig. 2). Add second short stringer, and glue to floor and lower landing. Install upper landing on top of partition G (Fig. 2). Glue inside stringer to wall, and fasten outside stringer with glue to lower and upper landing. Install upper short stringer. Attach risers first, then treads to stringers with glue. Drill ⅛-in. hole near end of each tread for balusters. Make balusters 2⅝ in. long from ⅛-in. dowel, and glue them into holes so they extend 2½ in. above treads. Make handrail out of ¼-by-¼ in. basswood. Round off top with sandpaper, and glue to balusters.

You'll need two pieces of ⅛-by-4-in. basswood 22 in. long and two 36-in. lengths of ⅛-in. dowels for both flights of stairs. Pattern for stair stringers is Fig. 15.

Add third-floor panel

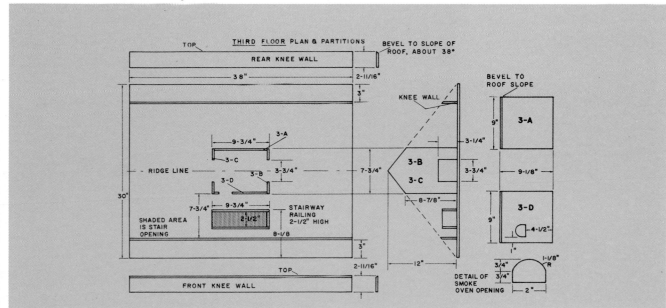

5. Cut opening for stairs, and attach panel to end panels. Install chimney enclosure. The pitch for the side pieces of this unit must match the pitch of the roof. Cut the two side pieces to correct width, then set them against end panel and use end panel as guide to mark correct angle for cut. Make openings for fireplace and smoke oven. Install knee walls. Bevel top edge of walls to about 38 degrees to match pitch of roof. Install stairs (Fig. 4). Use ⅛-in. dowels and ¼-by-¼-in. basswood for railing around stair opening.

Make front and rear hinged panels

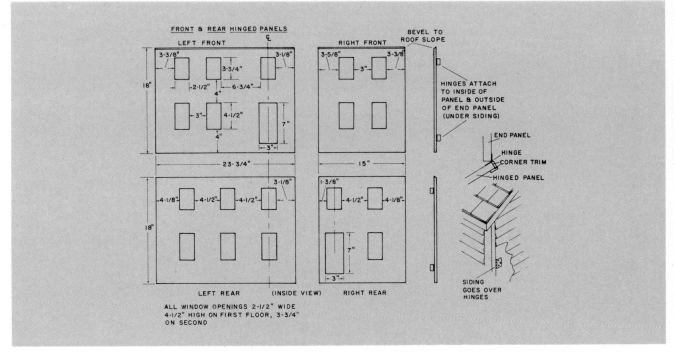

6. Cut both at same time, then cut each into two sections as shown in Fig. 6. Bevel top edge to about 38-degree angle to conform with roof angle. Cut opening for windows and doors. Center door openings on windows directly above. Attach panels to corners with two hinges per panel. Make up front and back doors (Fig. 14). Add outside steps made of 1 × 1.

Add roof and chimney

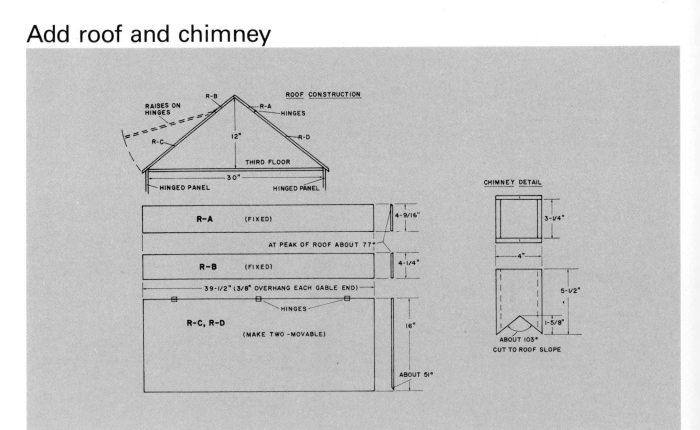

7. Install fixed section of roof, then attach movable sections of roof to fixed sections with three hinges per section. Install chimney (Fig. 7). If you cover it with chimney paper, apply before securing chimney to roof with glue and brads.

Make windows

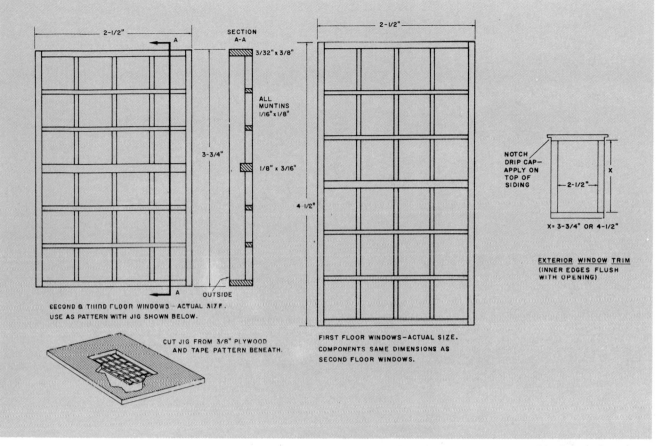

SECOND & THIRD FLOOR WINDOWS - ACTUAL SIZE.
USE AS PATTERN WITH JIG SHOWN BELOW.

CUT JIG FROM 3/8" PLYWOOD
AND TAPE PATTERN BENEATH.

FIRST FLOOR WINDOWS - ACTUAL SIZE.
COMPONENTS SAME DIMENSIONS AS
SECOND FLOOR WINDOWS.

EXTERIOR WINDOW TRIM
(INNER EDGES FLUSH
WITH OPENING)

8. These are made of three sizes of balsa—$\frac{3}{32}$-by-$\frac{3}{8}$-in., $\frac{1}{16}$-by-$\frac{1}{8}$-in., and $\frac{1}{8}$-by-$\frac{3}{16}$-in. An easy way to assemble the windows is to build a jig as shown in Fig. 8 out of $\frac{3}{8}$-in. plywood. Two jigs are required because the first-floor windows are higher than those on the second and third floors. Cut them out and lay them on the jig, and then cover with plastic so glue won't stick to the paper. Assemble all elements with glue. Install the windows and outside trim around them. If you are going to install clapboard siding, do not install the drip cap at top until after the siding is on. For each window and outside trim you will need one piece of $\frac{3}{32}$-by-$\frac{3}{8}$-in. balsa 36 in. long, $\frac{1}{16}$-by-$\frac{1}{8}$-in. balsa 25 in. long and $\frac{1}{8}$-by-$\frac{3}{16}$-in. balsa $2\frac{1}{2}$ in. long.

Apply the siding and roofing

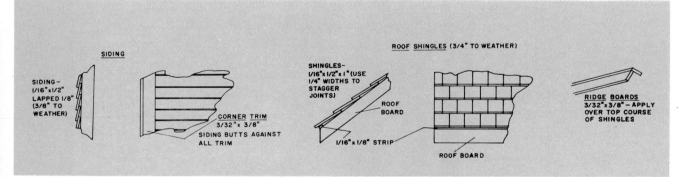

SIDING

SIDING—
1/16"x1/2"
LAPPED 1/8"
(3/8" TO
WEATHER)

CORNER TRIM
3/32" x 3/8"
SIDING BUTTS AGAINST
ALL TRIM

SHINGLES—
1/16"x1/2"x1" (USE
1/4" WIDTHS TO
STAGGER
JOINTS)

ROOF
BOARD

1/16"x1/8" STRIP

ROOF SHINGLES (3/4" TO WEATHER)

ROOF BOARD

RIDGE BOARDS
3/32"x3/8" – APPLY
OVER TOP COURSE
OF SHINGLES

9. First add the trim at corners. Manufactured dollhouse siding is available at many hobby shops, or it can be made with thin strips of balsa or thin cardboard cut from large sheets with paper cutter or utility knife. Paint siding before installing. Siding is easier to apply with staples than with glue. Install drip cap around windows after siding is on. You'll need four pieces of $\frac{3}{32}$-by-$\frac{3}{8}$-in. balsa 36 in. long for corner trim.

10. Apply $\frac{1}{16}$-by-$\frac{1}{8}$-in. eave board along edge of roof. Roof shingles should be $\frac{1}{2}$ in. wide and one-in. long laid $\frac{3}{4}$-in. to the weather. If table saw is available, cut $\frac{1}{16}$-in. strips out of $\frac{3}{4}$-in. cedar or pine and then cut to one-in. length with paper cutter. Shingles can also be made out of thin strips of cardboard. Dollhouse shingles are also available at many hobby shops.
  Apply shingles with staples or with glue. Install ridge boards and roof boards made of $\frac{3}{32}$-by-$\frac{3}{8}$-in. balsa.

Paneling

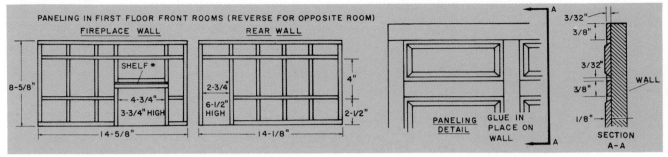

11. For paneling, install stiles and rails, then fit panels into place. Use utility knife to bevel edges of panels.

Fireplace

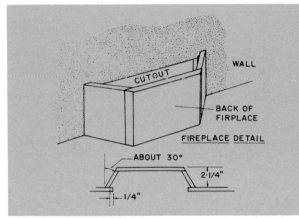

13. Fireplaces are made of three pieces of ⅜-in. plywood. Cut the edges of each piece at a slight angle so the sides will slant inward. Tack a piece of scrap to the floor inside the fireplace enclosure to hold the plywood pieces in place until glue has set. Paint inside of fireplaces black.

Front and back doors

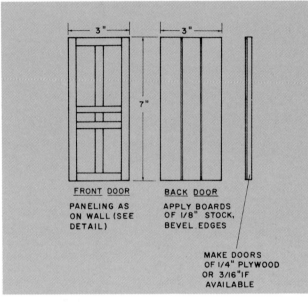

Molding and window molding

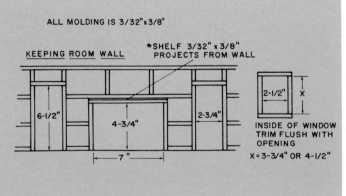

Pattern for stair stringers

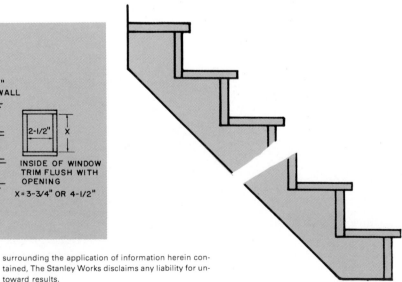

three-shelf bookcase

Construction Notes

This attractive bookcase is fairly simple to build and can be used in a living room, bedroom, or study.

The boards are ripped to size, with the shelves cut ¼ inch narrower than the sides to allow for the rabbet. The dadoes in the side pieces are made with the router or on the table saw. If a router is used, cut both sections at one time to ensure that the dadoes will be perfectly aligned. Fasten the pieces firmly to a flat surface, lay out the position of the dadoes, and clamp a straightedge to the work, allowing the proper clearance for the router base. Unless a hardwood is being used, the ¼-inch deep cut may be made in one pass. The tool should be fed slowly, and the base kept solidly against the straightedge.

After the dadoes are cut, the back edges of the side pieces are rabbeted. Then the curved sections are laid out and cut with a saber saw. After the sides are completed, rip the subtop to size. The widths of subtop and sides must match.

Before assembling the parts, a router with a rounding bit is used to round all exposed edges. The router must not be run through the dadoes, but should be stopped just short of them. Likewise, the rounding of the shelves should stop ¼ inch from the ends. Failure to do so will leave a gap at these points when the parts are later assembled.

Bore the screw and button holes as required, and then assemble the parts with glue and screws. The shelf ends should be glue-sized beforehand. The screws in the base piece are angled slightly into the end pieces, as shown in Detail E. The ends and front base piece are fastened with 1¼-inch FH screws driven from the inside. The base should be installed so that its upper edge is ¹⁄₁₆ inch above the bottom edge of the bottom shelf.

The subtop is fastened to the sides using two-inch finishing nails, driven from the topside into the rabbet.

Bore four ³⁄₁₆-inch screw clearance holes in the subtop one inch from the edges and two inches from each end. Fasten the top to the subtop with screws driven through these holes. Use 1¼″ FH screws. The top is centered from side to side, but it should project ¼ inch past the rear edge of the subtop. See Detail F.

Install the back panel with one-inch brads. Finish with stain and several topcoats of clear lacquer or varnish—*By John Capotosto.*

BILL OF MATERIALS

Except as noted, all lumber is pine.
All measurements are in inches.

Part	Description	Size	Qty.
1	Side	¾ × 9 × 42¼	2
2	Back, plywood	¼ × 33¾ × 40¼	1
3	Top	¾ × 8½ × 36¼	1
4	Subtop	¾ × 7 × 33¾	1
5	Skirt	¾ × 2¾ × 35½	1
6	Shelf	¾ × 8¾ × 33¾	3
7	Base	¾ × 4 × 36¼	1
8	Apron	¾ × 2 × 33¼	1
9	End	¾ × 4 × 9	2
10	Base, rear	¾ × 3¹⁵⁄₁₆ × 33¼	1
A	Screw	1½—8 FH	16
B	Screw	1¼—8 FH	4
C	Button	½ × ⅝	16
D	Finishing nail	2	4
E	Brad	1	18

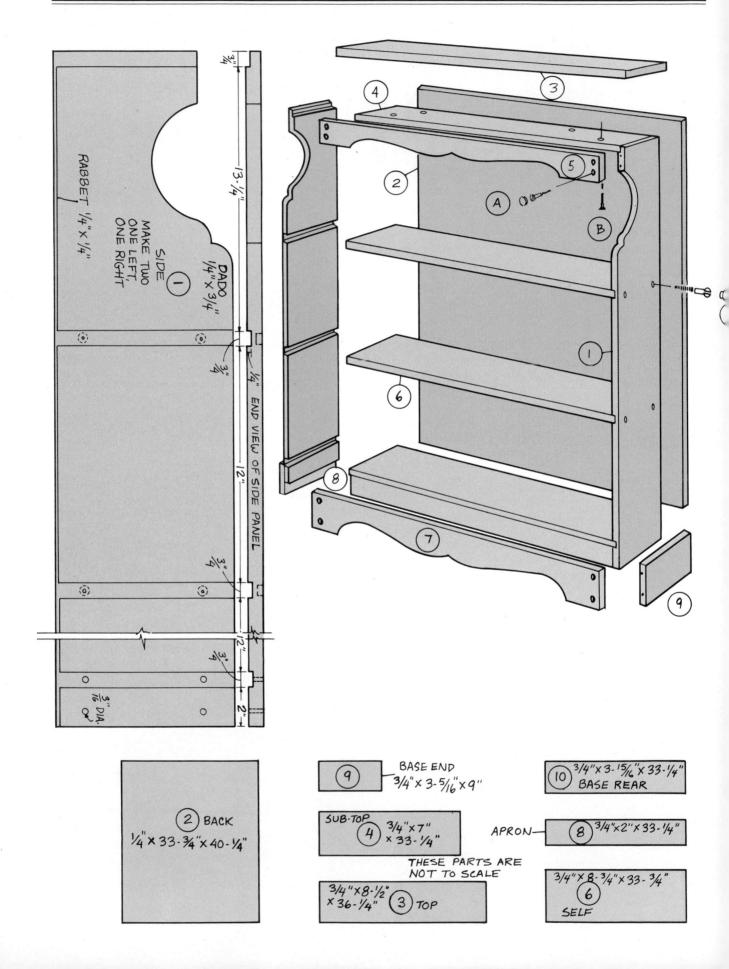

RABBET ¼" X ¼"

SIDE
MAKE TWO
ONE LEFT,
ONE RIGHT

DADO
¼" X ¾"

①

¾

13-¼"

¾"

¼"

END VIEW OF SIDE PANEL

12"

¾"

12"

¾"

2"

3/16 DIA.

② BACK
¼" X 33-¾" X 40-¼"

③
④
⑤
Ⓐ
Ⓑ
②
①
⑥
⑧
⑦
⑨

BASE END
3/4" X 3-5/16" X 9"
⑨

SUB-TOP
④ 3/4" X 7"
X 33-¼"

THESE PARTS ARE
NOT TO SCALE

3/4" X 8-½"
X 36-¼"   ③ TOP

⑩ 3/4" X 3-15/16" X 33-¼"
BASE REAR

APRON   ⑧ 3/4" X 2" X 33-¼"

3/4" X 8-¾" X 33-¾"
⑥
SELF

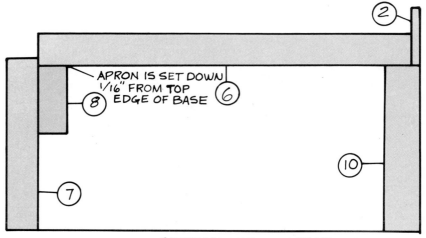

SECTION THROUGH BASE

APRON IS SET DOWN
1/16" FROM TOP
EDGE OF BASE

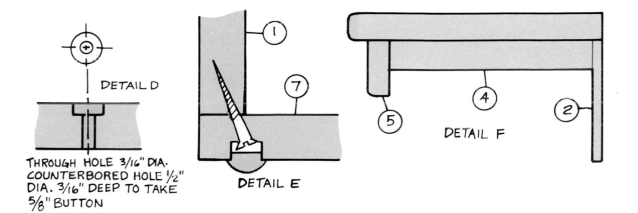

DETAIL D

THROUGH HOLE 3/16" DIA.
COUNTERBORED HOLE 1/2"
DIA. 3/16" DEEP TO TAKE
5/8" BUTTON

DETAIL E

DETAIL F

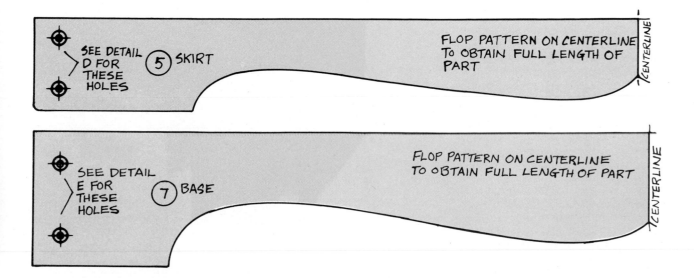

SEE DETAIL
D FOR
THESE
HOLES

SKIRT

FLOP PATTERN ON CENTERLINE
TO OBTAIN FULL LENGTH OF
PART

CENTERLINE

SEE DETAIL
E FOR
THESE
HOLES

BASE

FLOP PATTERN ON CENTERLINE
TO OBTAIN FULL LENGTH OF PART

CENTERLINE

working with waferboard

Waferboard is not particle-board or the old rough-faced chipboard, but a factory-sanded panel you can use anywhere you'd use plywood. It's formed of layers of wafers chipped from either hard-wood or softwood logs (usually aspen or poplar—woods of little other commercial value). These wafers are coated with wax and waterproof resin, deposited in layers, and fused under heat and pressure into various thicknesses. As with plywood, these range from ¼ to ¾ inches. Panels are then factory-trimmed to four-by-eight-foot sizes.

Waferboard is easier to buy than plywood since you needn't fret about choosing the right grade for the job: All panels are made the same way, so, properly finished, they're all appropriate for both indoor and outdoor projects. (Particleboard is meant for indoor use only.)

Unlike softwood plywood, whose wild surface grain must nearly always be tamed with pigmented sealer before you hide it under a coat of paint, a waferboard surface presents a mosaic of large hardwood chips that I find singularly attractive when varnished or shellacked.

You can, of course, get many special effects by letting a base-coat stain or paint dry thoroughly before brushing on a contrasting color and then wiping the surface, leaving the second coat only in the depressions. If you choose to enamel waferboard, you'll get a textured surface that suggests rough plaster.

Both treating edges and finishing exposed rear faces can be simpler than with most plywood. Since the panel is of the same layered-wafer structure throughout, you'll find no core voids or knotholes to fill.

I've worked with all standard panel materials, and I don't find waferboard any harder to handle than plywood or particleboard. Generally, it falls between those two in weight and workability, because it's between them in its wood-to-resin ratio. Since particle-board must use a lot of resin to bind its wood fragments, it's the heaviest panel—and the one that dulls cutting tools fastest. (A panel of ¾-inch waferboard weighs about 80 pounds.)

Use the same tools you'd choose for plywood. Waferboard saws, drills, and glues easily (its dense edge grain actually takes nails and screws better than plywood edges). A fine-toothed crosscut saw with little set will produce a smoother cut than a large-toothed rip blade with heavy set. A smooth-cutting carbide-tipped blade is

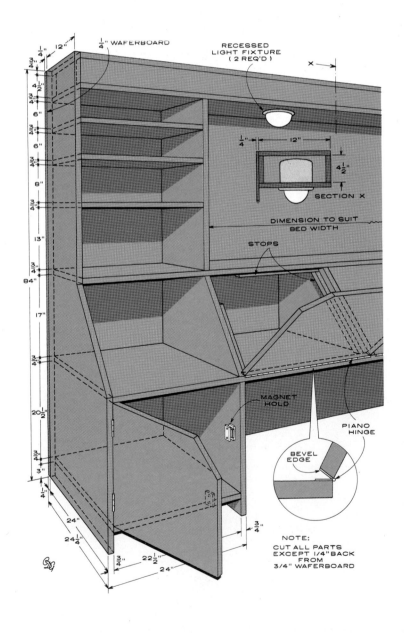

best for circular saws. In my saber saw, an extra-fine woodcutting blade breezed through a ¾-inch panel.

In using waferboard for indoor projects, should you fret about formaldehyde outgassing? No, say the makers: The phenolic resins used in waferboard don't have any significant formaldehyde emission levels.

In laying out your projects on a waferboard panel, you can forget about grain direction. Most panels are formed from a random placement of wafers, so there's equal strength in all directions. Since waferboard is regularly used in home building—as sheathing, underlayment, and roof decking—its strength and stability are well documented.

One caution, though: Surface wafers

Storage headboard is made of ¾-in. panels edged with lattice strips and backed with ¼-in. waferboard—all finished with clear sealer. Projecting handles on compartment doors have been eliminated by cutting corners to serve as finger grips.

Organ-pipe planters, cut from single ¾-in. column (as shown in sketch, next page), can be clustered in many arrangements. Planter faces are coated with an exterior sealer, then white enamel is applied to all exposed edges as an accent.

Barbecue cart is cut from ¾-in.-thick waferboard and painted with exterior enamels. Rough surfaces give textured effect. Edges are painted in contrasting terra cotta, as are shelf lips and dowel handle; cart is mounted on casters.

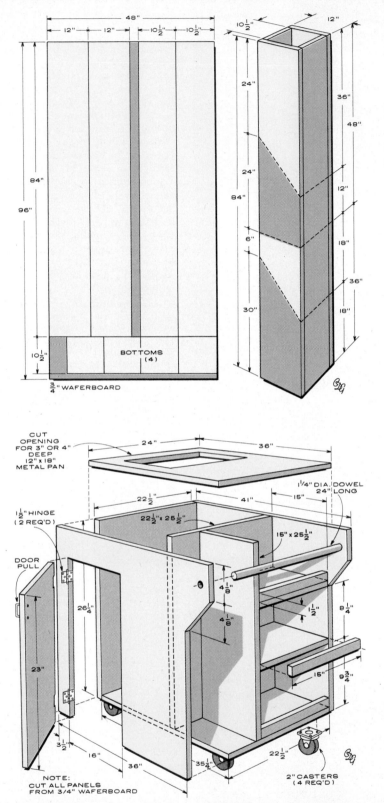

Pro woodworker Rosario Capotosto took these shots in his shop and offers these comments: (1) Face "good" side down when cutting panels with portable circular or saber saw; clamp straightedge for best cut. (2) Cabinet scraper with "turned" edge does quick job of removing saw ripples. (3) Gang-sand exposed edges to save time; broad edge offers flat surface for belt sander. (4) Cut mortises with saber saw, then true cuts with router and flush-trimming bit.

at the edges can be torn loose with rough handling, so don't drag panels around before you've got a protective finish on them. If a wafer lifts in sawing, you can fasten it back with glue and masking tape.

The major U.S. manufacturer of these panels is Louisiana-Pacific, under the brand name Waferwood. We asked L-P to create projects for us that would demonstrate the versatility and natural beauty of Waferwood; then we asked them to send panels for us to work with in our own shop. Our experience has confirmed our initial impression: Waferboard is a fine home-shop alternative to plywood—at a lower price—*By Al Lees*

cedar closet

I f you stash winter clothes just anywhere for the summer, moths or mildew could mean you'll need a new wardrobe in the fall. The cure is cedar. The natural aroma of the wood smells good to us, but not to flying feeders. It also discourages mildew. And cedar is flaked and pressed into four-by-eight-foot sheets—no need for the old tongue-and-groove boards that required time and a professional touch to assemble.

The free-standing closet shown is framed with 2×4 stock and covered with ⅝-inch exterior plywood. Nail the ply to the framing in order: floor, sides, back, and ceiling. Then, in the same order, line the closet—plus the door panels—with the cedar sheets, using nails or panel adhesive. The sheets must be cut with a saw—do not try to score and snap. Save the remnants to line shelves. Install the clothes rod at a convenient height.

Finally, add weatherstripping around the doors for an airtight seal. Magnetic catches will keep them closed yet allow them to be opened from the inside for safety. Once complete, don't finish or paint: This would seal the panels, making them useless.

Although a free-standing closet is shown here, it's even easier to construct a built-in cedar closet. For new construction, the panels are nailed or glued directly to open studding (if local building codes permit it). For installation over a finished wall, use 1¼-inch finishing nails spaced every 12 inches vertically at each stud position.

Cedar panels are available through local lumberyards, and more information—including an idea booklet and a panel sample—is available for 50 cents from Giles & Kendall, Box 188, Huntsville, Ala. 35804—*By William J. Hawkins. Drawing by Gerhard Richter.*

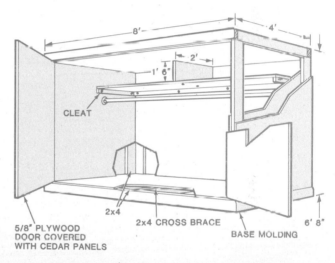

CLEAT

8'

4'

2'

1' 6'

5/8" PLYWOOD DOOR COVERED WITH CEDAR PANELS

2x4

2x4 CROSS BRACE

BASE MOLDING

6' 8"

home finance center

The design of this home finance center is based on the dimensions of a legal-size envelope (4¼ by 9½ inches). These envelopes containing receipts, statements, canceled checks, etc., can be filed in the top compartments. Movable dividers are provided for flexible organization. At the end of each year, all of the envelopes can be banded together and placed in the long-term storage compartment in the bottom of the cabinet. The shelves are movable to suit your storage needs.

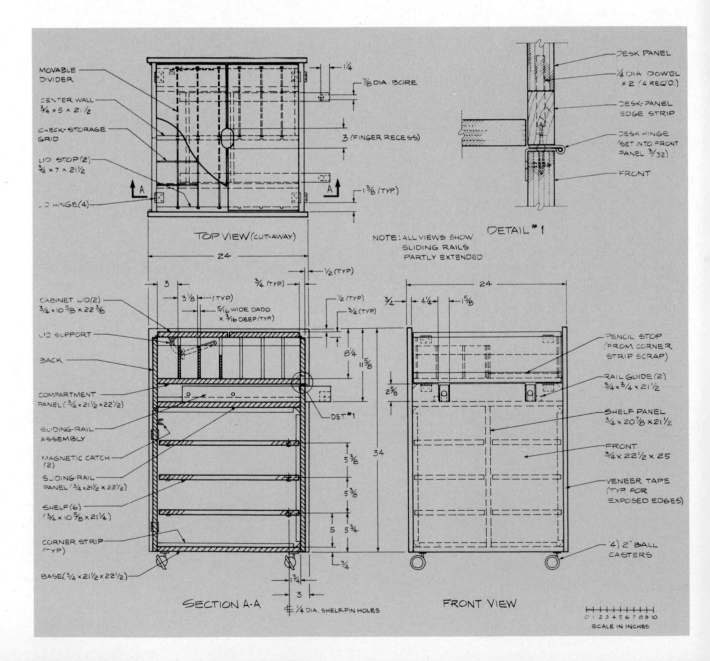

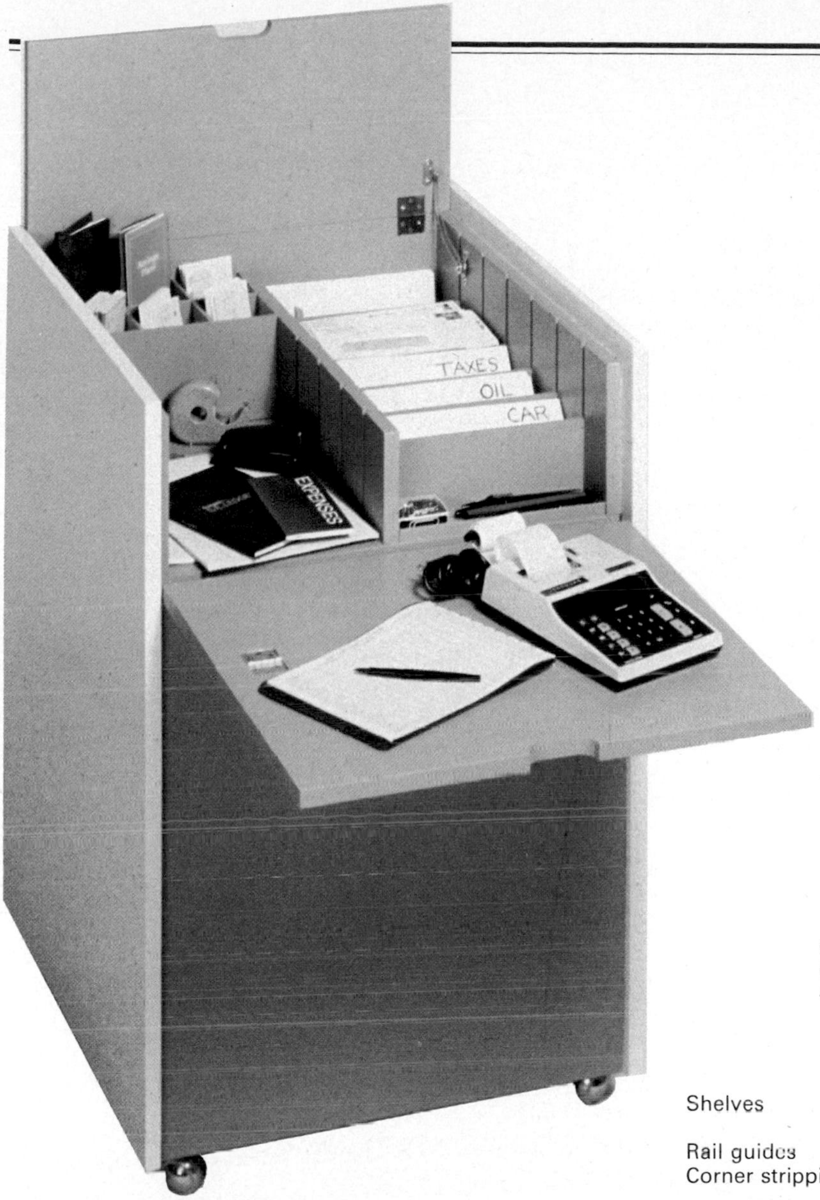

MATERIALS AND SPECIFICATIONS

Item	Quantity	Description
Sides	2	¾″ × 24″ × 34″ birch plywood
Front	1	¾″ × 22½″ × 25″ birch plywood
Back	1	¾″ × 11⅛″ × 22½″ birch plywood
Compartment panel	1	¾″ × 21½″ × 22½″ birch plywood
Lid stops	2	¾″ × 7″ × 21½″ birch plywood
Center wall	1	¾″ × 5″ × 21½″ birch plywood
Cabinet lids	2	¾″ × 10⅝″ × 22⅜″ birch plywood
Desk panel	1	¾″ × 6¼″ × 22⅜″ birch plywood
Storage doors	2	¾″ × 11⅛″ × 21½″ birch plywood
Base	1	¾″ × 21½″ × 22½″ A-C plywood
Sliding-rail panel	1	¾″ × 21½″ × 22½″ A-C plywood
Shelf panel	1	¾″ × 20⅞″ × 21½″ A-C plywood
Shelves	6	¾″ × 10⅝″ × 21¼″ A-C plywood
Rail guides	2	¾″ × ¾″ × 21½″ pine
Corner stripping	—	⅝″ × ⅝″ × 45° chamfer strip (200 linear inches)
Sliding rails	2	1½″ × 2½″ × 22¼″ pine
Cross ties	2	½″ dia. × 13¾″ wood dowel
Desk-panel edge strip	1	¾″ × 1½″ × 22⅜″ pine
Edge-strip dowels	4	¼″ dia. × 2″ wood dowel
Movable dividers	7	¼″ × 3½″ × 10⁷⁄₁₆″ hardboard

CHECK-STORAGE GRID

Item	Quantity	Description
Long walls	2	¼″ × 5″ × 10⁷⁄₁₆″ hardboard
Short walls	2	¼″ × 5″ × 6⅜″ hardboard
Lid hinges	4	1½″ × 2″ (open) brass hinges
Desk hinges (storage-door hinges)	6	1½″ wide offset cabinet hinge for ¾″ thick doors (brass plated)
Lid support	1	Right-hand brass-plated lid support
Door catches	2	Standard magnetic cabinet-door catches
Casters	4	2″ plate mounting brass-colored ball casters
Shelf supports	24	Plastic shelf pins
Veneer tape	—	¾″ wide birch veneer tape
Glue	—	Wood glue
Nails	—	3d finishing nails
	4	6d finishing nails
	—	1″ wire brads
Paint	—	Latex paint
Filler	—	Latex wood filler

Construction

1. Cut the sides to size.
2. On the sides, lay out the locations of the compartment panel, the base, the sliding-rail panel, the front and back, and the shelf-pin holes.
3. Drill ¼-inch-diameter holes ½ inch deep for the shelf pins.
4. Cut the front to size. Lay out and cut two 2⅝-inch-deep-by-1⅝-inch-wide notches in the top edge of the front to allow a passageway for the sliding rails.
5. Install two desk hinges on the top edge of the front, setting the hinges ³⁄₃₂ inch into the top edge.

12. Glue and nail the center wall to the compartment panel.
13. Cut the shelf panel to size.
14. Drill shelf-pin holes in the shelf panel.
15. Glue and nail the shelf panel between the sliding-rail panel and the base.
16. Cut the corner stripping (used to strengthen butt joints between panels) to size.
17. Glue and nail the compartment panel, the sliding-rail panel, the base, and the front to one of the sides. Do not attach the back. (You may find it easiest to attach corner stripping to the sides at this time, before assembly.)

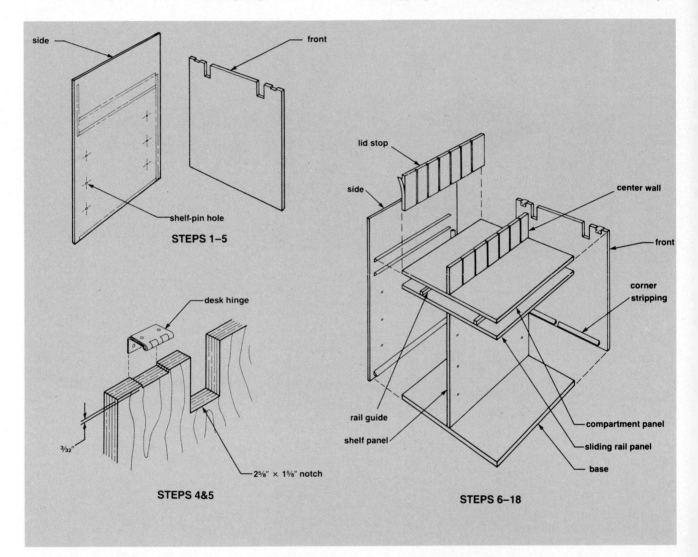

side

front

shelf-pin hole

STEPS 1–5

desk hinge

³⁄₃₂″

2⅝″ × 1⅝″ notch

STEPS 4&5

lid stop

side

center wall

front

corner stripping

rail guide

shelf panel

compartment panel

sliding rail panel

base

STEPS 6–18

6. Cut the back, the base, the sliding-rail panel, and the rail guides to size.
7. Attach the rail guides to the "C" side of the sliding-rail panel with glue and nails.
8. Cut the compartment panel, the lid stops, and the center wall of the top compartment to size.
9. Using an electric iron, apply veneer tape to the top and front edges of the center wall and the lid stops.
10. Machine six dadoes, ³⁄₁₆ inch deep and ⁵⁄₁₆ inch wide, on the inside face of each lid stop.
11. Machine six dadoes on both faces of the center wall. Make sure that the spacing of the dadoes from back to front is identical to that of the lid stops.

18. Glue and nail the other side in place. Glue and nail the lid stops in place.
19. Cut the sliding rails to size.
20. Drill two ½-inch-diameter holes through each sliding rail.
21. Cut the cross ties for the sliding rails to size.
22. Drill a ⅞-inch-diameter fingerhole 1¾ inches deep into the end of each sliding rail.
23. Drill a ⅞-inch-diameter hole into the bottom of each sliding rail intersecting the hole from Step 22.
24. Glue and nail the sliding rails onto the cross ties.
25. Insert the sliding-rail assembly between the compartment panel and the sliding-rail panel.

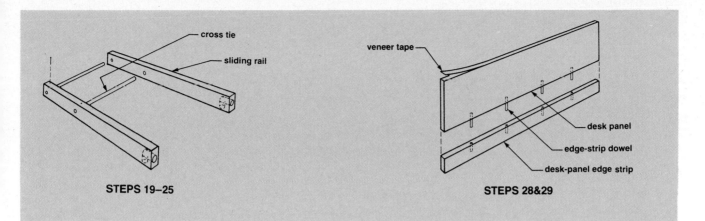

STEPS 19–25

STEPS 28&29

cross tie

sliding rail

veneer tape

desk panel

edge-strip dowel

desk-panel edge strip

26. Cut the cabinet lids to size.

27. Cut a finger recess into one edge of each lid.

28. Cut the desk panel and the desk-panel edge strip to size.

29. Attach the edge strip to the desk panel by drilling four ¼-inch-diameter holes into each and attaching with the edge-strip dowels.

30. Apply veneer tape to cover all end grain of lids and desk panel and the top edge of the back panel.

31. Hinge together the back panel and one of the lid panels. Set the hinges in ³⁄₃₂ inch, or until the crack between the panels is minimal.

32. Hinge together the desk panel with the second lid, setting the hinges as in Step 31. (All lid hinges will be removed for painting.)

33. Glue and nail the back panel in place.

34. Apply veneer tape to the exposed edges of the sides.

35. Cut the shelves to size. Trim one corner of each shelf as needed to clear the corner strips adjoining the front and side panels.

36. Cut the storage doors to size. Drill a ⅞-inch-diameter fingerhole in each door.

37. Cut the pencil stop to size. Glue and nail the pencil stop in the top compartment.

38. Cut the movable dividers of the top compartment and the long and short walls of the check-storage grid to size.

39. Cut two ¼-inch-wide by-2½-inch-long notches across each long wall of the check-storage grid. Cut notches, also ¼ inch wide and 2½ inches long at the center and at one end of the short walls of the grid.

40. Assemble the check-storage grid by gluing the long and short walls at the notches to form cross-lap joints.

41. Apply wood filler where needed, and sand all surfaces until smooth. Paint all parts the color of your choice.

42. Reinstall all lid hinges. Hinge the storage doors to the sides. Install a magnetic catch for each storage door and a lid support.

43. Install the shelf pins and shelves.

44. Install the casters on the base.

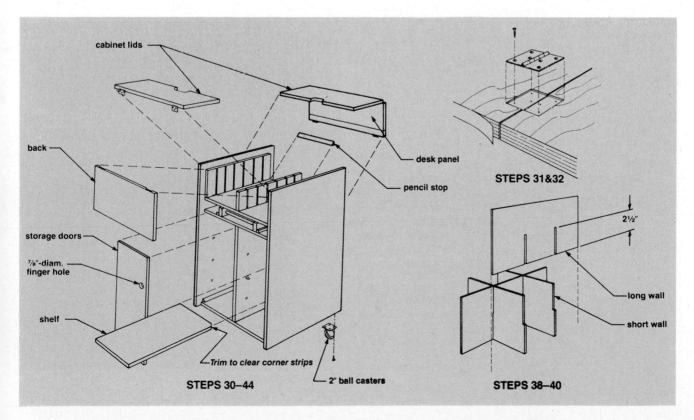

cabinet lids

back

storage doors

⅞"-diam. finger hole

shelf

desk panel

pencil stop

Trim to clear corner strips

2" ball casters

STEPS 30–44

STEPS 31&32

2½"

long wall

short wall

STEPS 38–40

queen anne corner table

This small Queen Anne table with its graceful and simple lines can add elegance to a corner of almost any room. As the table is decorated on all sides, it can also be reversed and used as an occasional table against a wall.

It is an easy piece of furniture to build because the legs are purchased. Our legs came from the Door Store of Washington, D.C. A set of three ash 27¼-inch Queen Anne legs costs $75, plus U.P.S. shipping. The address is 3140 M Street, Washington, D.C. 20007; phone (202) 333-7737.

There are other sources for Queen Anne legs, and you might be able to find them in mahogany or walnut. The shape of the legs are not standard, however, and buying the legs for your table should be the first step. You might have to change the dimensions of the apron pieces to match them.

You will need about four board feet of ¾-inch ash lumber for the top and aprons. Lay out all the pieces before doing any cutting. If possible, for easier clamping, leave the ends of the top pieces squared until after you glue up the top.

Sand the glued-up top flat, and dress the edges square and to accurate dimension for routing the edge thumbnail molding. I used a ball-bearing-piloted ½-inch radius corner rounding bit for the top and a piloted ¼-inch radius corner rounding bit for the bottom of the edge. Sand the edges to remove tool marks, and round off the corners for safety.

Blank the aprons, and dress them to ¹¹⁄₁₆-inch thickness (don't scroll the edges yet). Square and bevel the ends to the angles shown. The ¹¹⁄₁₆-inch thickness is necessary if the legs are to be attached to the aprons with three-inch hanger bolts—longer bolts will allow thicker aprons. Slot the aprons for the table-top fasteners. Draw full-size patterns for the lower edges, and saw the edges. A band saw, scroll saw, or saber saw can be used. Sand the edges with a drum sander.

The corner blocks can be made from any hardwood. Blank them, and bevel the ends as shown. Drilling mating holes for the screws must be done carefully if the table is to go together accurately. The angle of the holes is also important because the wrong angle will make driving the screws difficult. Initially, for No. 10 screws, drill pilot holes in the blocks using a No. 28 drill.

The tops of two legs have to be trimmed to match the 45-degree apron angle. Note that all this leg trimming is on the outside exposed surfaces—the sides of the legs that mate with the aprons are not touched. Remove material with chisel and Surform rasp, then sand smooth. Drill holes in the legs for the hanger bolts. Either size bolt can be used. For a neater job when threading in the hanger bolts, counterbore clearance holes in the legs ¼ inch deep before drilling the pilot holes.

The aprons and blocks must be positioned in a jig for assembly. To make a jig, I clamped a triangle of 2 × 2s to my bench, to surround the legs and aprons. The aprons were then clamped to the 2 × 2s, with ⅛-inch thick shims, as I wanted the aprons set back from the legs. The legs are used to line up the aprons, but they are not part of the assembly at this time and are not clamped. Check the ends of the aprons—the curve of the scrolled edges should flow into the curve of the legs nicely.

The corner table is finished on all sides and, therefore, can be reversed if desired.

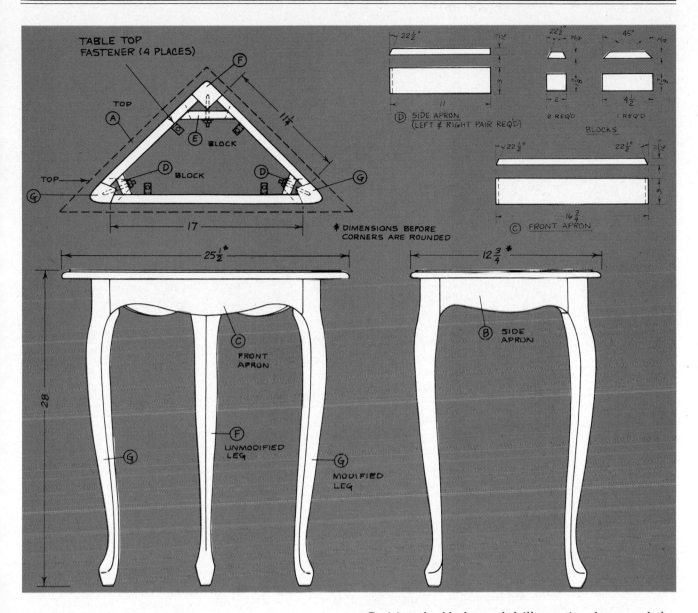

SHOPPING LIST

QUANTITY	ITEM
4 board feet	¾" ash
3	27¼" ash Queen Anne legs
4	¼" by 3" or ⁵⁄₁₆" by 3" hanger bolts
4	Steel table-top fasteners
—	Brown mahogany stain
—	Walnut paste filler
—	ZAR Quick Dry varnish
—	ZAR Gloss Polyurethane varnish

CUTTING LIST

KEY	QTY.	PART NAME	SIZE AND DESCRIPTION
A	1	Top	¾" ash, 12¾" × 25½"
B	2	Side apron	¾" ash, 3" × 11"
C	1	Front apron	¾" ash, 3" × 16¾"
D	2	Corner block	¾" hardwood, 1⅞" × 2"
E	1	Corner block	¾" hardwood, 1⅞" × 4½"
F	1	Back leg	27¼" ash Queen Anne leg
G	2	Front leg	27¼" ash Queen Anne leg (modified)

Position the blocks, and drill oversize clearance holes for the hanger bolts, then bolt the blocks in position with the nuts finger tight only. With the blocks held in position against the aprons, pass the No. 28 drill through the holes in the blocks and drill mating holes in the aprons.

Remove the blocks, drill body clearance holes, and countersink; then glue and screw the blocks to the aprons. When the glue is dry, you can glue the legs to the aprons if desired: I did not as I wanted to be able to disassemble the table.

We finished the table with brown mahogany stain, walnut paste wood filler, two coats of ZAR Quick Dry Varnish and two coats of ZAR Gloss Polyurethane varnish. Both varnishes were sanded between coats; the final coat was steel wooled (No. 000) before waxing. The underside of the top received all varnish coats to help prevent warping.

After finishing, the top is attached to the frame with steel top fasteners that seat into the slots in the inside surface of the aprons. These fasteners allow movement of the top relative to the apron with changes in humidity and prevent cracking.

A three-legged table has a unique advantage—even with an uneven floor, it won't wobble!—*By Thomas H. Jones. Drawings by Mel Erikson.*

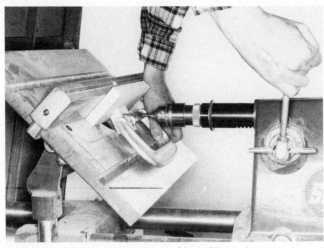

Drilling Screw Body Hole in Corner Block. Pilot holes are enlarged and countersunk after drilling mating holes in aprons. Body drill should produce a loose fit for screw. C-clamp provides safe handle for small part holding.

Corner Construction Detail

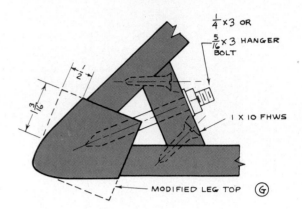

Table-Frame Assembly. A jig consisting of three 2 × 2s is clamped to the workbench to surround and position the legs and aprons. The aprons are clamped to the jig with ⅛-in. thick shims as shown to set back the aprons. The legs are held against the apron ends with the corner blocks and hanger bolts. Apron scrollwork is checked for fit against legs and trimmed if necessary.

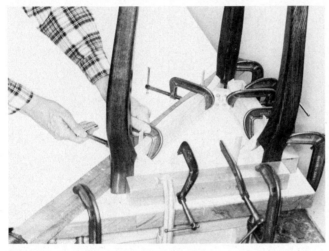

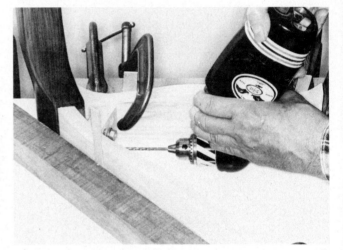

Drilling Screw Pilot Holes in Aprons. A No. 28 (for No. 10 wood screws) drill is run through previously drilled pilot holes in corner block and into the apron. The drilling angle is selected for electric drill and screwdriver clearance.

Top Attachment Detail

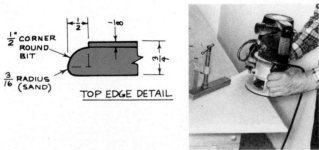

Routing Edge of Top. The thumbnail molding on the edge of the table top can be routed using a ball-bearing-piloted ½-in. rounding over bit from the top, and a piloted ¼-in. rounding over bit from the bottom.

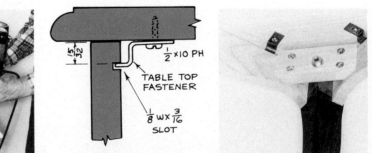

Table Construction. Aprons and corner blocks are assembled with screws and glue. Each leg is pulled tight against the ends of the aprons by means of a hanger bolt threaded into the leg and secured to the corner block with a nut and washer. The leg is not glued to the aprons. Steel table-top fasteners hooked in slots in the aprons attach the table top.

revolving jib crane

Construction Notes

This Revolving Jib Crane will bring many hours of joy to your young engineer. Made like the real ones, the crane rotates in a full circle on a ball-bearing swivel. The ratchet and pawl controls the angle of the boom. The handwheel raises and lowers the load, which hangs from the ball and hook.

All part numbers correspond to those in the materials list. Cut the lumber to size as per the list, then shape and work each piece as per the drawings. Assemble the parts as indicated in the exploded view. Note that the spacers are tapered slightly. Use a sander to make the taper after the pieces have been cut to size.

The ratchet was cut from a 2½-inch faced wheel the same as used elsewhere on the crane. If you do use such a wheel, be sure to make the notches for left- or right-hand use. See the note on the drawing.

The swivel can be mounted two ways—as shown or as suggested by the manufacturer. I think the method shown is the most practical. Proceed as follows: Locate the bearing on the platform (part 1) using the four inner holes, which are spaced 3³⁄₁₆ inches apart. For ease of installation, make screw starter holes using an awl then a small drill. Likewise, make similar holes on the underside of the base piece (part 3) using the four holes spaced 3⁹⁄₁₆ inches apart. Fasten the bearing to the top side of the platform, then, holding the superstructure upside down, place the platform (also upside down) in position over the base. Rotate as necessary to align the holes in the bearing with those in the base piece. Do this through the ⅝-inch clearance hole in the platform. As each screw is driven home, rotate to the next quadrant and repeat until the four screws are installed.

The wheels and axles are assembled with glue. Glue the hubs to the wheels first, then fasten the wheels to the axles. To mount the ball, drill a ¹⁄₁₆-inch hole through its center then counterbore the hole with a ³⁄₆₄-inch drill ¾ inch deep. Insert the twine, knot then pull through until the knot stops at the narrowed hole. Apply a little glue to the walls of the ³⁄₆₄-inch hole, then attach the screw hook. Run the twine over the pins as shown then through the hole in the shaft. Tie a small knot, then secure with a drop of glue.

Finish as desired. The unit shown was given two coats of clear lacquer then rubbed—*By John Capotosto.*

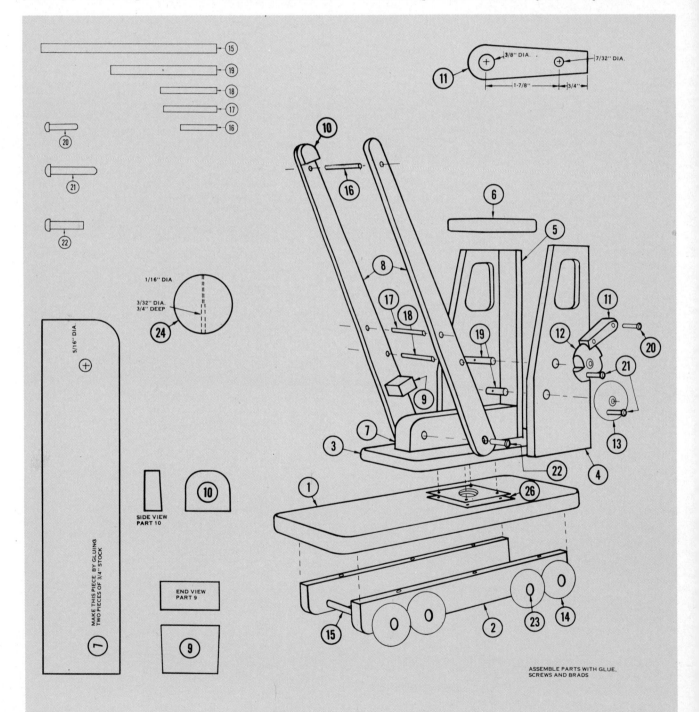

Note: Exploded view shows the controls installed for a left-handed child. If child is right-handed, place the controls on opposite side, as shown on page 89.

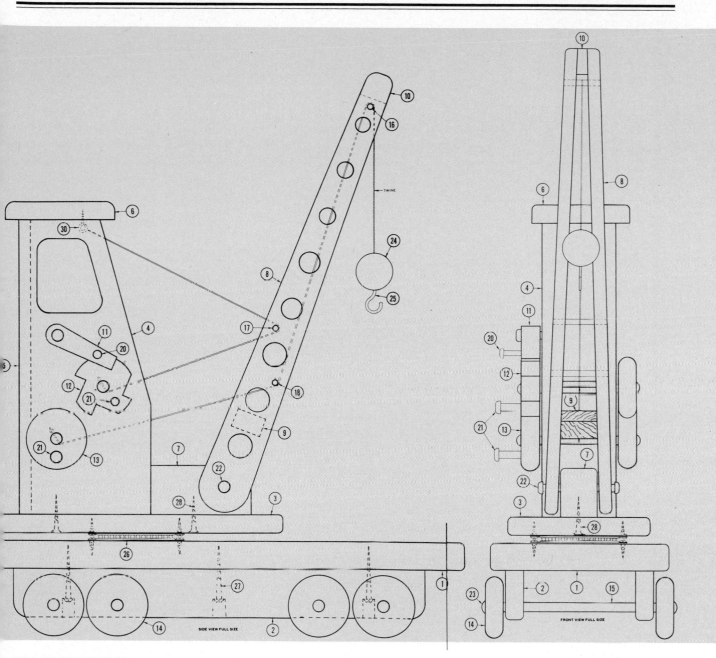

SIDE VIEW FULL SIZE

FRONT VIEW FULL SIZE

BILL OF MATERIALS

All measurements are in inches.

Part	Description	Size	Qty.
1	Platform	$1\frac{1}{8} \times 7\frac{1}{4} \times 20$	1
2	Axle support	$\frac{3}{4} \times 2 \times 17$	2
3	Base	$\frac{3}{4} \times 5\frac{3}{4} \times 12$	1
4	Side	$\frac{3}{4} \times 5\frac{3}{8} \times 12$	2
5	Rear	$\frac{1}{2} \times 1\frac{1}{2} \times 12$	1
6	Top	$4 \times 4\frac{1}{2}$	1
7	Boom support	$1\frac{1}{2} \times 2 \times 9$	1
8	Boom	$\frac{1}{2} \times 2 \times 19$	2
9	Spacer, lower	$\frac{3}{4} \times 1\frac{1}{4} \times 1\frac{1}{2}$	1
10	Spacer, upper	$\frac{7}{16} \times 1 \times 1\frac{1}{8}$	1
11	Pawl	$\frac{3}{4} \times \frac{7}{8} \times 3$	1
12	Ratchet wheel	$\frac{3}{4} \times 2\frac{1}{2}$ dia.	1
13	Hand wheel	$\frac{3}{4} \times 2\frac{1}{2}$ dia.	3
14	Wheel	$\frac{3}{4} \times 2\frac{1}{2}$ dia.	8
15	Axle	$\frac{3}{8} \times 7\frac{1}{4}$ dowel	4
16	Pin	$\frac{1}{4} \times 1\frac{1}{2}$ dowel	1
17	Pin	$\frac{1}{4} \times 2\frac{3}{16}$ dowel	1
18	Pin	$\frac{1}{4} \times 2\frac{5}{16}$ dowel	1
19	Shaft	$\frac{3}{8} \times 4\frac{3}{8}$ dowel	2
20	Handle	$\frac{7}{32} \times 1\frac{1}{8}$ (AP-1)	1
21	Handle	$\frac{5}{16} \times 2$ (AP-2)	2
22	Boom pin	$\frac{5}{16} \times 1\frac{3}{8}$ (AP-2)	2
23	Hub	$\frac{3}{8} \times \frac{1}{2}$ head (MWP)	13
24	Ball	$1\frac{1}{2}$ dia. (BA-1½)	1
25	Screw Hook	$\frac{5}{8}$ dia.	1
26	Lazy Susan bearing	4 (SWB-1)	1
27	Screw	2—8 RH	6
28	Screw	1½—8 FH	2
29	Nail	1½ finishing	14
30	Screw Eye	$\frac{3}{8}$	1

A parts kit consisting of wheels, axles, hubs, hooks, ball, twine, pegs, and swivel bearing is available from Armor Products, Box 290, Deer Park, NY 11729. Ask for Crane Kit No. 319 CK.

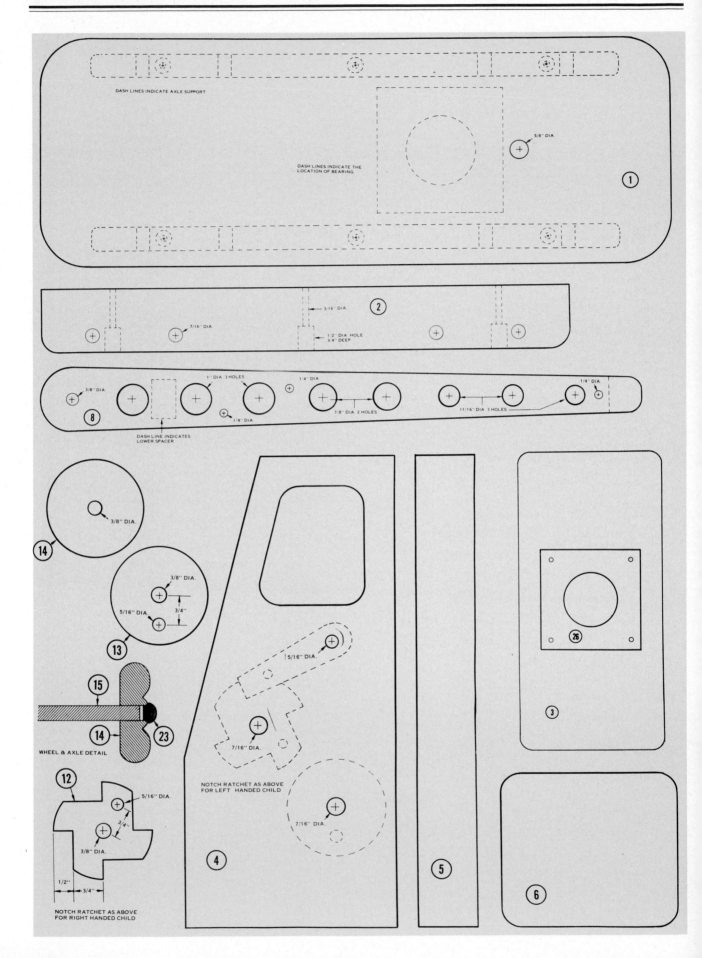

DASH LINES INDICATE AXLE SUPPORT

DASH LINES INDICATE THE
LOCATION OF BEARING

5/8" DIA

①

3/16" DIA

②

7/16" DIA

1/2" DIA HOLE
3/4" DEEP

3/8" DIA

1" DIA 3 HOLES

1/4" DIA

1/4" DIA

⑧

1/4" DIA

7/8" DIA 2 HOLES

11/16" DIA 3 HOLES

1/4" DIA

DASH LINE INDICATES
LOWER SPACER

3/8" DIA.

⑭

3/8" DIA.

5/16" DIA.

3/4"

⑬

⑮

⑭   ㉓

WHEEL & AXLE DETAIL

5/16" DIA.

NOTCH RATCHET AS ABOVE
FOR LEFT HANDED CHILD

7/16" DIA.

7/16" DIA.

⑫

5/16" DIA.

3/4"

3/8" DIA.

1/2"

3/4"

NOTCH RATCHET AS ABOVE
FOR RIGHT HANDED CHILD

④

⑤

⑥

㉖

③

log hauler

This 14-wheeler Log Hauling Truck will provide hours of enjoyment for the young lumberjacks of the family. Designed like a real one, the tractor features a realistic exhaust pipe and an air deflector above the cab. One-inch dowels are glued together and form an integral part of the truck frame. Lumber used is pine, but other species may be substituted. Size: seven by 25 inches.

Construction Notes

This 14-wheeler Log Hauler is made of pine and is easy to build. The "logs" are an integral part of the truck and serve to connect the tractor to the hitch at the rear. The logs, which are one-by-12-inch dowels, are glued to each other and to the log brackets, thus preventing them from constantly falling off and getting underfoot, which could be dangerous.

Before assembly drill the necessary holes as indicated. Join the parts with white glue and brads. The brads serve to hold the parts in place while the glue sets.

The exhaust pipe is made in three pieces: inner, outer, and cap. The inner pipe is a straight dowel with an axle peg inserted into one end. The outer pipe is drilled with numerous holes to give it a realistic appearance. Make it as follows: Draw four equally spaced lines along the length of the ¾-inch dowel. Since accuracy is not important, you can gauge the lines by eye. The ¼ inch holes are spaced and staggered as shown. Drill each hole about ¼ inch deep. Do not go through the dowel, as the exit hole will tear and splinter the wood. When all the ¼-inch holes are drilled, bore the ⁹⁄₁₆-inch center hole through the length of the dowel. Do this in steps starting with a ⅛-inch hole, then ¼ inch, ⅜ inch, and finally ⁹⁄₁₆ inch. If you use a lathe to bore the holes, you can drill straight through from one end. If you use a portable drill or drill press, it would be best to drill from both ends, meeting at the center—otherwise the drill may walk or wander off course.

The wheels are glued to the ⅜ axles (dowels) and the one-inch dowels are glued to each other and to the brackets. Stagger the logs lengthwise to add realism. The "ropes" consist of heavy shoelaces wrapped around the logs twice

and glued in place. Make the knot for the laces on the underside. Add a drop of glue to the knots to keep them from loosening.

Paint or finish clear as desired. Use non-toxic materials. The little people can be painted as shown. If you paint them, be sure to seal the wood first with shellac or other suitable sealer. The features are added with a felt marker—*Copyright 1983 John Capotosto.*

MATERIALS LIST

Except for dowels and wheels, lumber is pine. Wheels and dowels are maple. Measurements are in inches.

TRUCK

Part	Description	Size	Qty.
1	Side	¾ × 3½ × 9¾	2
2	Chassis	¾ × 2½ × 9¾	1
3	Hood	¾ × 2½ × 3	1
4	Roof	½ × 3 × 4½	1
5	Fender	¾ × 1½ × 6¼	2
6	Bumper	¼ × ¾ × 4½	1
7	Cab, rear	½ × 2¼ × 2½	1
8	Bracket	¾ × 1¼ × 4	1
9	Pin	⅜ × 1½ dowel	1
10	Axle	⅜ × 5⅝ dowel	1
11	Axle	⅜ × 7 dowel	1
12	Exhaust outer	¾ × 3 dowel	1
13	Exhaust inner	½ × 4¼ dowel	1
14	Exhaust cap	Axle peg, ⁵⁄₁₆ tenon	1
15	Deflector	¼ × 1⁹⁄₁₆ × 3	1
16	Bracket	¾ × ⅝ × 1	2
17	People	¾ × 2⁵⁄₁₆	2
18	Log	1 × 12 dowel	6

TRAILER

19	Side	¾ × 2 × 5⅜	2
20	Top	¾ × 1⅞ × 5⅜	1
21	Bracket	¾ × 1¼ × 4	1
22	Wheel	2¼ dia.	14
23	Axle	⅜ × 6⅝ dowel	2
24	Rope	Shoelace	2

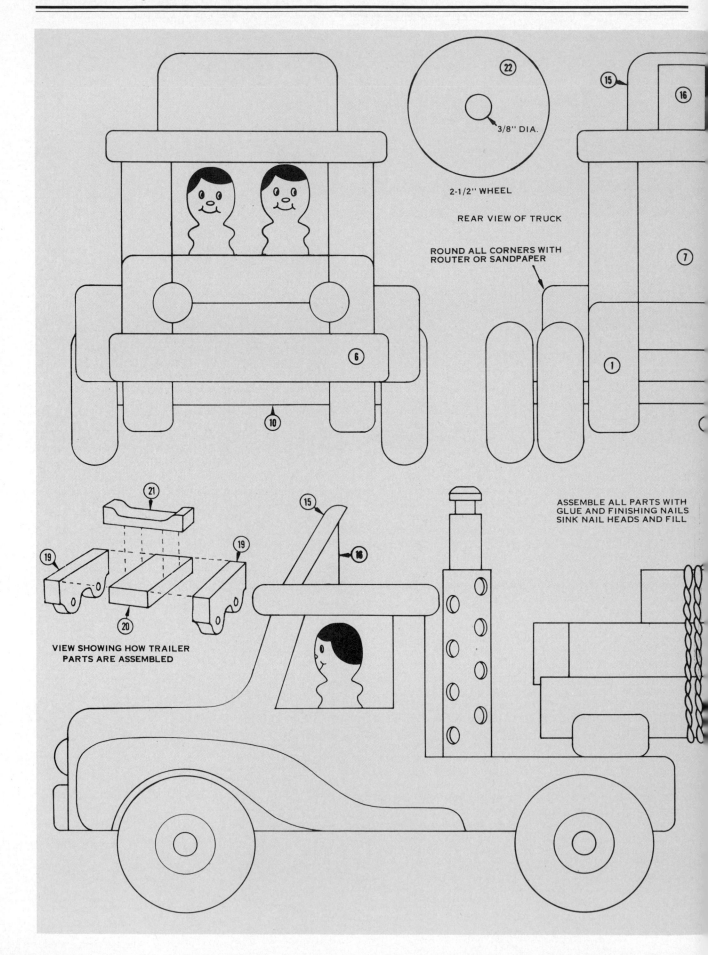

22

3/8'' DIA.

2-1/2'' WHEEL

REAR VIEW OF TRUCK

ROUND ALL CORNERS WITH
ROUTER OR SANDPAPER

ASSEMBLE ALL PARTS WITH
GLUE AND FINISHING NAILS
SINK NAIL HEADS AND FILL

VIEW SHOWING HOW TRAILER
PARTS ARE ASSEMBLED

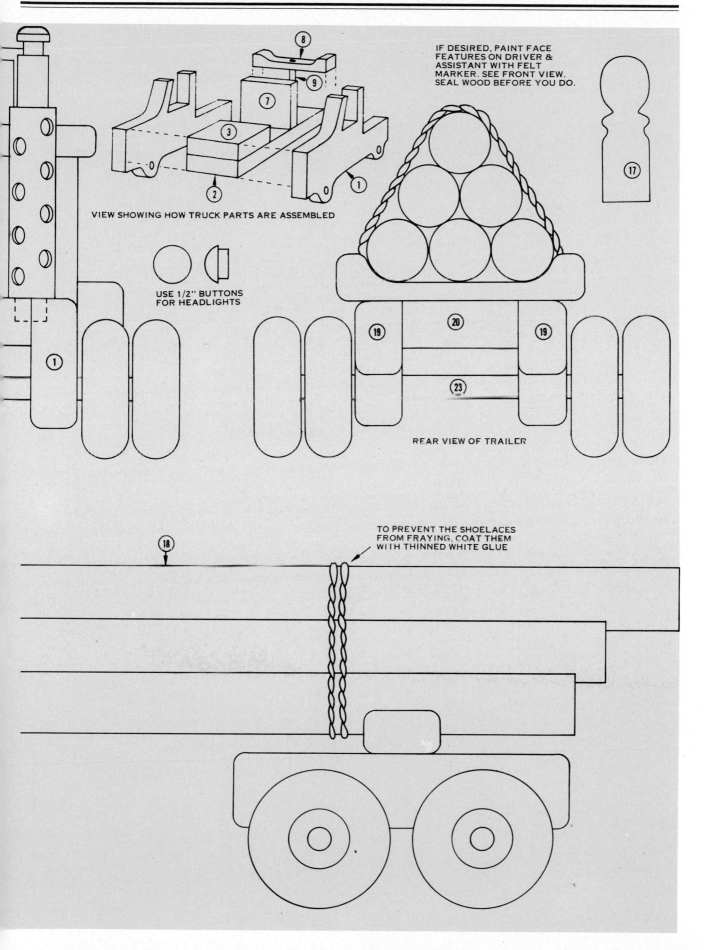

VIEW SHOWING HOW TRUCK PARTS ARE ASSEMBLED

USE 1/2" BUTTONS
FOR HEADLIGHTS

IF DESIRED, PAINT FACE
FEATURES ON DRIVER &
ASSISTANT WITH FELT
MARKER. SEE FRONT VIEW.
SEAL WOOD BEFORE YOU DO.

REAR VIEW OF TRAILER

TO PREVENT THE SHOELACES
FROM FRAYING, COAT THEM
WITH THINNED WHITE GLUE

Truck parts

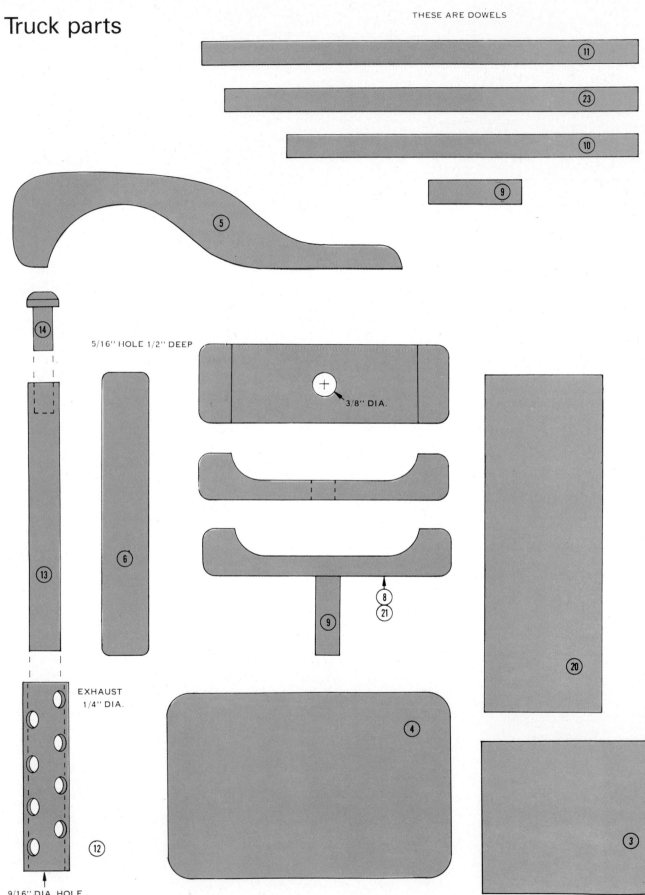

THESE ARE DOWELS

5/16" HOLE 1/2" DEEP

3/8" DIA.

EXHAUST
1/4" DIA.

9/16" DIA. HOLE
THROUGH DOWEL

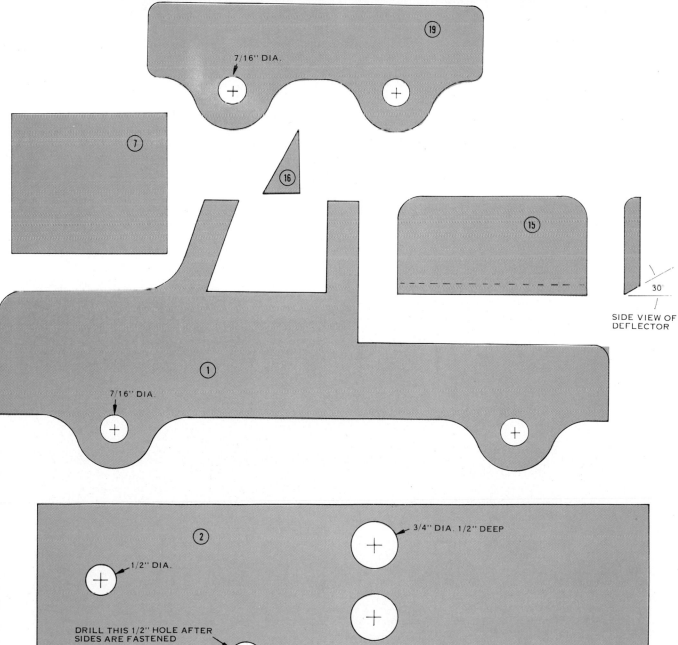

7/16" DIA.

⑲

⑦

⑯

⑮

30°

SIDE VIEW OF
DEFLECTOR

①

7/16" DIA.

②

3/4" DIA. 1/2" DEEP

1/2" DIA.

DRILL THIS 1/2" HOLE AFTER
SIDES ARE FASTENED

modern slat chair

Curved lines fit the contours of your body and sleek design fits any room of your home. A chair like this is so versatile, even the size can be adapted to fit any nook or lined up to make a sofa-like unit for any wall. However, a single chair should be no more than 24 inches wide.

If the chair will be viewed from the side, you may want to select a high-quality plywood, such as oak, or plan to cover it with a fabric that matches or coordinates with draperies. If several chairs will be lined up from wall to wall, a less costly material, such as a lower grade of plywood or a particleboard, would be a good option that would take paint well.

Drawing and Cutting

To start, carefully draw the first side-panel shape on the face side of a sheet of plywood or other building material, using a compass to make the curve of the seat.

Make a rough cut around this piece. It will later be trimmed to the lines you just drew. Now, tightly clamp the rough-cut piece to another part of the plywood sheet so reverse sides are together. Cut both sides of the chair at the same time using a circular saw for the straight sides. Be sure to use a good plywood blade. A saber saw will be needed for the curves. (You'll have the best luck using a saber saw with a splinter guard.)

Each time you move the clamps, make sure the cut sides and grain still match up.

Next, draw the radius for the corner pieces on the 2×2 and 2×4 material and use a table saw to rough cut the radius of the corner pieces as close to the dimensions on the drawing as possible. Sand the ridges off to make a smooth curve on the corner pieces.

Use the sanded corner pieces to draw the corners on the side pieces and make those curves with the saber saw.

Sand the side-panel edges, then band them with plywood edging. Roll

the tape as you go. Then sand so the edge of the tape is flush with the side of the plywood.

Make the cleats from 1×2 and 1×4 material. Mark the notches on the cleats with the corner pieces. On the side panels, measure in the width of a 1×2 on edge. Precision here is important because the chair slats will fit on top of the cleats. The bottom and back are measured in the width of a 1×2 laid flat.

Joining the Parts

Glue and screw or nail the cleats into place. Now connect the rounded 2×2 and 2×4 corner pieces to one side panel and then the other. Measure between the side panels for the back and bottom pieces. Glue and nail or screw these pieces on.

Cut chair slats, and sand them on one side. Starting at the bottom of the chair, glue and nail them on (sanded side out), working your way to the top

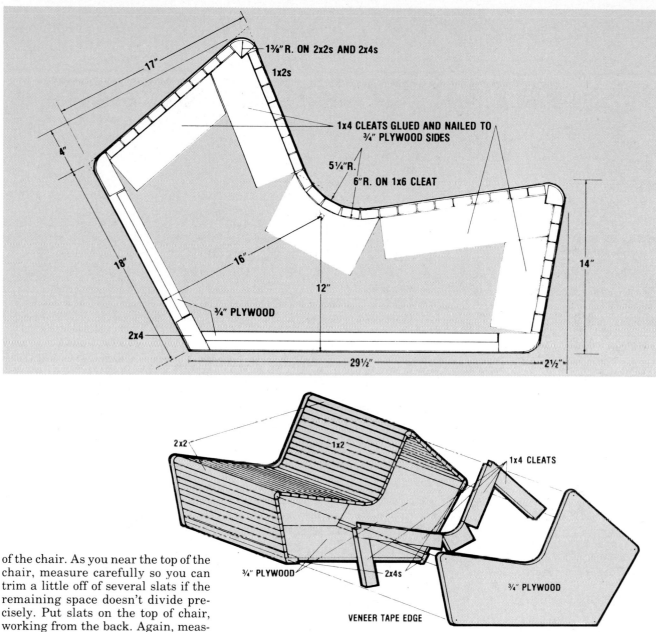

of the chair. As you near the top of the chair, measure carefully so you can trim a little off of several slats if the remaining space doesn't divide precisely. Put slats on the top of chair, working from the back. Again, measure carefully as you near the placement of the final slats.

Adding the Finishing Touches

Fill nail holes. Paint or stain. Add large pillows or a cushion that will be comfortable for sitting.

Add an Ottoman for Real Relaxation

Lean back, relax and put your feet up on the classy ottoman that matches your new chairs. Directions for the ottoman are the same as for the chair—only easier. The cleats and the slats will go on top, bottom, front, and back of the ottoman. For design coordination (and added comfort), top the ottoman with a cushion that matches the chair's pillows—*Courtesy of Georgia-Pacific Corporation.*

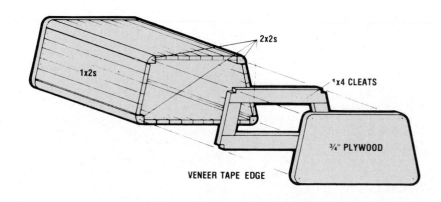

an affordable sauna

Do you drag home from work each evening, not an ounce of energy left in you? Does winter's cold seep so deeply in your bones you forget what it's like to be delightfully warm? This project offers the perfect panacea for these problems: A do-it-yourself indoor sauna.

The design costs over 85 percent less than comparable commercial units, yet can perform every bit as well. Instead of the many thousands you might expect to pay for a stripped-down sauna kit (one with no lights, benches, or bucket and ladle), the total cost to build your sauna, *including* the heater and all the luxuries that make it an efficient and comfortable room, is under $2000.

The sauna is framed with 2×4s, then insulated, drywalled, and paneled inside with tongue-and-groove cedar. (You can substitute redwood if it's more readily available or less expensive in your area.) This sauna is carefully designed to be tight enough so very little heat escapes through unseen cracks or crevices, but not so tight that the air quality inside will suffer. Also, careful use of materials helps to hold down costs. The door pulls, for example, are really trowel handles picked up at a local hardware store.

On these pages are listed materials needed, overall dimensions, and the basic construction steps for building the sauna. Blueprints, step-by-step illustrations, and instructions are available from: Project File #500, Box 155, Emmaus, PA 18049.

Construction

1. Frame the sauna's walls and ceiling with kiln-dried spruce 2×4s and 12d common nails.

2. CAUTION: All wiring must meet code specifications. Install the light fixture and switch box flush with the plane of the finished wall. Complete all rough wiring for the light, its switch, and the sauna heater. (All finish wiring will be completed after the drywall and paneling are installed.) Instructions for mounting the sauna heater are included in the owner's manual.

3. Install 3½″-thick × 15″-wide foil-faced insulation with the foil facing the inside of the sauna in the wall and ceiling frames. Staple the insulation in place.

4. Fasten ½″-thick drywall to the interior and exterior of the walls and ceiling. Apply tape and joint compound to all joints.

5. Panel the sauna's interior walls and ceiling with kiln-dried, V-joint, tongue-and-groove, clear cedar 1×6s. Lay out and cut an opening for the electrical box. Install filler pieces along the door's frame.

6. The following sauna accessories are built from kiln-dried redwood 1×4s and 2×4s:

Benches: Cut and assemble the frame of the upper bench (18″×77¾″) and the lower bench (24″×77¾″). Fasten 1″×3″ slats to the top of each frame for the seat surface. Fasten supports to the walls at each end of the sauna with ⅜″×4″ lag bolts to hold the benches in place.

Backrest: Assemble the backrest using two triangular 4″×18½″ sides, one 2¼″×12¾″ back and seven 2½″×15″ top slats.

Duck board: Assemble the duck board by fastening nine 2¼″×44″ slats to the tops of three 4½″×23½″ bottom support members.

7. A sauna door can be purchased ready to install. To cut costs, we built our own 2′×6′ insulated door. Frame the door with cedar 1×2s. Install rigid polystyrene insulation in the frame.

Safety Tips

1. We recommend that elderly persons, pregnant women, and people with heart conditions or high blood pressure consult a physician before using a sauna.

2. The sauna's door should swing out from the sauna. The door handle must be made of wood and no locking device should be used. Allow a ¾" airspace at the base of the door for ventilation.

3. Use only galvanized nails in the sauna, and be sure each is countersunk and filled.

4. Do not apply any finish to the wood surfaces in the sauna's interior.

5. Use only tempered insulating glass or clear sheet polycarbonate for the sauna's window.

6. Do not use carpeting on the sauna's floor.

7. Use only a vaporproof light fixture.

8. Avoid using any sapwood; the sap can heat up and cause burns.

9. Unless you're a skilled do-it-yourselfer, leave the electrical installations to a qualified electrician.

10. Most building codes insist that the sauna heater have a thermostat and 60-minute timer.

Fasten ³⁄₁₆" lauan plywood to both sides of the door frame. Cover the door's interior plywood surface with tongue-and-groove interior siding. Finish the exterior plywood door surface with filler and paint. Attach hinges (including one spring hinge) and door pulls. Construct the jamb, stop, and trim of the door of ¾" inch clear cedar.

8. The window's jamb, stop, and trim are also constructed from ¾"-inch clear cedar. Install a 10½" × 52½"

Thermopane window and ⅛" × 1" blocks to hold the glazing securely in place.

9. Install interior and exterior clear cedar trim as needed.

10. Install the sauna heater. Construct a heater guard of clear cedar 1 × 3s to protect bathers from accidental contact with the heater.

Adapted from *Rodale's New Shelter* magazine
Copyright 1984 Rodale Press, Inc.
All rights reserved.

MATERIALS LIST

Insulation	
Door	One 1½" × 24" × 96" sheet extruded polystyrene
Ceiling and walls	Two 75'-long rolls 3½" × 15" foil-faced insulation
Walls	Six ½" × 48" × 96"-drywall panels
Door	One ³⁄₁₆" × 48" × 96" sheet lauan plywood
Window	10½" × 52½"-tempered Thermopane
Framing	Forty-three 8'-long spruce 2 × 4s
Benches and posts	Seven 8'-long redwood 2 × 4s
Jambs	Four 8'-long clear cedar 1 × 6s
Paneling and door siding	Sixty 8'-long T & G clear cedar 1 × 6s
Benches, backrest, duck board, heater guard, stops, and trim	Forty 8'-long clear cedar 1 × 3s

Sauna heater available from many sources, including Sears, Roebuck, & Co.

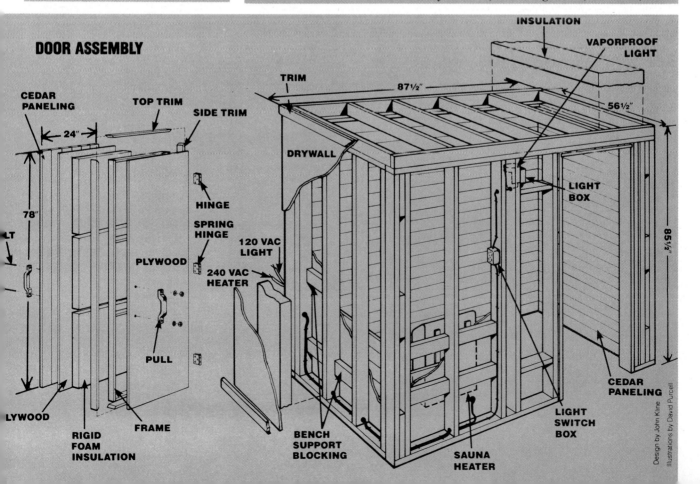

DOOR ASSEMBLY

CEDAR PANELING — TOP TRIM — SIDE TRIM — 24" — HINGE — SPRING HINGE — 78" — PLYWOOD — PULL — LT — 120 VAC LIGHT — 240 VAC HEATER — PLYWOOD — RIGID FOAM INSULATION — FRAME — BENCH SUPPORT BLOCKING — SAUNA HEATER — LIGHT SWITCH BOX — CEDAR PANELING — INSULATION — VAPORPROOF LIGHT — TRIM — 87½" — 56½" — DRYWALL — LIGHT BOX — 85½"

Design by John Kline
Illustrations by David Purcell

round victorian table

The round tables made of oak by American manufacturers and craftsmen of the early Victorian period are very popular once again. There are many different styles of these tables. They range from simple tables with square-cut legs and pedestals to the one featured in this project. It has the more heavily carved claw foot and turned pedestal post. Although early round tables were made of walnut, mahogany, and oak, oak seems to be the choice of most collectors, and so it has become traditional for these tables.

Construction

Although the table appears to be quite complicated, it's not particularly hard to build. You will need a good heavy-duty lathe for turning the large hollow post and a good band saw for cutting many of the shaped pieces. Cutting and fitting the apron board pieces is one of the hardest parts of the project.

The top is made of two halves, joined with dowel guide pins between them. Table extensions fasten to the underside of the top so that table-top leaves can be added. Two drop-down legs (hinged to the underside of the top) provide extra support when the table is fully extended.

Support Column. Construction starts with the support post. This is a hollow wooden column made by cut-

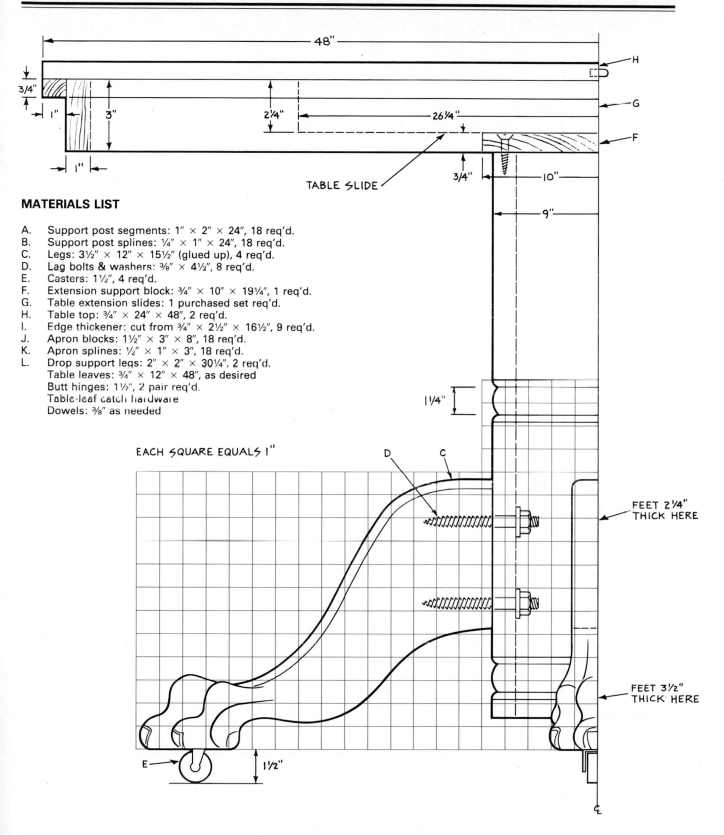

MATERIALS LIST

A.   Support post segments: 1″ × 2″ × 24″, 18 req'd.
B.   Support post splines: ¼″ × 1″ × 24″, 18 req'd.
C.   Legs: 3½″ × 12″ × 15½″ (glued up), 4 req'd.
D.   Lag bolts & washers: ⅜″ × 4½″, 8 req'd.
E.   Casters: 1½″, 4 req'd.
F.   Extension support block: ¾″ × 10″ × 19¼″, 1 req'd.
G.   Table extension slides: 1 purchased set req'd.
H.   Table top: ¾″ × 24″ × 48″, 2 req'd.
I.   Edge thickener: cut from ¾″ × 2½″ × 16½″, 9 req'd.
J.   Apron blocks: 1½″ × 3″ × 8″, 18 req'd.
K.   Apron splines: ½″ × 1″ × 3″, 18 req'd.
L.   Drop support legs: 2″ × 2″ × 30¼″. 2 req'd.
     Table leaves: ¾″ × 12″ × 48″, as desired
     Butt hinges: 1½″, 2 pair req'd.
     Table-leaf catch hardware
     Dowels: ⅜″ as needed

EACH SQUARE EQUALS 1″

ting a number of wood segments (A) to the angles shown in the drawing. These are then fitted with a wood spline (B) in slots that have been cut in their joining, angled, edges.

Once all pieces have been cut to size and shape, insert glue on the splines and join the segmented circle together. Use band clamps to clamp the column securely, and allow the glue to set up overnight.

Remove from the clamps and cut nine-inch-diameter circles from ¾-inch plywood to fit over each end. Locate the exact center of the circles. Fasten these end caps in place with wood screws over the ends of the column, making sure they align properly.

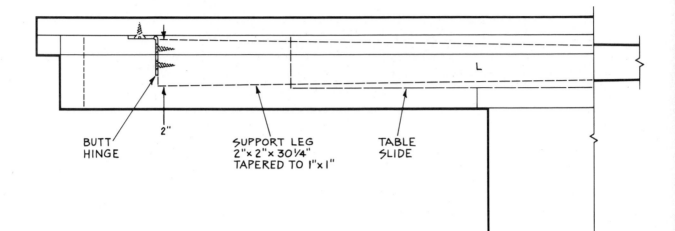

BUTT HINGE   2"   SUPPORT LEG
2"x 2"x 30¼"
TAPERED TO 1"x1"   TABLE SLIDE   L

Then place the large hollow column in your lathe, and rough it in at a very slow speed. Finish the decorative turning, and sand smooth while still in the lathe.

After the piece has been turned to the proper size and shape, remove it from the lathe. Using a small square, divide the bottom plywood holding circle into four equal parts. Mark these lines down the sides of the hollow post. This will locate the position for each of the four legs (C) around the outside of the circle. Then remove the plywood end caps from the hollow post.

Legs. The legs (C) are made by gluing stock to make up the thickness. Then enlarge the squared drawing, cut the leg to shape on a band saw, and carve the claw-foot portion to shape. With a Dupli-Carver you can easily duplicate the carving from one foot onto the others; this saves a great deal of time and effort.

After carving the legs, shape their concave, inside faces (these fit up against the hollow post). Locate the holes for the holding bolts (D), and bore them. Then bore matching holes in the lower part of the hollow post.

The holding bolts are special lag bolts. They have a screw thread cut on one end, which is turned into the leg. The opposite end is threaded for a nut. After turning the lag bolts into the legs, fasten the legs to the hollow post with washers and nuts.

Table Slides. The table slides are purchased, but you could also make them up. Use slotted dovetails to cre-

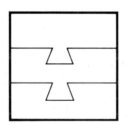

ate the slides, as shown in the detail. Cut the slide holding block (F) to size, and shape and install the slides on top of it with screws. Then fasten the slide and block assembly to the hollow post with screws driven down through the holding block.

Table Top. Construction of the top (H) itself is fairly simple, but the apron is more complicated. The top is two separate pieces made of solid stock glued up from smaller-width stock. This can be done with tongue-and-groove or dowel joints. In any case, glue up to the rough size. Then use a large shop-made compass (or trammel point) to create a cutting line for the round outer edge of the top halves.

Saw the top pieces using a band saw or saber saw. You can make a band-saw-table extension and guide-pin jig to insure the circle is cut perfectly round.

The edge of the table top is thickened with an additional layer of stock glued to the underside of the edge. This "thickener" (I) is made using the same segment method employed on the center post. Cut the segment pieces to the rough shape and size, as shown in the drawing. Then make a pattern for the circumference, transfer this to the segment pieces, and cut them to shape on the band saw. Fasten these in place to the underside of the top with glue and screws. Make sure their mating edges join smoothly and perfectly.

Apron. The apron (J) is one of the hardest parts of the table to build. On the original, it was cut from one solid piece, steamed and bent to shape. But you will probably want to make it from segmented pieces. You can make these of solid oak and let the joint lines show, or you can cover the outside of the apron with oak veneer.

Saw the segment pieces (J) to size and rough shape; then create an exact pattern for cutting each of the segments to shape. Saw the segment angles, and then make a slot for the joining splines (K). Use a dado blade in a table or radial-arm saw. Finally, cut the outside rounded edge of each segment using a band saw. You can also make up this large segmented circle with the blocks in the rough, temporarily fasten it to a piece of plywood with screws, and then use a table extension and pin guide on your band saw to cut the circle. This will result in a truer, more finished appearance.

Sand the apron as smooth as possible, and fasten to the underside of

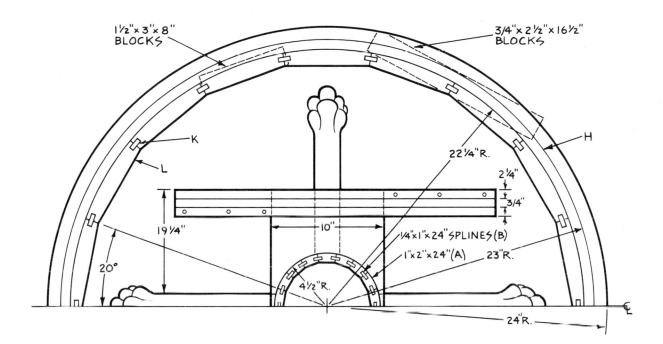

the table top and thickener with glue and countersunk screws. You might also want to add glue blocks for extra strength.

Bore the pin-guide holes for the table-top leaf halves, and smooth the ends of a couple of dowels. Glue one end of each dowel permanently in the holes in one side. They mate with holes bored into the opposite half of the table.

Assembly

Turn the top upside down on a smooth, flat surface, and then put the post assembly down in place over it. Fasten the extensions to the table top to secure the two assemblies together.

Drop Support Legs. Cut the drop legs (L) to size, joint their edges, and sand smooth. Then install on the underside of the table top with butt hinges. Install the table-leaf catch. Make up as many leaves as needed. Sand the entire project smooth, stain, and finish—By Monte Burch. Drawings by Gerhard Richter.

cane-bottomed chair

This classic country-style chair is very popular today for use in kitchen or dining room. Almost any hardwood can be used; however, oak has become the typical choice for these chairs.

Construction

Although the chair looks fairly simple to build, the bending required for legs and other parts makes it somewhat complicated.

Legs. The first step in construction is to turn the back (B) and front (A) legs. Then bend them into the shape shown in the squared drawings. Bending wood works most easily if the wood to be used is green and unseasoned. It should be straight grained and without any knots or weak spots. The usual method of bending wood uses steam to make the wood more pliant. Steamed wood pieces are then bent and fastened over a form.

There are several homemade shop steamers that can be constructed for steaming wood pieces. Or, you can steam in the old-fashioned way with a simple outdoor fire and boiling water to create the steam. You can even make up a smaller unit to use on your kitchen stove (for steaming small parts).

Regardless of which method you use, the wood should be steamed for at least one hour for each inch of thickness. Then remove it from the steam using heavy rubber gloves, being careful not to burn yourself, and clamp it to the form as quickly as possible. Note that the bend in the form must be a bit more pronounced than the final curve you want in the bending stock.

Dry wood as fast as possible with a heat lamp, but do not expose it to direct sunlight. It will take a bit of experimentation to get the form curved properly for each individual piece, type of wood, and size of stock.

Once the legs are bent and dried, locate and bore the counterbored holes in the sides of the back legs for countersunk screws to hold the seat board to the legs.

Back splats. Cut the top back splat (L) to shape. Enlarge the squared drawing and carve to the proper pattern. Then bend it to shape as well. Cut the lower back splat (K) to size and shape and bend it to fit.

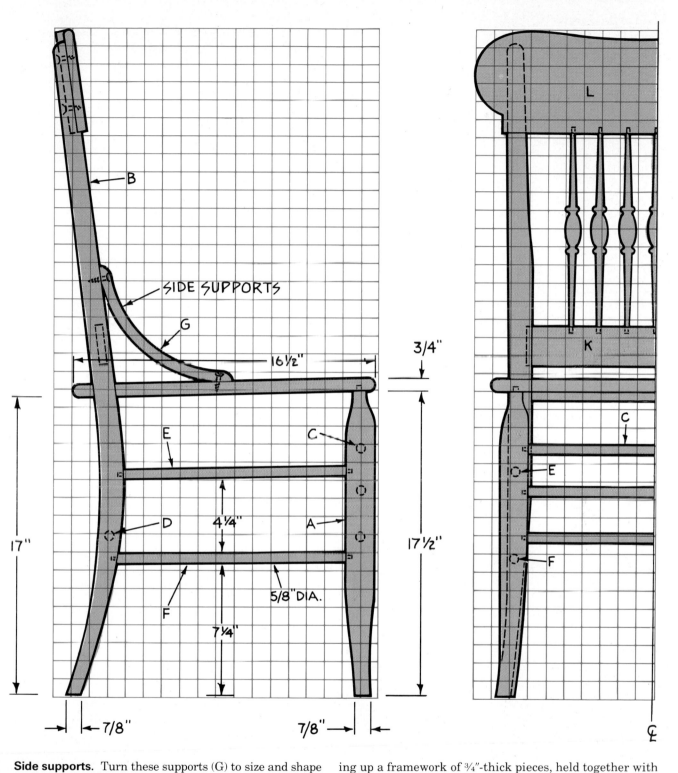

Side supports. Turn these supports (G) to size and shape on a lathe, then bend them into the required shapes. It will take a great deal of work to get both of these in the exact shape and bend needed to match them up. But this must be done correctly or they can force the chair out of square during assembly.

Bore holes for the back spindles (M) in the bottom edge of the top splat (L) and the upper edge of the bottom splat (K).

Rungs. Turn all the rungs (C-F) to shape and size. Be sure to make tenons on each end of each rung.

Seat Board. The seat board (H-J) is made by first mak-

ing up a framework of ¾"-thick pieces, held together with dowels and glue (see detail drawing). Then rout a recess in the top inside edge of the framework for the cane and spline. Using a saber saw or coping saw, round the corners of the seat board and cut the back recesses for the back legs (see detail drawing). Then sand the edges round on both top and bottom of the seat board. Bore the holes for the front legs (A) in the bottom of the seat to the angle shown.

Assembly

Proper sizing of the tenons, dowel ends, and the holes in

MATERIALS LIST

A. Front Legs: $1\frac{3}{4} \times 1\frac{3}{4} \times 17\frac{1}{8}$", 2 req'd.
B. Back Legs: $1\frac{3}{4} \times 1\frac{3}{4} \times 36$", 2 req'd.
C. Front Rungs: $\frac{5}{8} \times \frac{5}{8} \times 14\frac{1}{2}$", 3 req'd.
D. Back Rung: $\frac{5}{8} \times \frac{5}{8} \times 14\frac{1}{2}$", 1 req'd.
E. Top Side Rungs: $\frac{5}{8} \times \frac{5}{8} \times 12\frac{3}{4}$", 2 req'd.
F. Bottom Side Rungs: $\frac{5}{8} \times \frac{5}{8} \times 13\frac{1}{4}$", 2 req'd.
G. Side Supports: $\frac{5}{8} \times \frac{5}{8} \times 11\frac{1}{2}$", 2 req'd.
H. Seat Board, Front: $\frac{3}{4} \times 3\frac{1}{2} \times 18$", 1 req'd.
I. Seat Board, Back: $\frac{3}{4} \times 3 \times 15$", 1 req'd.
J. Seat Board, Sides: $\frac{3}{4} \times 3\frac{1}{2} \times 9\frac{1}{2}$", 2 req'd.
K. Lower Back Splat: $\frac{3}{4} \times 2\frac{1}{4} \times 15$", 1 req'd.
L. Top Back Splat: $\frac{3}{4} \times 5\frac{1}{2} \times 21\frac{1}{2}$", 1 req'd.
M. Back Spindles: $\frac{3}{4} \times \frac{3}{4} \times 11\frac{1}{4}$", 7 req'd.
   Cane to fit

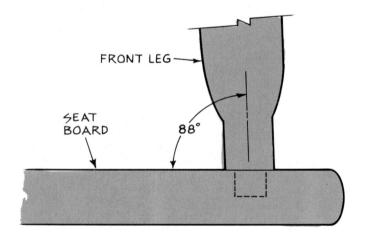

FRONT LEG

SEAT BOARD

88°

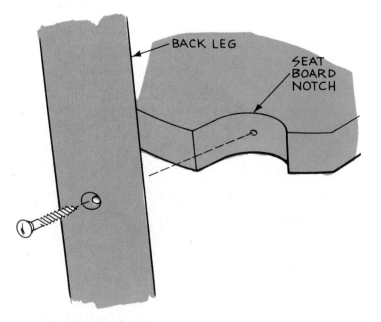

BACK LEG

SEAT BOARD NOTCH

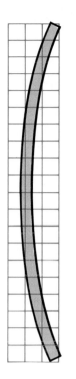

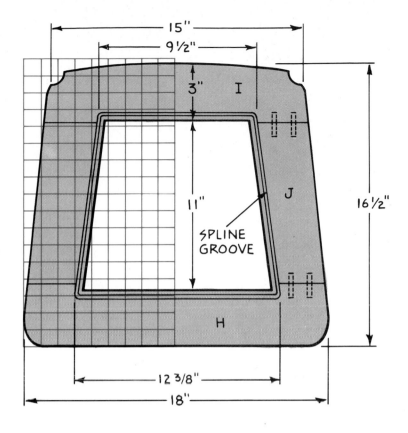

which they fit is very important for a properly constructed, long-lasting chair. Tenons and dowels should be snug, but they should not have a hard "drive-on" fit or there will be no room for the glue that holds the parts securely. Place glue on each tenon or dowel end before insertion, but not so much that it squeezes onto the surrounding wood surface.

Assembly starts with the front legs (A). Insert their doweled ends up into holes bored in the seat bottom. Then place the front rungs (C) between them and temporarily clamp together. Put this assembly aside for a few moments and assemble the lower back leg assembly. Put the lower back splat (K) and the back lower rung (D) between the back legs (B), and clamp this assembly together. Fit the side rungs (E, F) in the back leg assembly. Then put the front leg assembly in place, with side rungs in their correct holes. Locate the correct position for the back edges of the seat board and fasten in place with countersunk wood screws inserted through the counterbored holes in the back legs.

Stand the leg assembly on a smooth, flat surface and make sure it doesn't rock on its legs. Clamp the entire assembly together with band clamps. Install the side support pieces (G) with screws into the seat board and back legs.

Upper back assembly. To assemble the upper back, insert the back spindles (M) into the holes in the lower splat and then slide the top back splat (L) down over their ends. Anchor it to the back legs with countersunk ovalhead wood screws driven through the back legs. Make sure none of the screws break through.

Stain and finish after a thorough sanding, then install cane. To do this, buy cane pre-woven (many do-it-yourself stores and catalogs supply it), cut larger around than the seat opening. Soak according to directions supplied with cane. Place the cane into the groove routed in the seat-board, and hammer the spline in place. Make sure to stretch the cane tightly. Finish the cane seat according to the instructions supplied with the pre-woven cane—*Monte Burch. Drawings by Gerhard Richter.*

breakfast table

Not much free time on your hands? Here's a project as quick and easy to make as the three-minute egg you'll be eating on it. The size of the table can be adjusted to your needs. Just be sure to increase or decrease the width of the base in proportion to the diameter of the tabletop. The tabletop is plastic laminate, so you can select the right color for your decor. Design by Jim Eldon.

Construction

Illustration A

1. Cut the horizontal base members to size.
2. Lay out and cut two ⅜″ deep × 2″-wide dadoes in each horizontal member.
3. Face-glue the horizontal members together in pairs, forming four horizontal units. The dadoes on each pair of horizontal members should match to form two mortises in each unit.

Illustration B

4. Lay out and cut a 2½″ radius on the corners of each horizontal unit.
5. Lay out and cut a 1½″-wide × 1¼″-deep edge half-lap joint at the center of each horizontal unit. Join the horizontal units to form two "X" units.
6. Drill and countersink two holes at the intersection of each "X" unit to accept #10 × 1½″ flathead wood screws. Fasten each "X" unit together with glue and #10 × 1½″ flathead wood screws.
7. Machine a ¼″ radius on all edges of the "X" units.

Illustration C

8. Cut the vertical base members to size.

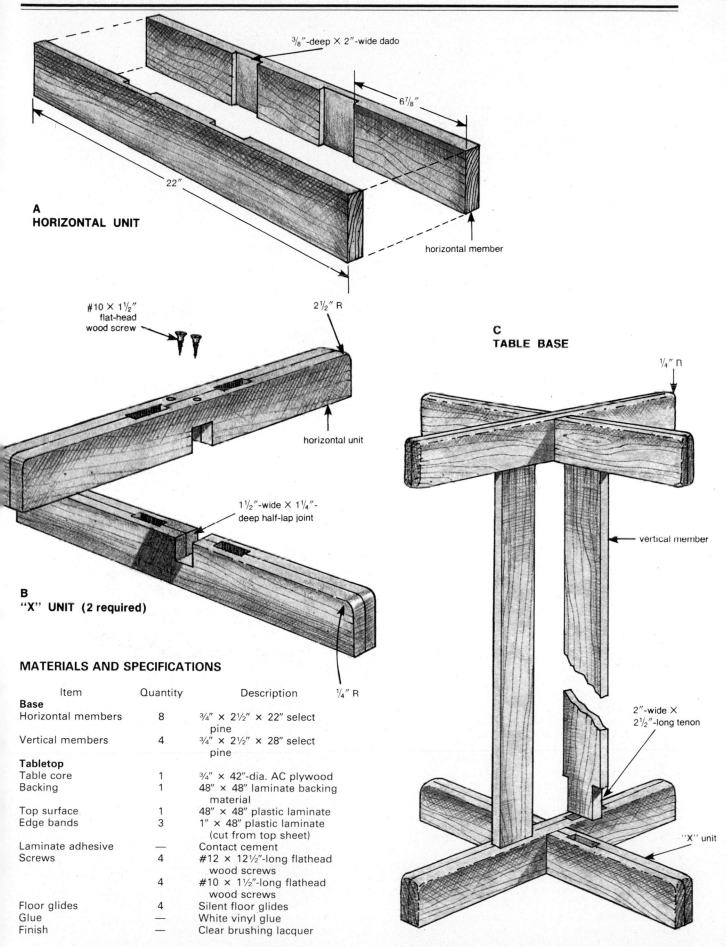

A HORIZONTAL UNIT

3/8"-deep × 2"-wide dado

6 7/8"

22"

horizontal member

#10 × 1 1/2" flat-head wood screw

2 1/2" R

C TABLE BASE

1/4" R

horizontal unit

1 1/2"-wide × 1 1/4"-deep half-lap joint

vertical member

B "X" UNIT (2 required)

1/4" R

2"-wide × 2 1/2"-long tenon

"X" unit

MATERIALS AND SPECIFICATIONS

Item	Quantity	Description
Base		
Horizontal members	8	3/4" × 2 1/2" × 22" select pine
Vertical members	4	3/4" × 2 1/2" × 28" select pine
Tabletop		
Table core	1	3/4" × 42"-dia. AC plywood
Backing	1	48" × 48" laminate backing material
Top surface	1	48" × 48" plastic laminate
Edge bands	3	1" × 48" plastic laminate (cut from top sheet)
Laminate adhesive	—	Contact cement
Screws	4	#12 × 12 1/2"-long flathead wood screws
	4	#10 × 1 1/2"-long flathead wood screws
Floor glides	4	Silent floor glides
Glue	—	White vinyl glue
Finish	—	Clear brushing lacquer

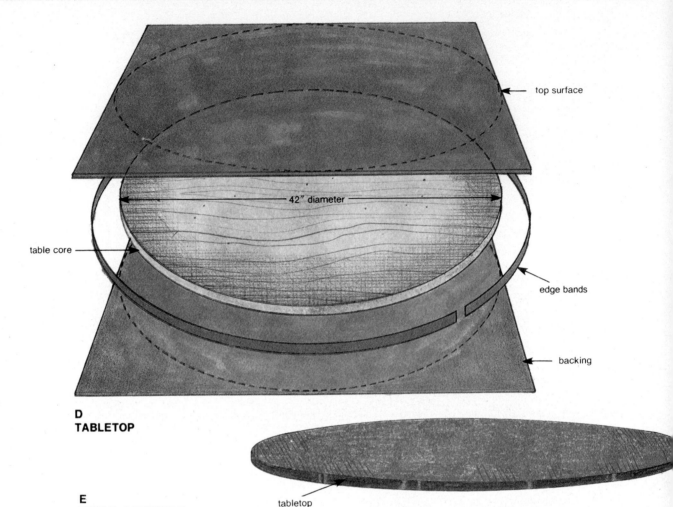

D
TABLETOP

top surface

42″ diameter

table core

edge bands

backing

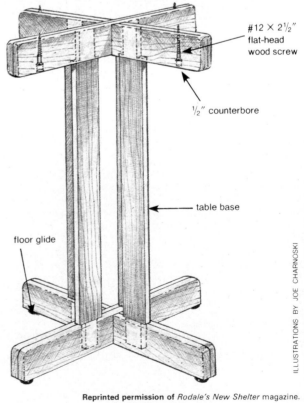

E
TABLE ASSEMBLY

tabletop

#12 × 2½″
flat-head
wood screw

½″ counterbore

table base

floor glide

9. Lay out and cut a 2″-wide × 2½″-long tenon on both ends of each vertical member.

10. Machine a ¼″ radius on the exposed edges of each vertical member.

11. Glue and clamp the vertical members into the "X" units to form the table base.

12. Apply a clear finish to the table base.

Illustration D

13. Cut the table core and backing to size.

14. Fasten the backing to the underside of the table core using contact cement.

15. Machine the backing flush with the edge of the table core using a laminate trimmer.

16. Cut the edge bands to size.

17. Fasten the edge bands to the table core with contact cement. Trim the edges flush.

18. Cut the top surface to size.

19. Attach the top surface to the top side of the table core with contact cement.

20. Machine the top surface flush with the edge of the tabletop.

Illustration E

21. Drill and counterbore the top horizontal members of the base to accept #12 × 2½″ flathead wood screws.

22. Attach the assembed tabletop to the table base using #12 × 2½″ flathead wood screws.

23. Attach the floor glides to the bottom of the table base.

davenport desk

A Davenport desk is small, with the prototype believed to have been a shipboard desk ordered by a Captain Davenport in the early 19th century in England. It was a very popular style in the early and middle Victorian years.

Although there was considerable variety of design, all Davenport desks had drawers in the side (one or both sides), rather than in the front. The writing surface was usually a hinged compartment-lid, but some desks had pull-out writing surfaces. Many early Davenport desks had secret compartments, swing out drawers, and compartments with small drawers and pigeon holes that rose above the desk top when a catch was released. The desks tended to be elaborately decorated. Ours is made of cherry, with Carpathian elm burl veneered panels. The panel trim is walnut.

The dimensioning of this desk started with a modern hanging file. The lower double drawers will each accommodate these useful files. You could quite properly have drawers on one side only, with dummy drawer fronts on the other side, or a combination of drawers that ran the full width of the desk with some that didn't. Dummy drawer fronts can be made up that are attached to the drawer rails so you could easily reverse the side with the drawers when the desk is moved to a different location.

Opportunities are endless for tailoring this desk to your exact needs. Plans are given for an interior compartment with drawers and pigeon holes if you want them in your desk; materials for the compartment, however, have not been included in the cutting list.

You will need about 35 board feet of ¾″ cherry lumber for the desk. Begin by planning how to get all the parts out of your lumber. When you blank the parts, leave some extra al-

lowance on lengths for squaring and fitting. (Dimensions are given assuming nominally ¾″ thick wood; when you surface sand the wood, it usually ends up less than ¾″ thick.)

Begin construction with the front and back frames of the drawer case. Rabbet top rails, bottom rails, and stiles to receive the veneered plywood panels. Assemble the frames with dowels. Four drawer frame assemblies are required. They are identical except that the top one does not have drawer guides. Rails and guides can be doweled, rather than mortise and tenoned

as shown. The back drawer rail is doweled in place after the rails and guides are assembled.

When laying out dowel hole locations note that the bottom drawer frame assembly is spaced up ¼″ from the bottom of the case and the space is to be filled with a filler block. This was done to keep the face of the bottom drawer rails clear of the base cove molding.

The center drawer guides are positioned with a gap between them for inserting a piece of plywood to serve as a drawer stop. Shims can be added

to the face of the plywood for exact drawer positioning.

The ends of the parts for the base frame and the sides, and the ends of the front and back of the box should all be formed at one time. Both the base and the box use identical lock miter joints. I prefer this joint to a splined miter (a plain miter would not be strong enough for the desk) as it is far easier to clamp. Alignment of the joint is positive and you only have to clamp from one side. Follow the steps shown to make the joints, and start with several pieces of scrap the same thickness as your stock for test cuts.

After forming the lock miter joints, cut the grooves in the inside of the box sides, front, and back for the bottom panel, and in the base frame parts for glue blocks and cleats.

Rabbet and dado the base frame parts and do a trial assembly, then glue. Do not assemble the box at this time.

All of the moldings for the base and box should be formed at one time with one setup. For safety in handling, I glued the box trim strips and the base back and front strips back-to-back to waste pine. Follow the sequence shown to form the molding.

Miter the base top parts and assemble them with reinforcing dowels. Use the base frame as a jig to get the parts cut correctly. When glued, drill all screw holes for attachment to the base frame cleats. Next, position the base top on the inverted drawer case and drill for screws.

Before the box is assembled make jigs and rout out the recesses in the sides, front, and back for the veneered panels. These recesses should be 5/16″ deep. The bottom panel is made narrower than the front to back opening and glued only at the front to allow expansion and contraction with changes in humidity. With normal humidity change, the top can be doweled to the sides and back.

To assemble the box, glue the bottom panel to the box front, then glue up all corner joints immediately. After the box is glued, rabbet around all sides to receive the molding, which can be mitered and glued to the box. The rabbet provides a better looking joint, and allows more thickness to be left on the molding for safer ripping from the blank.

Turn the two columns following the pattern. The top of the column is fitted with a short hanger bolt that threads into a steel threaded insert in the bottom of the box. A longer hanger bolt in the bottom of the column passes through clearance holes in the base

Base Frame

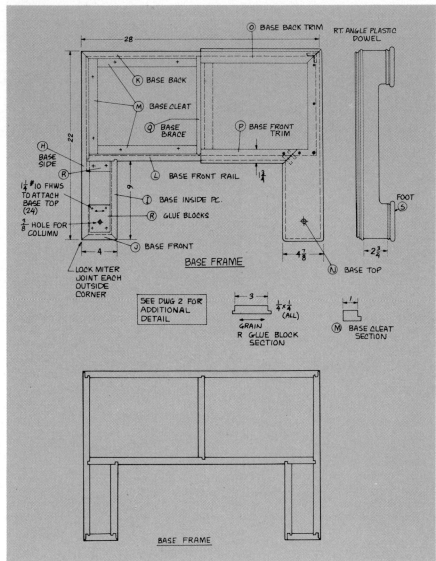

Lock Miter Joint Detail

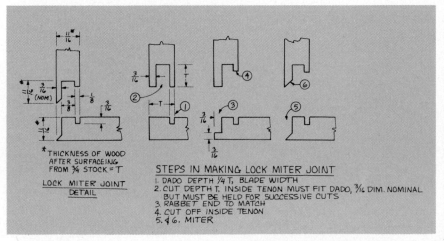

Molding Detail

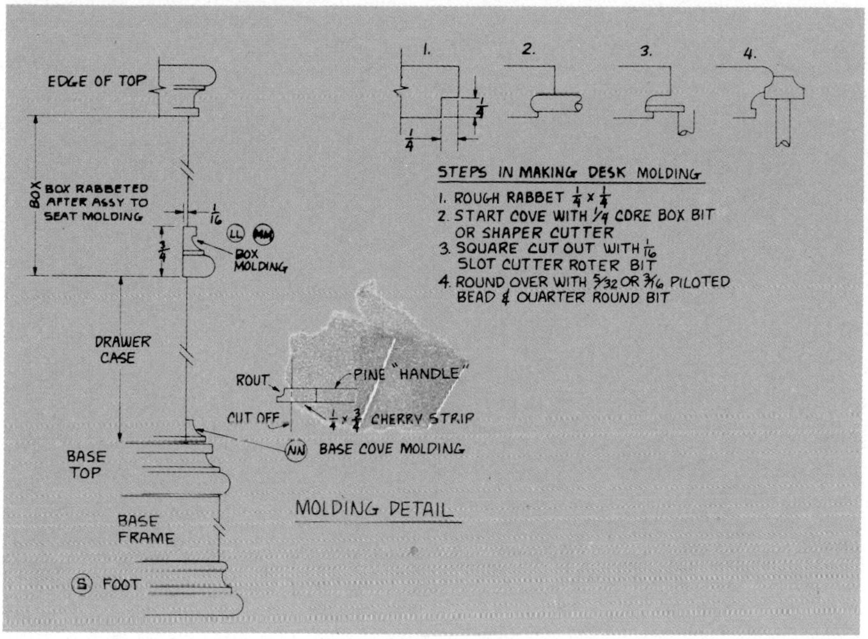
EDGE OF TOP
BOX
BOX RABBETED AFTER ASSY TO SEAT MOLDING
1/16
3/4
LL MM
BOX MOLDING
DRAWER CASE
BASE TOP
BASE FRAME
S FOOT
1. 2. 3. 4.
1/4
STEPS IN MAKING DESK MOLDING
1. ROUGH RABBET 1/4 x 1/4
2. START COVE WITH 1/4 CORE BOX BIT OR SHAPER CUTTER
3. SQUARE CUT OUT WITH 1/16 SLOT CUTTER ROTER BIT
4. ROUND OVER WITH 5/32 OR 3/16 PILOTED BEAD & QUARTER ROUND BIT
ROUT
PINE "HANDLE"
CUT OFF
1/4 x 3/4 CHERRY STRIP
NN BASE COVE MOLDING
MOLDING DETAIL

CUTTING LIST All dimensions in inches

Key	Part Name	Qty.	Material	Dimensions
A	Top rail	2	¾ Cherry	3⅜ × 19
B	Bottom rail	2	¾ Cherry	3⅝ × 19
C	Stile	4	¾ Cherry	4⅜ × 21¼
D	Drawer rail	8	¾ Cherry	2 × 10½
E	Drawer support	8	¾ Hardwood	1¼ × 23½
F	Drawer back rail	4	¾ Hardwood	3 × 8
G	Drawer guide	6	¾ Hardwood	1⅛ × 12½
H	Base side	2	¾ Cherry	2¾ × 22
I	Base inside piece	2	¾ Cherry	2¾ × 9¼
J	Base front	2	¾ Cherry	2¾ × 4
K	Base back	1	¾ Cherry	2¾ × 28
L	Base cross brace	1	¾ Cherry	1⅞ × 27
M	Base cleat	6	¾ Hardwood	1¼ × 12
N	Base top	2	¾ Cherry	4⅞ × 23
O	Base back trim	1	¾ Cherry	1¾ × 29
P	Base front trim	1	¾ Cherry	1¾ × 24
Q	Base brace	1	¾ Hardwood	1⅞ × 12
R	Base glue blocks	3	¾ Hardwood	3 × 3 (split one)
S	Foot	4	¾ Cherry	4⅞ × 4⅞
T	Box side	2	¾ Cherry	7½ × 21
U	Box front	1	¾ Cherry	4 × 27
V	Box back	1	¾ Cherry	7½ × 27
W	Box top	1	¾ Cherry	6 7/16 × 27⅞
X	Box lid	1	¾ Cherry	16⅝ × 27⅞
Y	Box bottom	1	¾ Cherry	20 × 26
Z	Panel	2	¼ Plywood	15 × 19
AA	Drawer front	6	¾ Cherry	5 3/16 × 10⅜
BB	Lower drawer side	4	½ Oak	11 × 13
CC	Lower drawer back	2	½ Oak	11 × 10⅜
DD	False rail	2	¾ Cherry	¾ × 10⅜
EE	Middle drawer side	4	½ Oak	5 3/16 × 13
FF	Middle drawer back	2	½ Oak	5 3/16 × 10⅜
GG	Top drawer front	2	¾ Cherry	1¾ × 10⅜
HH	Top drawer side	4	½ Oak	2 × 13
II	Top drawer back	2	½ Oak	2 × 10⅜
JJ	Drawer bottom	6	¼ Birch Ply	9⅞ × 12¾
KK	Drawer runner	6	½ Hardwood	2¼ × 13
LL	Box side molding	2	¾ Cherry	½ × 23
MM	Box front, Back molding	2	¾ Cherry	½ × 29
NN	Base cove molding	3	¼ Cherry	5/16 × 28
OO	Column	2	Cherry	3 × 3 × 24

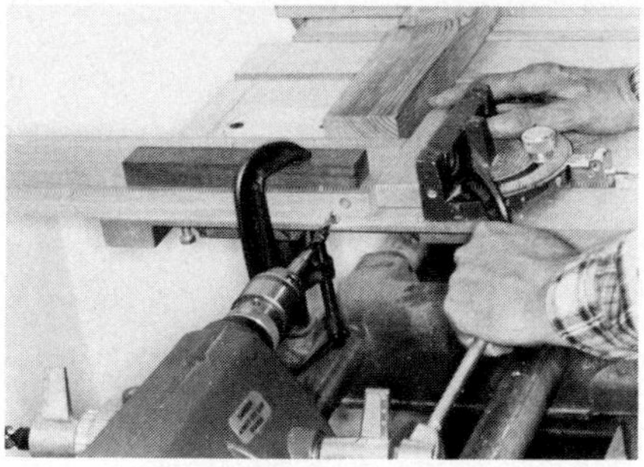

Drilling dowel holes requires accuracy. The best way to do it is in a horizontal boring setup, such as can be done on a Shopsmith. No matter how you jig up to drill dowel holes, always work with only one side of the stock as the reference surface. This way, when you are slightly off the centerline, the parts won't be twisted when you dowel them together.

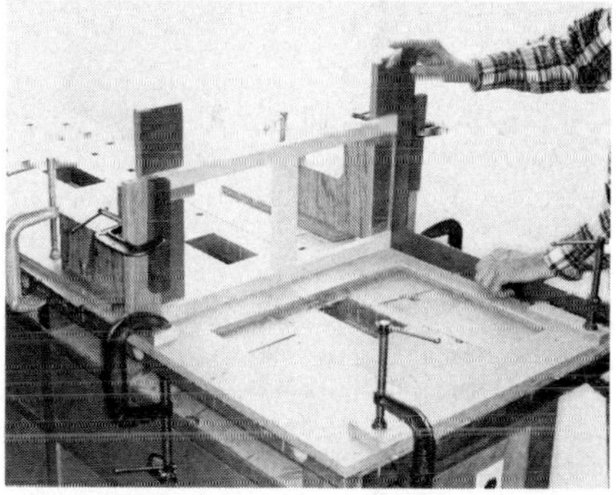

Assembling the drawer case. Before doing any gluing, completely assemble the case dry. When gluing, it is absolutely essential that the first joint is true. The top drawer frame is being glued and aligned to one side with a pair of shop-made right angle gluing jigs, and double-checked with a carpenter's square. As each successive frame is added, it will be aligned by having the free side (top) dry-dowelled to the other side of the case.

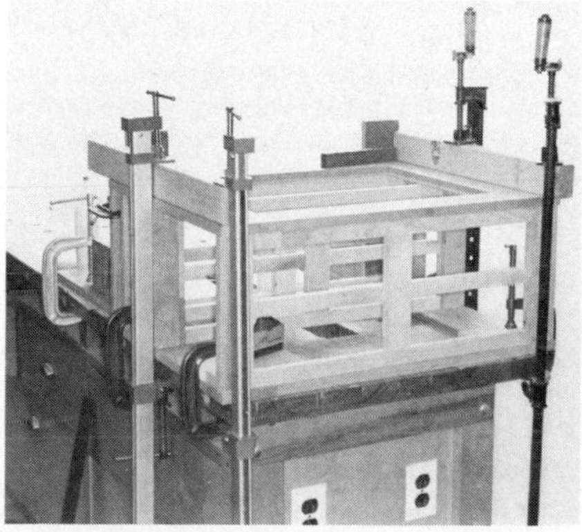

The drawer case completely assembled. Gluing the second side to all of the frames involved 16 dowels—assistance is a good idea for this gluing. The frame-to-side joints are reinforced with screws.

Gluing up the base frame. Lock miter joints are easy to assemble; alignment is positive, and clamping is required in one direction only.

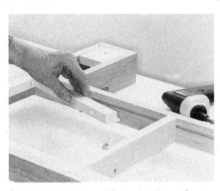

Cleats are tenoned into the base frame after being drilled for attaching the base top.

Fingerboards help hold the box top against the fence for making the first rabbet (see drawings, step 1 in forming the molding).

Drawers

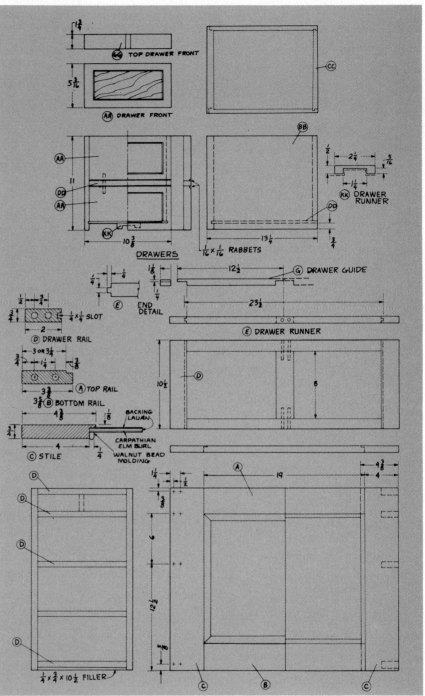

top and glue block and is secured with a washer and nut.

The two large drawer fronts are given the appearance of being two drawers. The fronts and dummy rails are glued up with dowels. Before gluing, rout a ¹⁄₁₆″ by ¹⁄₁₆″ rabbet in the drawer fronts as shown to enhance the two-drawer appearance. If either of the big drawers is going to contain a hanging file, notch the sides for the

support rails before you assemble the drawers. The drawer fronts are routed out a depth of ⁵⁄₁₆″ to receive the Carpathian elm burl panel. The panel should be glued into the drawer after routing the dovetails and before drawer assembly. I used a thin walnut bead molding strip ripped from scrap wood.

The drawers otherwise are built conventionally. Sides, front, and back

are joined with router-jig dovetails. The drawer bottom is slotted into the sides and front, but passes under the back. The runner is doweled or mortised into the drawer front and nailed to the drawer back.

The Carpathian elm burl veneer was a real problem to handle: It would not lay flat and was extremely brittle. It was difficult to cut without breaking, and impossible to clamp flat to

Box Frame Corner Joints

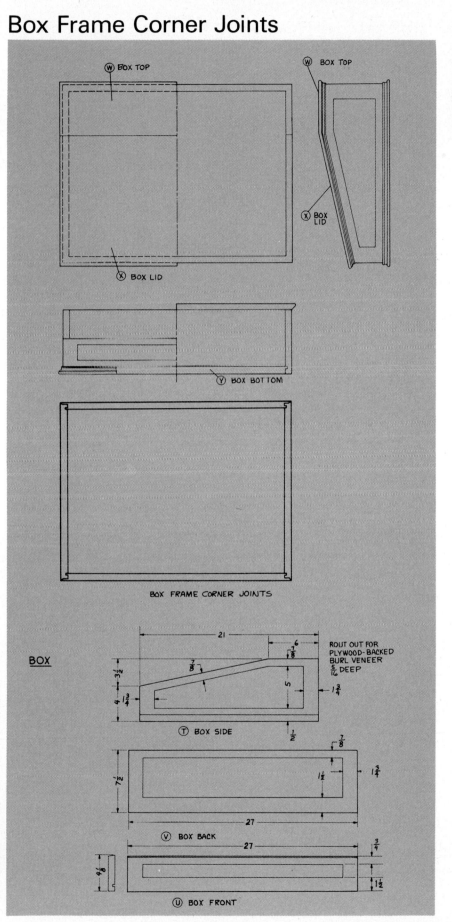

A Rockwell tenoning jig is invaluable for holding workpieces while forming the lock miter joint tenon on a table saw (see drawings, step 2 in making lock miter joint).

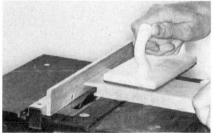

The Dremel table saw is hard to beat for precise cuts on small workpieces, such as cutting off the inside stub tenon while forming a lock miter joint (drawings, step 4). I also used the Dremel to make the miters.

true the edges for book-matching the large drawer case panels.

To get the veneer to lie flat, it had to be treated with the following mixture: 3 parts plastic (urea) resin glue (powder), 4 parts cold water, 2 parts glycerine (drug store), 1 part denatured alcohol.

Measurements are by volume. The plastic resin glue must be fresh; the powder goes bad in the can. Mix the powder and water, add the other two ingredients. The dilute glue sizes the veneer to add strength, the glycerine provides flexibility. The alcohol speeds drying. Soak the veneer in the solution for two minutes, drain dry, wipe the surfaces and put the veneer between sheets of aluminum foil, stack between boards and weight the pile to flatten. Drying will take several days. The veneer will come out flat, flexible and able to be easily cut.

Quarter-inch lauan plywood was used for the large drawer case panels, and the backside was veneered with low-cost veneer to balance out any warp. Veneer for the small panels inset in the drawers and box were glued to 1/8" plywood. No veneer was added to the backs as these panels will be glued into the drawers. All of the veneered panels were trimmed with walnut bead molding.

Typical Drawers and Pigeon Holes

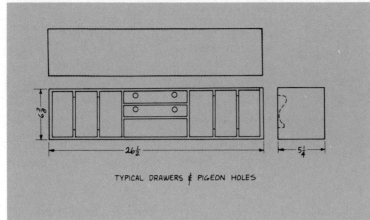

TYPICAL DRAWERS & PIGEON HOLES

Gallery

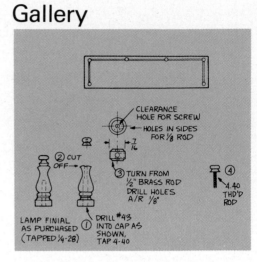

Base Frame

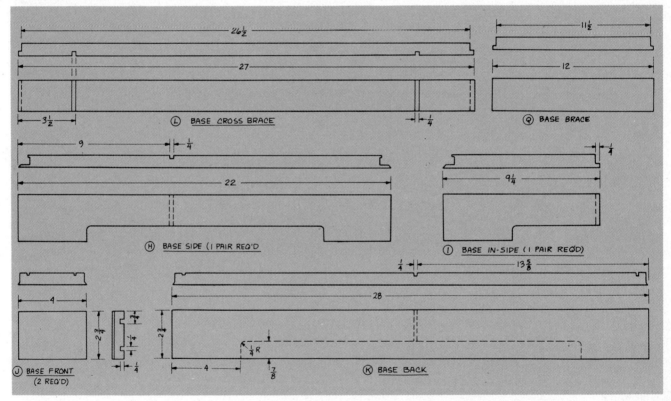

Column

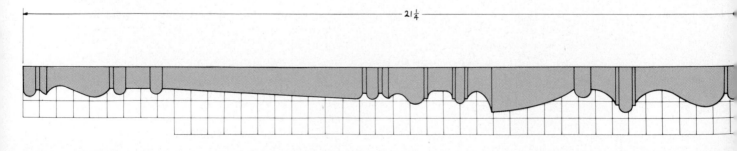

The undercut cove part of the desk molding was formed on a Shopsmith set up for shaping as I did not have the correct bit for routing.

The squared edge of the cove part of the molding was cleaned out with a slotting cutter with the router set up in a shaping table.

The box is attached to the drawer case with brass screws through the box bottom into the top drawer rails.

The gallery was made using inexpensive brass table lamp finials for posts. Drill the finials from the bottom to 1/16″ from the top with a #43 drill, then tap the hole for 4-40 threads. Cut off the tops of the finials as shown and dress the cut edges. Turn the rail post sections from 1/2″ brass rod, and drill for 1/8″ diameter brass rod rails, and a clearance hole for a 4-40 threaded rod. Attach the posts to the desk top by threading 1/4-28 threaded rod into the wood. Thread the finial onto the rod. Cut 1/8″ rod for the rails and insert in post rail sections. Secure these sections to the finials with the finial tips and 4-40 threaded rod.

The wood can either be stained, or allowed to naturally darken with age. I stained, using fruitwood stain on the cherry, walnut stain on the walnut, and a light-colored oak stain on the Carpathian elm burl. All the parts can be stained and varnished completely before assembly, which makes the task a lot easier. The top coat consisted of two coats of UGL's ZAR Quick Dry polyurethane coating lightly sanded between coats to knock off any dust particles, etc., followed by three coats of their Gloss ZAR with more thorough sanding between coats. All coats were applied with foam brushes which inherently lay on a thinner and smoother coat than you will get with a brush—*By Thomas H. Jones.*

Carpathian elm burl veneer is not normally flat and easy to cut. The selection purchased for the desk was especially curled and brittle. Before use, it was treated (see text) to add strength and flexibility. After

the veneer was pressed flat and dried, the greater ease of use was amazing.

To dress veneer edges for butt joint, I clamp the stacked veneer between boards and sand it on a bench disc sander.

The desk was built in modules—base frame, base top, drawer case, and box.

Attaching the box to the drawer case with brass screws—brass, because the ones at the front of the sides will show.

After the box top and lid have been mortised for hinges, the top is attached to the box with dowels.

three redwood gazebos

Whether you use it as a place to entertain, as a garden shed or poolside cabana, or merely as a shady retreat from the summer sun, a backyard shelter makes an enticing addition to any home. An octagonal gazebo with latticework painted white is an American tradition, but these variations—designed and built by Homecrafters of California for homes in Fresno—show how tradition can be updated.

That customary white treatment must be renewed every few seasons to prevent decay. Today's chemically treated woods will stand up to outdoor conditions for many years. But garden-grade redwood is naturally resistant to insects and decay—and dimensionally stable. These qualities, combined with its warm and rustic visual appeal, make redwood a natural choice for garden and poolside shelters.

The California Redwood Assn. lists four garden grades of redwood; these are less expensive than the architectural grades but have knots and are not kiln-dried. Construction heart and merchantable heart grades contain no

Curved Pool Pavilion

sapwood, and thus are recommended for structural members and for use in or near the ground. Construction common and merchantable grades, which do have sapwood streaks, are good choices for decking, fencing, trellises, and similar uses. Merchantable grades contain larger knots than construction grades. The wood will weather differently depending on the finish. Unfinished, it will gradually turn gray; with a water repellent applied, the wood will stabilize at tan; to keep its red tone, you'd have to apply a deck stain—*By Daniel Ruby. Photos by Karl Riek. Drawings by Eugene Thompson*

Three inviting shelters are variations of basic post-and-beam design. Curved pool pavilion (left) has a flat slatted roof and airy crisscross latticework. A side door opens into the house. Classic garden gazebo (right) takes on a rustic look when built with garden-grade, knot-patterned redwood. Its shingled pyramid roof keeps out rain; lattice walls screen the sun. Angular pool shelter (below) has a shed-type slat roof that leaves part of the diagonal deck exposed to sun, part shaded.

Garden Gazebo

Angular Pool Shelter

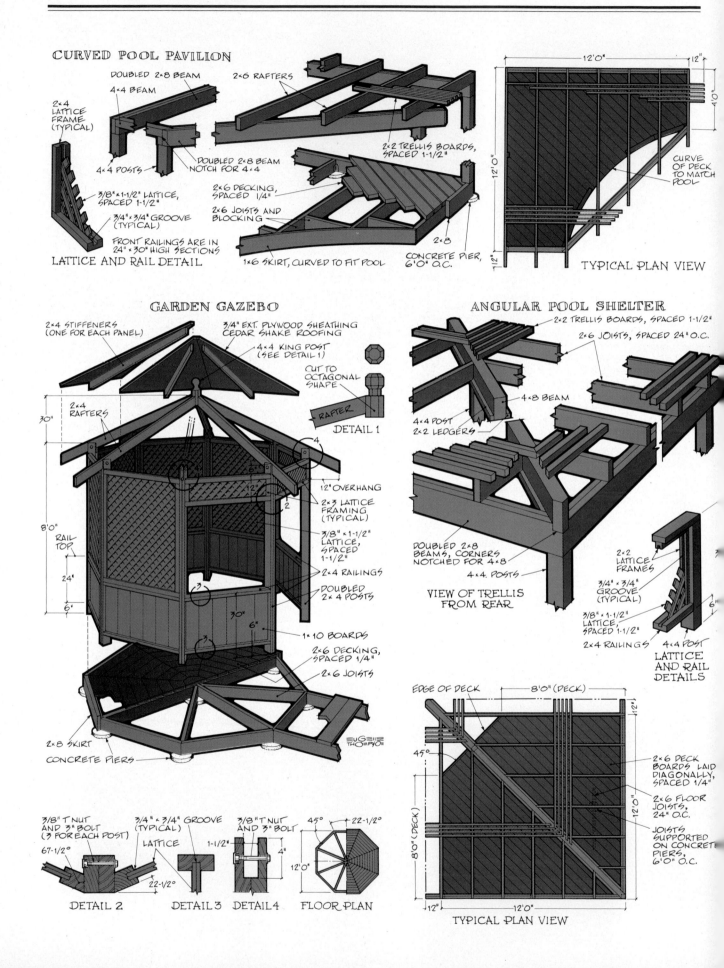

CURVED POOL PAVILION

2×4 LATTICE FRAME (TYPICAL)

DOUBLED 2×8 BEAM

4×4 BEAM

2×6 RAFTERS

4×4 POSTS

DOUBLED 2×8 BEAM NOTCH FOR 4×4

2×2 TRELLIS BOARDS, SPACED 1-1/2"

3/8"×1-1/2" LATTICE, SPACED 1-1/2"

3/4"×3/4" GROOVE (TYPICAL)

2×6 DECKING, SPACED 1/4"

2×6 JOISTS AND BLOCKING

FRONT RAILINGS ARE IN 24"×30" HIGH SECTIONS

LATTICE AND RAIL DETAIL

1×6 SKIRT, CURVED TO FIT POOL

CONCRETE PIER, 6'0" O.C.

2×8

12'0"

4'0"

12'0"

12"

1/2"

CURVE OF DECK TO MATCH POOL

TYPICAL PLAN VIEW

GARDEN GAZEBO

2×4 STIFFENERS (ONE FOR EACH PANEL)

3/4" EXT. PLYWOOD SHEATHING CEDAR SHAKE ROOFING

4×4 KING POST (SEE DETAIL 1)

CUT TO OCTAGONAL SHAPE

RAFTER

DETAIL 1

30"

2×4 RAFTERS

8'0"

RAIL TOP

24"

6"

12" OVERHANG

2×3 LATTICE FRAMING (TYPICAL)

3/8"×1-1/2" LATTICE, SPACED 1-1/2"

2×4 RAILINGS

DOUBLED 2×4 POSTS

30"

6"

1×10 BOARDS

2×6 DECKING, SPACED 1/4"

2×6 JOISTS

2×8 SKIRT

CONCRETE PIERS

ANGULAR POOL SHELTER

2×2 TRELLIS BOARDS, SPACED 1-1/2"

2×6 JOISTS, SPACED 24" O.C.

4×8 BEAM

4×4 POST

2×2 LEDGERS

DOUBLED 2×8 BEAMS, CORNERS NOTCHED FOR 4×8

4×4 POSTS

VIEW OF TRELLIS FROM REAR

2×2 LATTICE FRAMES

3/4"×3/4" GROOVE (TYPICAL)

3/8"×1-1/2" LATTICE, SPACED 1-1/2"

2×4 RAILINGS   4×4 POST

LATTICE AND RAIL DETAILS

3/8" T NUT AND 3" BOLT (3 FOR EACH POST)

67-1/2°

3/4"×3/4" GROOVE (TYPICAL)

LATTICE

22-1/2°

DETAIL 2

1-1/2"

DETAIL 3

3/8" T NUT AND 3" BOLT

4"

DETAIL 4

45°

22-1/2°

12'0"

FLOOR PLAN

EDGE OF DECK

8'0" (DECK)

12"

45°

8'0" (DECK)

12'0"

2×6 DECK BOARDS LAID DIAGONALLY, SPACED 1/4"

2×6 FLOOR JOISTS, 24" O.C.

JOISTS SUPPORTED ON CONCRETE PIERS, 6'0" O.C.

12"   12'0"

TYPICAL PLAN VIEW

EUGENE THOMPSON

framework for a modular garden

The traditional vegetable garden, with neat rows of vegetables stretching on and on, is a poor strategy for people with limited space. What's more, the pathways between the rows end up compacted, leaving the soil less able to absorb as much moisture as it needs. Raised bed planting is a far better way to utilize your garden space, and it's better for the plants in many ways.

The biggest problem in any garden is getting the full advantage of the local growing season. By enclosing your raised beds, you gain extra weeks of growing and precious protection against wind and rain damage. Most gardeners I know prefer to frame their beds with wood. Wood-framed beds are easier to care for and look much neater. Cheap, construction grade pine is sufficient, provided you treat it with a wood preservative such as Cuprinol. Avoid creosote as a preservative: It's toxic to plants and isn't very good for humans, either.

To give your bed plenty of height, 2×8 or 2×10 lumber is best. One-inch boards tend to warp quickly, and the edges aren't particularly comfortable to kneel on. You can make the beds as narrow as you like, but they shouldn't be much wider than 4 feet, or you risk falling in when trying to reach the vegetables in the middle of the bed. 4' × 4' beds are nearly ideal, being an easy size to maintain.

These plans incorporate a basic raised-bed frame with a removable cold frame and trellis. Both accessories fit into the sides of the bed frame that are made from two 1 × 10s with spacers in between. The cold frame can be used early in the season, to protect young plants from the cold; as the

The grow frame with glazing flaps down and doors off. Inside, the crop (lettuce here) gets a little breather.

Framework for a Modular Garden

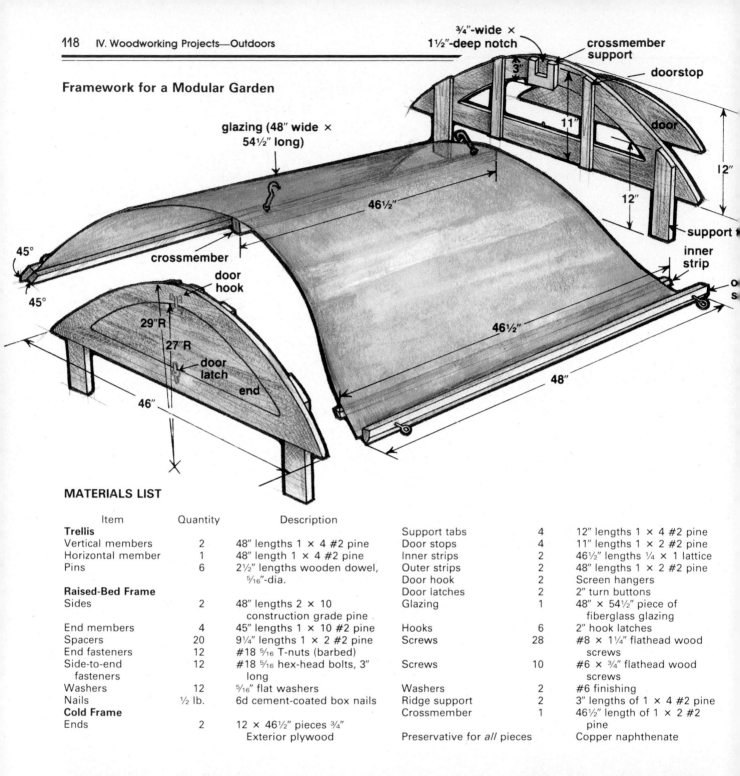

¾"-wide × 1½"-deep notch

crossmember support

doorstop

glazing (48" wide × 54½" long)

crossmember

door hook

door latch

end

45°

45°

29"R

27"R

46"

46½"

46½"

48"

12"

11"

12"

door

support

inner strip

MATERIALS LIST

Item	Quantity	Description
Trellis		
Vertical members	2	48" lengths 1 × 4 #2 pine
Horizontal member	1	48" length 1 × 4 #2 pine
Pins	6	2½" lengths wooden dowel, 5⁄16"-dia.
Raised-Bed Frame		
Sides	2	48" lengths 2 × 10 construction grade pine
End members	4	45" lengths 1 × 10 #2 pine
Spacers	20	9¼" lengths 1 × 2 #2 pine
End fasteners	12	#18 5⁄16 T-nuts (barbed)
Side-to-end fasteners	12	#18 5⁄16 hex-head bolts, 3" long
Washers	12	5⁄16" flat washers
Nails	½ lb.	6d cement-coated box nails
Cold Frame		
Ends	2	12 × 46½" pieces ¾" Exterior plywood

Item	Quantity	Description
Support tabs	4	12" lengths 1 × 4 #2 pine
Door stops	4	11" lengths 1 × 2 #2 pine
Inner strips	2	46½" lengths ¼ × 1 lattice
Outer strips	2	48" lengths 1 × 2 #2 pine
Door hook	2	Screen hangers
Door latches	2	2" turn buttons
Glazing	1	48" × 54½" piece of fiberglass glazing
Hooks	6	2" hook latches
Screws	28	#8 × 1¼" flathead wood screws
Screws	10	#6 × ¾" flathead wood screws
Washers	2	#6 finishing
Ridge support	2	3" lengths of 1 × 4 #2 pine
Crossmember	1	46½" length of 1 × 2 #2 pine
Preservative for *all* pieces		Copper naphthenate

Raised-Bed Frame

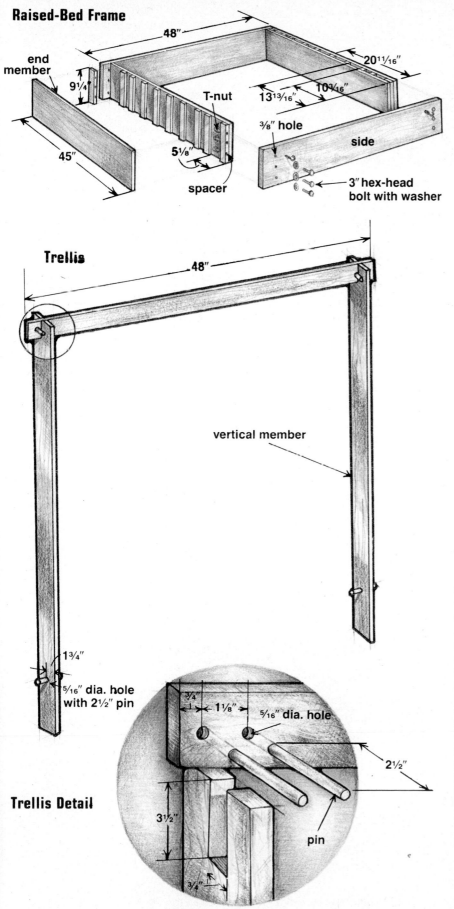

end
member

48"

9¼"

20¹¹⁄₁₆"

T-nut

13¹³⁄₁₆"   10³⁄₁₆"

45"

⅜" hole

side

5⅛"

spacer

3" hex-head
bolt with washer

Trellis

48"

vertical member

1¾"

⁵⁄₁₆" dia. hole
with 2½" pin

Trellis Detail

¾"

1"   1⅛"

⁵⁄₁₆" dia. hole

2½"

3½"

pin

¾"

season progresses, to protect new plants of later crops; and even in the fall, to extend the season for a late planting of salad greens or to keep the chill off a bed of cold-sensitive crops. It also features removable side doors which act as vents to help regulate the temperature within the frame. In summer, the glazing can be replaced with netting to shade plants and fend off hungry birds.

The trellis allows you to plant more intensively by utilizing the space above the garden to grow climbing plants. It can be as high as you'd like, but 6 feet is probably as much as you'll need. This one is made from three lengths of 1 × 4: Two risers, and a crosspiece that fits into slots at the top. You can staple string, wire, or netting in the middle to give the plants something to grab on to.

Construction

To build this 4' × 4' raised-bed frame, simply gather all that's specified in the materials list and assemble it as shown in the accompanying diagram. After you cut all pieces to size and drill ⅜" holes for the T-nuts, paint all lumber with a copper naphthenate wood preservative (such as Cuprinol). Then hammer T-nuts into the holes of the end spacer sandwiches with nails. Bolt them to the 2 × 10 sides, and you're finished.

The cold frame is trickier. Start by cutting the plywood ends. Lay out the 29" radius first and cut it with your saber saw to give a half-moon shape to the ends. Then cut out a door along a 27"-radius. Cut the pine members as specified on the materials list: You'll need to further modify the support tabs and door stops by cutting a radius on top to match the plywood ends. Also, you'll need to rip two 45-degree angles along the outer glazing strips, so that the bottom edge of each strip comes to a point. (A table saw is almost essential for these cuts.) When the glazing top is in place, one of the 45-degree edges will lie flat on the raised-bed frame's top edge; the other will be parallel with the raised bed side. Paint all lumber with copper naphthenate before assembly. For the glazing, use any flexible, thin plastic sheet, such as Filon's Solar Plate or Solar Components Corporation's Sun-Lite Premium II.

The trellis is very straightforward (see illustrations)—*Michael Lafavore*

Adapted from *Rodale's New Shelter* Magazine
Copyright 1983, Rodale Press Inc.
All rights reserved.

adjustable trellis/sun shade

Don Weber, a Colorado builder, wanted a deck outside his sun room. The room doubles as a passive solar collector, so Weber didn't want to screen out winter sun. Yet he needed summer shade for both the deck and the room.

His solution was an adjustable trellis. This structure has removable slats, which slip in or out of the frame easily, so you can adjust the amount of shade to the season.

"When the sun starts getting strong in the spring, you start by slipping every third board into the frame," Weber told me. "As the sun gets stronger, you go to every other board. By summer, you have them all in."

The adjustable trellis also lets you vary the amount of shade that falls on the deck and where it falls. "If you want full shade close to the house—say, for shade-loving plants—you put all the boards in at the beginning of the season and leave them there," Weber said.

But if you want direct sun on one part of the deck for sunbathing, it's a simple matter to slip out some slats. "It takes probably 10 seconds per slat," Weber said, "and about 20 minutes to take them all down."

In fact, Weber dismantles the whole trellis for the winter. "Only the support posts stay up," he said. "I do it that way to get maximum solar gain. I don't want even the shadow from a 1×8 falling on the glass."

Building the deck and trellis was a fairly straightforward task, Weber says, once he determined the correct angle for the slat slots. After studying insolation tables, he decided that slanting the boards at 40 degrees would provide the best midsummer shade.

"I first erected the corner support posts," explained Weber. "Next I lag-screwed a nailer to the house, then nailed galvanized joist hangers on it for deck joists. After laying the decking, I attached an upper nailer to the house for the trellis framework."

The two inner supports have slat blocks and 1×2 stops nailed to *both* faces, as shown in the diagram below. These angle-cut blocks hold the slats at the correct pitch.

For the joists, decking, and support posts, Weber found it sensible to use construction heart redwood, a textured "garden grade" that is rot resistant and dimensionally stable yet costs less than the architectural redwood grade.

For the trellis slats, he used clear all-heart redwood. "It's better-looking," he explained, "and these boards are the most visible."

Weber made the slats four feet long. "Any longer and they might have too much sag," he warned. He added that the slats may sag anyway as they dry. In that case, "all you do is take them out, turn them around, and put them back in," he said. "They'll straighten right out."

Weber says the adjustable trellis has worked well for him—and for the many homeowners who have since commissioned him to build similar trellised decks. "I must have built 50 of them since I did mine," he said, "and I haven't changed the design at all—just altered the deck to fit the space available"—*By Susan Renner-Smith.*

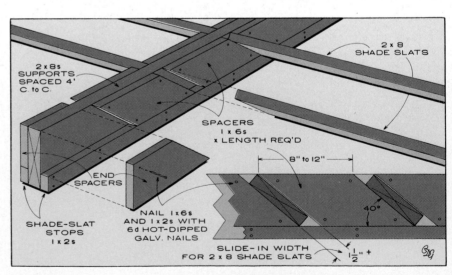

Trellis slats slip into grooves formed by spacer blocks nailed inside the support frame. Cut blocks to identical angles and nail them to the 2×8s, flush with their top edges. Trellis slats fit snugly in gaps between spacer blocks and are held in place by a 1×2 stop nailed below. Galvanized hardware was used throughout.

Lifting out a louver (above) adds a sunny spot to the well-shaded deck (right). Removable slats allow winter sun to heat the skylighted sun room (top). Designer Weber estimates that it takes only about 10 seconds to remove or replace each board.

outdoor swing

This outdoor swing exemplifies passive cooling at its rudimentary best. After a grueling day at the office or a few hours of gardening and lawn work, nothing is more soothing than rocking to and fro.

Our outdoor swing offers tradition with a modern twist. Every edge of the swing is rounded and sanded smooth, providing added comfort and visual appeal. The swing is constructed with clear cedar, but redwood, oak, maple, or any other available hardwood that is free from knots can also be used. To protect the swing from the weather and decay, be sure to finish all parts with an exterior polyurethane or paint.

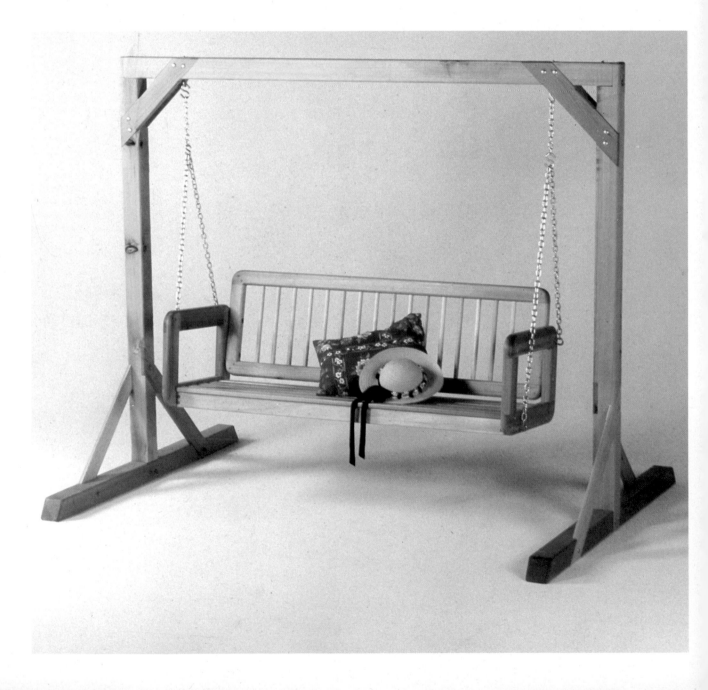

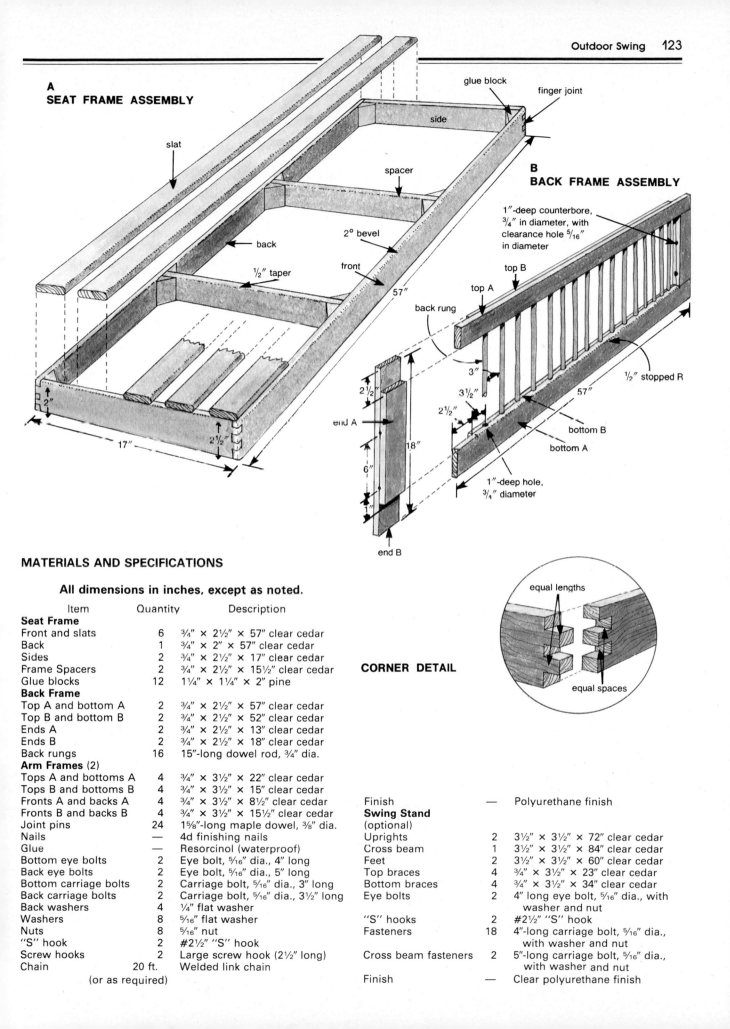

A
SEAT FRAME ASSEMBLY

slat

glue block

finger joint

side

spacer

2° bevel

back

½" taper

front

57"

2"

17"

2½"

B
BACK FRAME ASSEMBLY

1"-deep counterbore, ¾" in diameter, with clearance hole ⁵⁄₁₆" in diameter

top B

top A

back rung

½" stopped R

57"

2½"

3"

3½"

2½"

end A

18"

6"

1"

bottom B

bottom A

1"-deep hole, ¾" diameter

end B

CORNER DETAIL

equal lengths

equal spaces

MATERIALS AND SPECIFICATIONS

All dimensions in inches, except as noted.

Item	Quantity	Description
Seat Frame		
Front and slats	6	¾" × 2½" × 57" clear cedar
Back	1	¾" × 2" × 57" clear cedar
Sides	2	¾" × 2½" × 17" clear cedar
Frame Spacers	2	¾" × 2½" × 15½" clear cedar
Glue blocks	12	1¼" × 1¼" × 2" pine
Back Frame		
Top A and bottom A	2	¾" × 2½" × 57" clear cedar
Top B and bottom B	2	¾" × 2½" × 52" clear cedar
Ends A	2	¾" × 2½" × 13" clear cedar
Ends B	2	¾" × 2½" × 18" clear cedar
Back rungs	16	15"-long dowel rod, ¾" dia.
Arm Frames (2)		
Tops A and bottoms A	4	¾" × 3½" × 22" clear cedar
Tops B and bottoms B	4	¾" × 3½" × 15" clear cedar
Fronts A and backs A	4	¾" × 3½" × 8½" clear cedar
Fronts B and backs B	4	¾" × 3½" × 15½" clear cedar
Joint pins	24	1⅝"-long maple dowel, ⅜" dia.
Nails	—	4d finishing nails
Glue	—	Resorcinol (waterproof)
Bottom eye bolts	2	Eye bolt, ⁵⁄₁₆" dia., 4" long
Back eye bolts	2	Eye bolt, ⁵⁄₁₆" dia., 5" long
Bottom carriage bolts	2	Carriage bolt, ⁵⁄₁₆" dia., 3" long
Back carriage bolts	2	Carriage bolt, ⁵⁄₁₆" dia., 3½" long
Back washers	4	¼" flat washer
Washers	8	⁵⁄₁₆" flat washer
Nuts	8	⁵⁄₁₆" nut
"S" hook	2	#2½" "S" hook
Screw hooks	2	Large screw hook (2½" long)
Chain	20 ft.	Welded link chain
	(or as required)	

Item	Quantity	Description
Finish	—	Polyurethane finish
Swing Stand (optional)		
Uprights	2	3½" × 3½" × 72" clear cedar
Cross beam	1	3½" × 3½" × 84" clear cedar
Feet	2	3½" × 3½" × 60" clear cedar
Top braces	4	¾" × 3½" × 23" clear cedar
Bottom braces	4	¾" × 3½" × 34" clear cedar
Eye bolts	2	4" long eye bolt, ⁵⁄₁₆" dia., with washer and nut
"S" hooks	2	#2½" "S" hook
Fasteners	18	4"-long carriage bolt, ⁵⁄₁₆" dia., with washer and nut
Cross beam fasteners	2	5"-long carriage bolt, ⁵⁄₁₆" dia., with washer and nut
Finish	—	Clear polyurethane finish

Construction

Illustration A

1. Cut the seat-frame front, back, and slats to size.

2. Cut or plane a 2° bevel along the top edges of the seat-frame front and back.

3. Cut the seat-frame sides to size.

4. Lay out and cut a ½" taper on the top edge of each side.

5. Lay out and cut a finger joint at each corner of the seat frame (see Corner Detail).

6. Glue and clamp the seat frame.

7. Cut the seat-frame spacers to size.

8. Lay out and cut a ½" taper (to match the sides' taper) along the top edge of each spacer. Fasten the spacers in place, using glue and 4d finishing nails.

9. Cut the glue blocks to size. Fasten the blocks in the corners of the seat frame and in the spacer corners with glue.

10. Machine a ¼" radius along all edges of the seat frame, spacers, and slats.

11. Fasten the slats to the seat frame, using glue and 4d finishing nails.

Illustration B

12. Cut the back-frame tops (A and B) and bottoms (A and B) to size.

13. Face-glue top A to top B and bottom A to bottom B, leaving a 2½" step at each end of top and bottom A for a half-lap joint. These assembled pieces are the top and bottom of the back frame.

14. Machine a ½" stopped radius along the inside edges of the top and bottom.

15. Lay out and drill 16 holes, ¾" diameter, 1" deep, in the inside edge of the top and bottom to accept the back rungs.

16. Cut the back-frame ends A and B to size.

17. Face-glue an end A to an end B, leaving a 2½" step at the top and bottom of the end B for a half-lap joint. Repeat the procedure for the other end of the back frame.

18. Locate and drill two counterbores, ¾" diameter and 1" deep, with clearance holes, 5/16" diameter, in each of the end pieces to accept 3"-long carriage bolts.

19. Cut the back rungs to size. Glue the back rungs into the ¾" holes drilled in Step 15.

20. Glue and clamp the ends to the top and bottom, forming half-lap joints at each corner of the back frame.

Illustration C

21. Cut eight joint pins to size. Lay out and drill two holes, ⅜" diameter, through each of the four corner joints of the back frame to accept the joint pins. Glue the joint pins in place.

22. Lay out and cut a 2" radius along the four corners of the back frame.

23. Finish machining the ½" radius along all edges of the back frame.

Illustration D

24. Cut the arm-frame tops (A and B) and bottoms (A and B) to size.

25. Face-glue top A to top B and bottom A to bottom B for each arm frame, leaving a 3½" at each end of top and bottom A for a half-lap joint. These assembled pieces are the tops and bottoms of the arm frames.

26. Cut the arm frame's fronts (A and B) and backs (A and B) to size.

27. Face-glue front A to front B and back A to back B for each arm frame leaving a 3½" step at the top and bottom

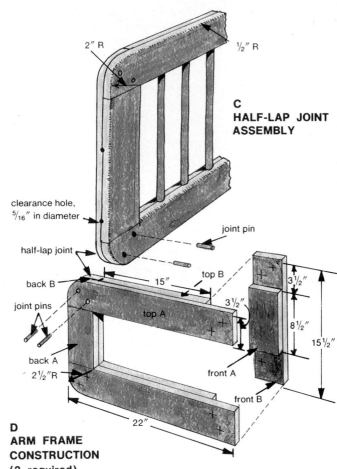

C HALF-LAP JOINT ASSEMBLY

2" R

½" R

clearance hole, 5/16" in diameter

joint pin

half-lap joint

back B

top B

15"

joint pins

top A

3½"

3½"

8½"

15½"

back A

2½" R

front A

22"

front B

D ARM FRAME CONSTRUCTION (2 required)

of front and back B for a half-lap joint. These assembled pieces are the fronts and backs of the arm frames.

28. Glue and clamp the front and back to the top and bottom, forming half-lap joints at each corner.

29. Cut sixteen joint pins to size. Lay out and drill two holes, ⅜" diameter, through the corner joints of both arm frames. Glue the joint pins in place.

30. Lay out and cut a 2½" radius at the four corners of each arm frame.

31. Machine a ½" radius along all edges of the arm frames.

Illustration E

32. Clamp an arm frame to each end of the seat frame.

33. Drill two holes, 5/16" diameter, at the base of the arm frame and through the seat frame, one at the back to accept a carriage bolt, and one at the front to accept an eye bolt.

34. Lay out and drill a hole, 5/16" diameter, through the upper back corner of each arm frame aligned with the top hole already located at each end of the back frame to accept an eye bolt. Drill a second hole through the back of each arm frame aligned with the lower hole on each end of the back frame to accept a carriage bolt.

35. Sand the seat, back, and arm frames, and apply a polyurethane finish.

36. Open the eye in four eye bolts.

37. Cut two pieces of chain, 40" long, and two pieces of chain, 32" long. (The amount of chain required may vary depending on the location of the swing.) Fasten the ends

of each piece of chain to an eye bolt by closing the eye around the chain.

38. Assemble the swing using the eye bolts and carriage bolts with washers.

39. Fasten two large screw hooks (at least 2½″ long) into overhead joists. (If the swing stand is going to be used, two ⁵⁄₁₆″ × 4″ eye bolts with an "S" hook will be used instead of the screw hooks.)

40. Hang the swing and adjust the height and balance to a comfortable position using additional chain and an "S" hook.

Illustration F (Swing Stand (optional)
1. Cut the uprights to size.
2. Lay out and cut a 1¾″ notch for a half-lap joint on the bottom of each upright. Cut a 2¾″-deep shoulder at the top of each upright.
3. Cut the cross beam to size.
4. Position the cross beam in the shoulders of the uprights. Counterbore and drill a clearance hole at an angle through the cross beam and each upright to accept a ⁵⁄₁₆″ × 5″ carriage bolt.

E
PORCH SWING ASSEMBLY

F
SWING STAND ASSEMBLY

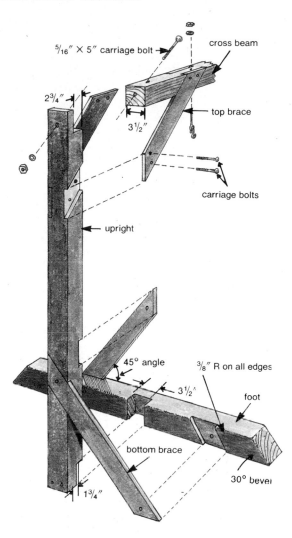

5. Cut the feet to size. Lay out and cut a 30° bevel on both ends of each foot.
6. Lay out and cut a 1¾″ × 1¾″ half-lap on each foot to accept the uprights.
7. Connect the feet to the uprights forming a half-lap joint, using two carriage bolts for each foot.
8. Cut the top and bottom braces to size.
9. Position the braces from the uprights to the feet and cross beam at 45° angles. Scribe lines on both sides of each brace indicating the proper cutting lines on the uprights, feet, and cross beam.
10. Hollow out the appropriate notches in the feet and uprights to accept the bottom braces, and in the cross beam and uprights to accept the top braces.
11. Mark and cut each brace to its finished shape.
12. Drill holes for carriage bolts and fasten braces to uprights, cross beam, and feet.
13. Machine a ⅜″ radius on all edges of the stand. Some of the fasteners may have to be removed for this step.
14. Sand the assembled stand and apply a polyurethane finish.

Adapted from *Rodale's New Shelter* magazine

kids' backyard play centers

1. Swing Set with Playhouse

My son and his buddies spend much of their time in a geodesic-dome playhouse (perched 6½ feet above the ground) or sliding, swinging, and climbing on the play equipment below. I designed and built the structure rather than settling for a standard bolt-together set of steel tubes, swings, and slides. My main objection to those: They tend to rust after a few years and become a maintenance problem. And commercial wooden swing sets are rather expensive. I built this wooden play center for less than $400.

Except for the playhouse siding, all the wood is Wolmanized for easy upkeep and durability. The geodesic-dome playhouse is easily assembled with the help of Starplate connectors (see drawing, following page). Its frame is of 2 × 4s; its siding is ½-inch exterior-grade chipboard. A coat of preservative helps protect the walls.

I began the construction by sinking the 4 × 4 posts in the ground to below the frost line. I used a full bag of ready-mix cement to stabilize each one. Then I built the frame for the deck by attaching four 2 × 8s to the posts (see diagrams, following page) with four-inch lag screws. Next, I put joists of 2 × 6s on 24-inch centers between the 2 × 8s and planked the deck with 2 × 6s, trimming the edges after the dome was in place.

Dome construction was simple. The instruction booklet that comes with the Starplate connectors tells how to

make any size dome. I built the dome on the ground, then, with helpers, lifted it to the deck and attached it securely with nails and lag screws.

The swings hang from a 2×6 beam, which I fastened to the tops of two base posts using eight-inch galvanized spiral spikes. The swing is a piece of 2×8 hung by galvanized chain from large screw eyes. I also made a glider-type swing for adults.

I made the slide of 18-inch-wide galvanized metal (the kind used for ductwork). It's nailed to a base made of two 2×8s assembled edge-to-edge with bracing. The sides of the slide are also made of 2×8s, rabbeted to cover the nailheads. I left extra metal on the top of the slide and attached it to the playhouse deck with decking nails. I notched the edges of the slide to fit tight against the deck at the appropriate angle. Two scrap 4×4s, set about 18 inches deep in cement, anchor the bottom of the slide.

The ladder is made completely of 2×4s. Its legs are mounted in cement. I made the steps 13 inches apart to keep toddlers from climbing up.

To make the railing, I ripped 2×4s in half for the uprights and placed them about every seven inches. A 2×4 nailed along the top and another along the side just below complete it.

After I had finished the construction, I took a router and rounded all edges. This wasn't just for looks. Even treated lumber will crack and split slightly as it ages. With the edges rounded, I'm less likely to have to pluck splinters from small fingers and toes—*By Bryan P. Shumaker.*

2. Swing Set for a Slope

Like many backyards, ours isn't exactly pool-table flat. In fact, it's a ravine with a 25 percent slope—that is, one foot of drop for every four horizontal feet. A further complication: Even that space is of limited size. When we set out to buy outdoor play equipment for our young son, it quickly became apparent that off-the-shelf swing sets, jungle gyms, slides, and so-called customized play equip-

ment just couldn't be used.

So I decided to apply my architectural training to the problem. The result is a unique play structure (next page) that uses its hillside location to advantage. It provides opportunity for many activities, and it cost me much less than a comparable manufactured play set. Materials came to about $150 (three years ago).

The entire structure is cantilevered from five 4×4 wood posts. These are set in a concrete slurry in holes dug about 24 inches deep into the sloping ground. I assembled the structural elements with carriage bolts and a few joist hangers. I used pressure-treated lumber for durability. Its natural wood tone blends with the wooded site.

The plan and elevation on the following page show the design in detail. All materials used are readily available, and you can adapt the design to your site—*By James Calhoun.*

1. Swing set with playhouse

Starplate connectors (detail) are used at all intersections of the dome's frame. The 2×4 struts are inserted in all five sleeves at roof joints but only in four at the base. Author used four-ft. struts to give the dome a diameter of about six ft.

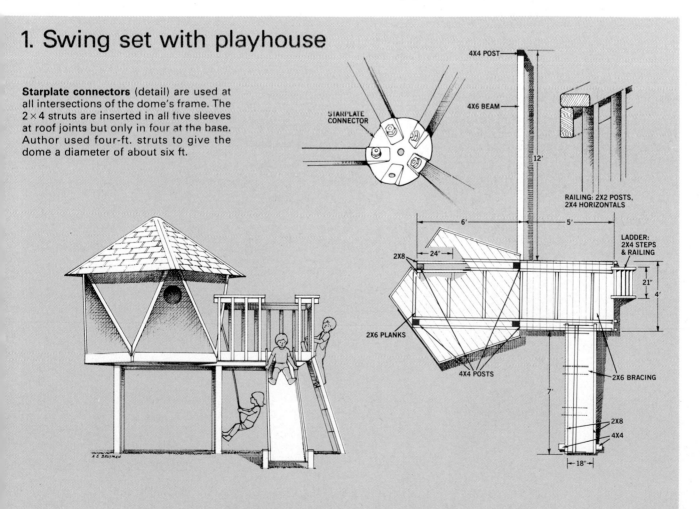

STARPLATE CONNECTOR

4X4 POST

4X6 BEAM

12'

6'

5'

RAILING: 2X2 POSTS, 2X4 HORIZONTALS

2X8

24"

LADDER: 2X4 STEPS & RAILING

21"

4'

2X6 PLANKS

4X4 POSTS

2X6 BRACING

7'

2X8

4X4

18"

2. Swing set for a slope

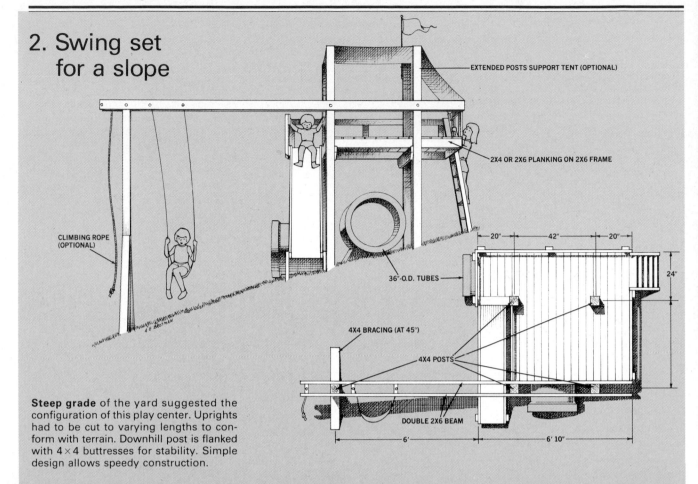

EXTENDED POSTS SUPPORT TENT (OPTIONAL)

2X4 OR 2X6 PLANKING ON 2X6 FRAME

CLIMBING ROPE (OPTIONAL)

36"-O.D. TUBES

4X4 BRACING (AT 45°)

4X4 POSTS

DOUBLE 2X6 BEAM

20"   42"   20"

24"

6'   6' 10"

Steep grade of the yard suggested the configuration of this play center. Uprights had to be cut to varying lengths to conform with terrain. Downhill post is flanked with 4×4 buttresses for stability. Simple design allows speedy construction.

boat trailer you can build

After years of creating a variety of wooden boats, we've finally designed a wooden trailer for towing them. Our trailer's chassis is considerably stiffer than a comparable commercially made metal one. Yet the wooden trailer is light for its rigidity. The trailer also tracks well, takes corners nicely, and backs easily.

Before building the chassis, we talked to some old-timers who used wooden trailers back in the '50s to tow ski boats. To handle these 3,000 pound inboards, the rugged trailers had a stressed frame with bent side rails.

We borrowed that idea for our trailer. But instead of trying to find perfect 3×8s and bend them, we laminated the rails from 1×8 stock (see diagram). This made bending easy, and the three layers make a stiff rail.

To stiffen the chassis, we attached all cross members with standard, heavy-duty joist hangers.

The only design problem was how to make a really rugged tongue and hitch. For this, we chose a steel beam (inset, left.) The beam extends from the first cross member through the chassis front. There it's through-bolted to the frame to stiffen against yaw stress. The rails in turn are sandwiched between top and bottom plates and through-bolted for pitch stress.

We mounted the chassis on a brand-new standard trailer suspension that cost us $250. One assembled from junkyard parts would work as well. The chassis cost us about $230. (Plans cost $5 from Stevenson Projects, Dept RT5, Box 584, Del Mar, Calif. 92014.)

We knocked this trailer around for a whole season and found just one disadvantage: It floats. That means you've got to move the boat onto it fast when leaving the water. But we think the trailer's strength and light weight compensate for this minor glitch—*By Susanne and Peter Stevenson.*

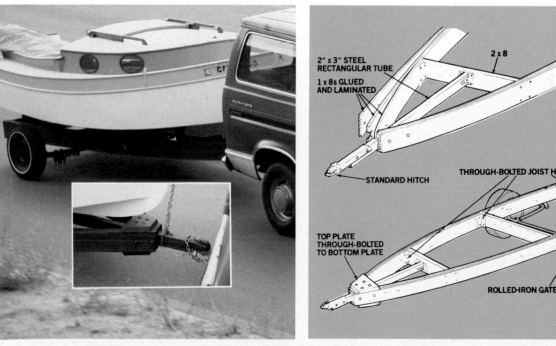
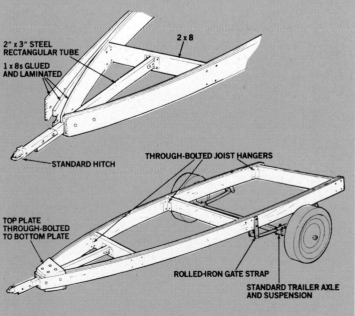

three-way day tripper

On past visits to Hawaii we've longed for a boat of our own. But we were torn between a sailboat (all those enticing trade winds) and a small powerboat for chugging up Kauai's little rivers. We also wanted to drift quietly along the banks to savor the breathtaking beauty of birds and flowers. For that, we'd need a rowboat.

Preparing for this visit, we built a boat that would let us do all three things. We translated the traditional lines of the old Greek sponge boat into a practical pleasure craft using light, easily worked modern materials. The Triad is a versatile 12-footer that gave us far more fun than we'd hoped for.

We spent countless wonderful hours sailing through the crystal-clear waters. When we came to reefs, we stowed the dagger board under the foredeck and flipped the rudder to its beaching position (see diagram). Even in this position the rudder gave us control, and the full-length keel let us sail where we wanted.

The locals couldn't believe we were stupid enough to try sailing over a reef. But we cruised in depths of one to three feet with ease.

Wheeling the boat to water is easy with a small cradle under the keel (inset) and oars slipped under the stern tie-down hooks used for car topping. With the oars as handles, one person can trundle the fully rigged boat to water.

An easy rower (left) thanks to the full-length keel, the Triad also sails smartly (above), even with its dagger board up. It tacks to windward with keel alone and skims safely through shallows. A wide, flat bottom makes the craft stable under power or when unloading gear (above right). The wood hull is naturally buoyant but has room for optional foam flotation.

In deeper waters we used the boat as a stable swim and dive platform. To clear the decks for scuba gear, we folded boom and gaff vertically up against the mast and tied them in place. The rudder assembly unhooked in seconds, and we looped a rope ladder over the transom hooks for easy access from the water.

The Triad sailed easily with four adults aboard. When we switched to power or oars, there was room for five, with ample freeboard.

The price of this versatility? Our costs were $389 for a painted boat, rigged with sail and fitted with launch cradle. Construction was simple: We used only hand tools and lumberyard stock—*By Susanne and Peter Stevenson. Photos by the authors. Illustrated by Gene Thompson.*

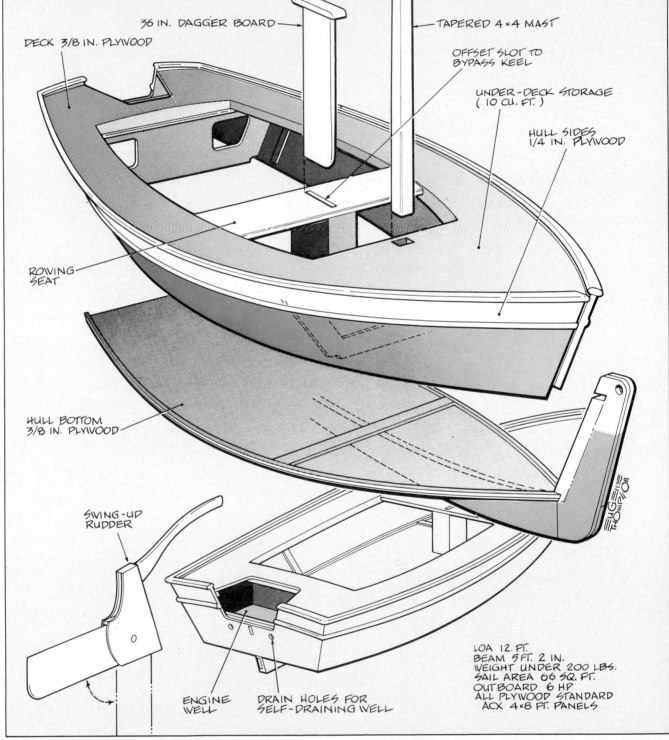

36 IN. DAGGER BOARD

TAPERED 4×4 MAST

DECK 3/8 IN. PLYWOOD

OFFSET SLOT TO BYPASS KEEL

UNDER-DECK STORAGE (10 CU. FT.)

HULL SIDES 1/4 IN. PLYWOOD

ROWING SEAT

HULL BOTTOM 3/8 IN. PLYWOOD

SWING-UP RUDDER

ENGINE WELL

DRAIN HOLES FOR SELF-DRAINING WELL

LOA 12. FT.
BEAM 5 FT. 2 IN.
WEIGHT UNDER 200 LBS.
SAIL AREA 66 SQ. FT.
OUTBOARD 6 HP
ALL PLYWOOD STANDARD
ACX 4×8 FT. PANELS

A tapered plywood box, the Triad is selfaligning as you build. Just line up deck, hull bottom, and bulkhead center lines; the boat comes out straight without resorting to jigs. All materials are standard lumberyard stock—there's no fancy marine hardware or tubing to find. Boom and gaff are made from 2×3 lumber. Sail is rugged polyethylene ripstock sold for tarps. There's no sewing needed—spars slip into pocket seams made by lacing string through punched holes. For detailed Triad plans, send a $10 check to Stevenson Projects, Dept. T-3, Box 584, Del Mar, Calif. 92014.

latticework bench

The arresting, striped-and-slatted look of this corner bench is achieved by spacing the redwood structural members with thinner stock. The idea is practical, too, since it allows fast drainage and drying after a rain. (The same technique can be applied to a straight version as shown in the first sketch. For a materials list, write California Redwood Assn., 591 Redwood Hwy., Mill Valley, Calif. 94941.)

For the latticework top, first rough-cut to length six 2 × 4s for each "wing" of the bench (note how they lap at the corner). Next, cut all spacers from 1 × 4 stock in the two lengths shown. To assemble the herringbone corner, nail up a 90-degree work frame of two long, straight 2 × 4s with a cross brace. Working on the outside of this frame, butt-join the shortest 2 × 4s and the six-inch corner spacers as shown. Nail from the face of both corner spacers into the end of the lapping 2 × 4, using 16-penny nails. Next, nail the three 12 inch spacers to the faces of the 2 × 4s, using 10-penny nails. Proceed with the next pair of 2 × 4s and their spacers, using 16-penny nails throughout, but alternating the triangular nailing pattern through the spacers. Repeat this procedure with four more pairs of 2 × 4s.

At the outer bench corner, trim down one spacer as shown so the projecting leg insert will snug under it after this spacer is nailed flush with the top edge of the last 2 × 4s.

When assembly is complete, trim the open ends of the 2 × 4s even and proceed with the outer frame. For the butt-joined version shown at the left end of the assembly sketch (and in the sketch of the straight version), cut the end 2 × 4s the width of the latticework, including outer spacers. Attach these to each 2 × 4 end with one 16-penny nail, in a zigzag pattern. Next, trim four side-frame members to lap the end frame, and attach with three nails per bench spacer plus two nails into each frame end.

For legs, assemble pairs of 14½-inch 2 × 6s with spacers as shown. Place the four-inch spacer flush with the foot and the six-inch spacer projecting two inches above the top. Clamp the assembly, and drill one center hole per spacer. Insert a ¼-by-four inch carriage bolt, snugging it up with a washer and nut on the inside face. Now, fit the leg projection into an end slot so that the leg's 2 × 6s are flush with the ends of the bench. Join the leg to the bench top with right-angle brackets. (There's no projection at the top of the inside corner leg; attach with six corner angles, as shown.)

Finish with two coats of water repellent, two weeks apart.

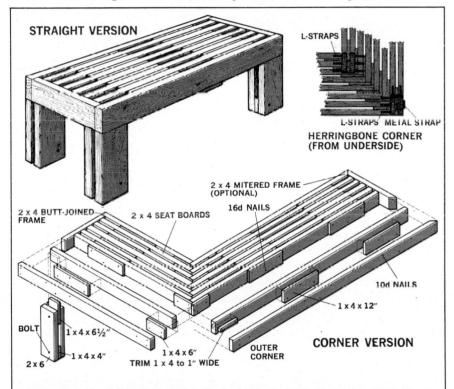

STRAIGHT VERSION

L-STRAPS

L-STRAPS METAL STRAP

HERRINGBONE CORNER
(FROM UNDERSIDE)

2 x 4 MITERED FRAME
(OPTIONAL)

16d NAILS

2 x 4 BUTT-JOINED FRAME

2 x 4 SEAT BOARDS

10d NAILS

1 x 4 x 12"

BOLT

1 x 4 x 6½"

1 x 4 x 4"

2 x 6

1 x 4 x 6"

TRIM 1 x 4 to 1" WIDE

OUTER CORNER

CORNER VERSION

Expensive-looking bench is actually crafted from garden-grade redwood. This has more knots and sap streaks than top grades but is nearly as durable.

post lamp and mail center

Architects are often dissatisfied with ordinary fixtures around their homes—inside or out. Julia Sturdevant, a landscape architect in Portland, Ore., is no exception. She saw no reason to stick a traditional mailbox—a 4 × 4 with a galvanized metal box on top—out in front of her contemporary home.

Her solution was an elegant design that combines a mailbox, an outdoor light, and a newspaper box in one project. The lamp and mail center was built of Douglas fir that was stained and sealed. Underground wiring for a low curb light was already in place, so it was only necessary to set a concrete footing and extend the wire and conduit up between the posts to the fixture (see drawing on facing page for construction details). Then the posts and wood parts were assembled around the conduit and secured to the footing.

Note that custom-built mailboxes require prior approval from your local postmaster before you can substitute them for existing types. Boxes are generally 3½ to four feet above the roadway (not the top of the curb), but it's a good idea to check with your postmaster for an exact height and what, if any, street or box numbers need to be inscribed on the side of the box—*By Paul Bolon. Julia Lundy Sturdevant and Ralph Cereghino, designers.*

The appearance is striking, yet lamp and mail center blends with surroundings because of all-wood construction.

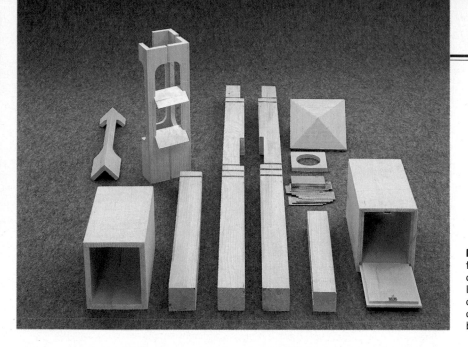

Major frame pieces are shown at left before assembly, except for decorative chamfers to be cut on posts. Wiring for light comes from house via underground conduit; switch is in house. Light bulb is changed by removing peaked cap. Photos by Western Wood Products Assn.

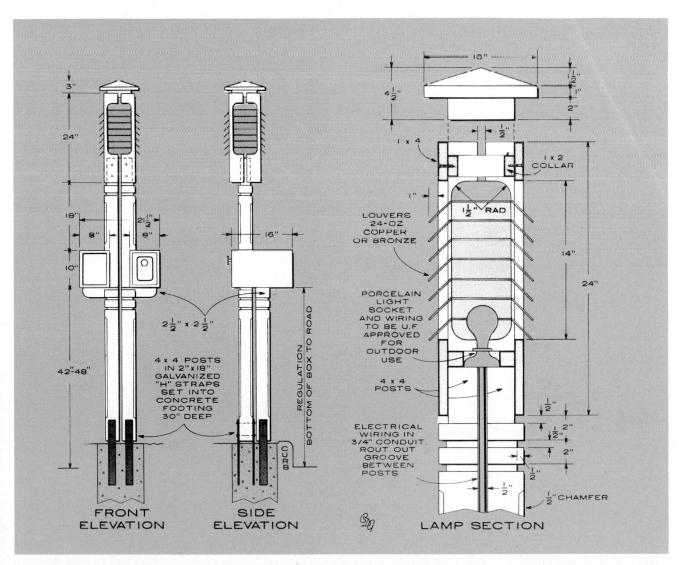

FRONT ELEVATION

SIDE ELEVATION

LAMP SECTION

3"

24"

18"

8"

10"

42"-48"

21½"

8"

2½" x 2½"

4 x 4 POSTS IN 2"x18" GALVANIZED "H" STRAPS SET INTO CONCRETE FOOTING 30" DEEP

16"

REGULATION BOTTOM OF BOX TO ROAD

CURB

10"

4½"

1½"
1"
2"

1 x 4

½"

1 x 2 COLLAR

1"

1½" RAD

LOUVERS 24-OZ COPPER OR BRONZE

PORCELAIN LIGHT SOCKET AND WIRING TO BE U.F. APPROVED FOR OUTDOOR USE

4 x 4 POSTS

ELECTRICAL WIRING IN 3/4" CONDUIT. ROUT OUT GROOVE BETWEEN POSTS

14"

24"

½"
2"
2"
½"

½"

½" CHAMFER

Backbone of lamp post is two full-length 4×4s secured by galvanized straps embedded in concrete footing. Dadoes for conduit are routed in post's mating faces; decorative chamfer is also routed. Boxes fit in notches in tall posts and are supported by crossmember atop third, short post. Light socket is special porcelain model for outdoor applications. Copper or bronze louvers are cemented in slots with small amount of exterior-type epoxy. Box sides and back are rabbeted together and screwed to posts and crossarm support. Check with local postmaster for height from road to box bottom.

solar wood dryer

If you gather and split wood in spring, will it be dry enough for your stove or fireplace when the first cold snap hits? Probably not. Even short, split logs need up to six months to reach an acceptable moisture level (less than 25 percent).

But there's a way to accelerate the process: Put the sun to work by building a shed from clear FRP. A solar wood dryer can cut your drying time by 50 percent or more.

In my design, dry air enters the shed through the gap between the walls and ground, picks up heat and moisture as it circulates around two cords of sun-warmed logs, and exits as moist air through the top vents.

I used Filon's Type 416 Standard Clear corrugated panels in the six-ounce-per-square-foot weight. You could use lighter material if snow loads aren't a problem; for very heavy loads, frame the roof with 2×4s. My panels cost about $200, and I spent an additional $125 on lumber and hardware.

The hinges on the walls let you fold the shed for storage or relocation. The two cross-buck doors hang from an aluminum track. Treat or paint all wood before attaching Filon. When fastening the panels, I didn't use the customary filler strips. This allows greater air circulation, but it means you must nail through the corrugation

bottoms. Common nails are okay for walls, but on the roof use nails with neoprene washers to prevent leaks. Follow the panel overlap pattern (drawing) for a proper fit—*By Jeffrey Milstein.*

Six stakes hold dryer walls three to five in. above ground. After positioning them, move frame away so you can swing clear (right). To fasten panels (far right), pre-drill holes at bottom of corrugations; carriage bolt makes good nailset. If you overdrive, Filon will craze, so practice on scrap. Space nails every other corrugation along edges, every third one across center. On verticals, nail every eight to 10 in. For roof panels, use Filon nails with neoprene washer for a tight seal.

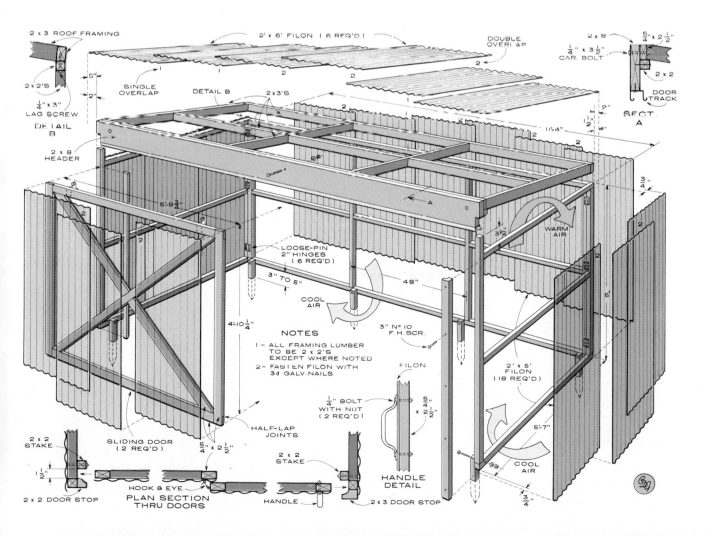

2 x 3 ROOF FRAMING

2 x 2'S

1/4" x 3"
LAG SCREW

DETAIL
B

2 x 8
HEADER

2' x 6' FILON (6 REQ'D)

DOUBLE
OVERLAP

SINGLE
OVERLAP

DETAIL B

2x3'S

2 x 8

1/4" x 3 1/2"
CAR. BOLT

5/4" x 2 1/2"

2 x 2

DOOR
TRACK

SECT.
A

11 1/4"

WARM
AIR

3 1/2"

3/4"

LOOSE-PIN
2" HINGES
(6 REQ'D)

3" TO 5"

48"

COOL
AIR

3" N° 10
F.H. SCR.

4'-10 1/4"

NOTES
1 - ALL FRAMING LUMBER
TO BE 2 x 2'S
EXCEPT WHERE NOTED
2 - FASTEN FILON WITH
3d GALV. NAILS

2' x 5'
FILON
(18 REQ'D)

5'-7"

FILON

1/4" BOLT
WITH NUT
(2 REQ'D)

5/4"
x 2 1/2"

COOL
AIR

3/4"

2 x 2
STAKE

1 1/2"

2 x 2 DOOR STOP

SLIDING DOOR
(2 REQ'D)

5/4" x 2 1/2"

HOOK & EYE

PLAN SECTION
THRU DOORS

HALF-LAP
JOINTS

2 x 2
STAKE

HANDLE

HANDLE
DETAIL

2 x 3 DOOR STOP

upgrade your walkways

The walk in front of my house had been getting shabby, to put it mildly. The undergrowth was taking over, and the stepping stones of precast concrete on a bed of marble chips made walking difficult for visitors at night.

My solution was a new duckboard walk, which I designed in removable modules so I could get to a septic cleanout in front of my house. Also, by making the walk in sections, it was easy to build modules away from where they were to be placed—where I had access to power tools—and then move them to their final position.

You can adapt this design to suit your home, but use weather-resistant materials throughout. I used unpainted pressure-treated lumber (I'll allow it to weather) and heavily creosoted railroad ties, which bound the walk on either side.

My walk goes down to the bottom of a rise at the side of my house, where the boundary ties meet with others to form a wall on a 90-degree turn down to the driveway.

At the 90-degree turn there's a step down to a lower walk. It's actually a four-foot-square module placed on top

Completed modules are ready to be moved. Each board is secured with two galvanized nails at lifters to prevent distortion.

Ground beneath the walk is sloped slightly for runoff. The photo shows railroad ties in position, anchored by rebar.

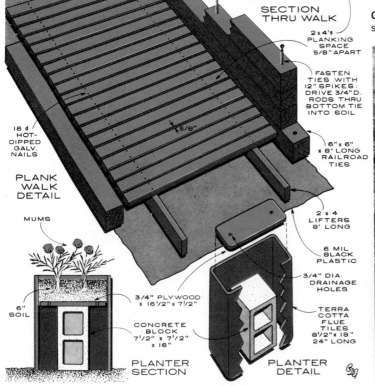

SECTION THRU WALK

48"

2 x 4's 8' LONG

2 x 4's PLANKING SPACE 5/8" APART

FASTEN TIES WITH 12" SPIKES. DRIVE 3/4" D. RODS THRU BOTTOM TIE INTO SOIL

5/8"

16 d HOT-DIPPED GALV. NAILS

6" x 6" x 8' LONG RAILROAD TIES

PLANK WALK DETAIL

2 x 4 LIFTERS 8' LONG

6 MIL BLACK PLASTIC

3/4" DIA. DRAINAGE HOLES

MUMS

3/4" PLYWOOD x 16½" x 7½"

6" SOIL

TERRA COTTA FLUE TILES 8½" x 18" 24" LONG

CONCRETE BLOCK 7½" x 7½" x 16"

PLANTER SECTION

PLANTER DETAIL

Entry walk from driveway to front of house is shown above. The half step is created by a smaller, four-foot-square module. Photo at left shows finished walk with landscaping of evergreen bushes and pine-bark chips. Below the duckboard is a sheet of six-mil-thick black plastic. Septic cleanout is in the center of the walk under a removable duckboard module.

of an eight-foot one. A fascia board covers the end of the smaller unit. In effect, there's a half step down to the lower level of the walk.

I nailed all the ties together with 12-inch spikes and anchored the boundary ties (and the bottom course of ties in the wall) with three-foot-long ¾-inch rebars.

The modular duckboard fits snugly between the firmly anchored railroad ties, so there's little danger of the walk upending if someone steps on the edges.

I used planters made of sections of chimney-flue tile to border the railroad ties, positioning them so that if a modular unit must be removed, the planters won't get in the way. This is a good feature, particularly with my house: If I ever needed to get to my septic system for extensive repairs, a large hole in the front would obliterate a concrete walk and planter.

The flue tile shouldn't be filled all the way to the bottom with dirt; otherwise, in a prolonged spell of freezing weather, moisture in the soil might expand and cause the tile to crack. I used a false bottom of plywood (see diagram).

A helpful hint: The best way to ensure that the duckboard doesn't curl or warp is to place the wood so that the end grains arch upward—that way water can drain instead of pooling in the middle of the board.

Thus far, I've enjoyed the walk. Future plans include low-voltage lighting to highlight the planters and front of the house, and a trellis at the front door.—*By W. David Houser. Photos by the author.*

router-gear roundup

For all its power and speed, a router by itself is pretty limited. But team it with the right accessories, and you can perform operations never before possible. You can cut threads in wooden dowels, for example, or form a perfect dovetail joint. You can cut rabbets, grooves, and dadoes—circular, oval, or straight. You can decorate kitchen-cabinet doors or duplicate a pattern—even a piece of sculpture—in wood.

There is a near-avalanche of router attachments on the market; the intent here is to sort them out. In the tables on the following pages, they are grouped into 17 categories. The photos illustrate the most useful ones.

To get the best performance from router attachments, you should keep a few principles in mind. Most attachments have linkages, slides, or pivots with inherent clearance and "give." Make sure everything is tight when you put the attachment together; check it before each use. Cutters must be in top-notch shape. Extend cutter bits no farther than necessary from the collet. Consider carbide-tipped cutters when available; in my opinion they are well worth the extra cost.

You should read—and follow—the instructions and safety information included with each attachment. As a minimum, wear safety glasses and hearing protectors. Also, wear a face shield when chips are flying and a respirator when there's dust—*By Mack Philips. Photos by the author.*

Beall threader uses a veining bit in the router to cut screw threads in three sizes of dowel stock (note dowel sizer at rear). Threader comes with taps for cutting female threads in mating parts. Care is needed in adjusting depth, but the threader operates easily. Use it to make clamps, mechanism models, knockdown furniture, toys, and moldings.

Leigh's dovetail jig has infinitely variable layout of pins and tails and allows precise adjustment of joint tightness. Less-costly jigs don't have such flexibility, but they guide dovetail cutter through joining members to ensure fit.

Panel guide acts as fence to guide router when making long, straight cuts. Black & Decker Cutting Guide (also used with portable saws) has non-marring clamps and provides rigid eight-ft.-long guide for edge joining and dadoing.

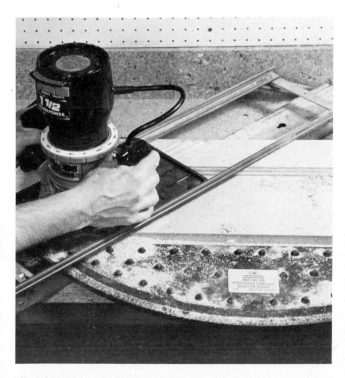

Miter base lets you cut slots, grooves, and dadoes at 45 deg. and other angles. Most bases, such as this from Vermont American, also can be used with portable saws. Tool mounts on a slide that locks into slots in a calibrated base.

Router table holds router underneath and can do some of the same jobs as a costly spindle shaper or jointer-planer (grooving, dadoing, and edge shaping, for example). A fence controls cut depth. The position of the cutter is controlled by the router's depth adjuster.

Craftsman Edge Crafter, used with router table, makes wavy-edge or piecrust table tops and other oval or circular items up to a 30-in. diameter. Pilot and template cam are attached to work. Cam follower on overarm moves work in and out as cutter forms edge.

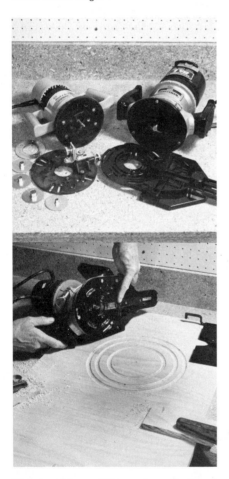

Universal-base kits such as Vermont American's (top photo) fit nearly all routers and adapt them to use edge guides and standard guide bushings (supplied in three sizes) required by many attachments. Also included is a roller edge guide for trimming laminates and edging irregular shapes. Craftsman router guide (photo above) allows straight or contour edge guiding and circular routing with trammel point.

Attachment	Brand	Model/ description	Approx. price ($)	Size/ capacity	Special features	Comments
Bowl lathe	Craftsman	9GT25194L Bowl Lathe	80	2½" dia. × 5¼" high to 10" dia. × 3½" high	Supplied with template patterns for bowls, plates, candlestick holders, glasses, egg cups, shakers, etc.	Uses Sears routers, ¾ hp and larger; requires special cutters (extra)
Dovetail jig	Black & Decker	U52331 Dovetail Kit	74	½" dovetails	Includes everything needed to equip router to make dovetails	Accessories available to cut ¼" dovetails
	Craftsman	9GT2571 Dovetail Joint Fixture	45	½" dove-tails on drawers to 12" deep	Accessory ¼" template available	Requires special cutters and guide bushings (extra)
		9GT2570 Dovetail Joint Fixture	30	¼" and ½" dove-tails on drawers to 8" deep		Same as above
	Leigh	TD 515 Dovetail Jig	150	¼" and ½" dove-tails on drawers to 12" deep	Infinitely variable lay-out of pins and tails; complete handbook included	Guide bushings are extra; requires special cutters (extra)
	Porter-Cable	5008 Dovetail Template	68	½" dove-tails on drawers to 12" deep		Bits, guide, and nut are extra; requires special cutters (extra)
	Vermont American	860 Dovetail Fixture	23	¼" and ½" dove-tails on drawers to 8" deep	Includes guide bushings	Requires special cutters (extra)
Edge crafter	Craftsman	9GT25188	30	Round, oval shapes to 30" dia.	Includes four templates	Must use with router table; requires special bits (extra)
Guide	Black & Decker	76-230 Straight and Circular Guide	9			Fits all B&D routers
		U52332 Slot and Circle Guide	13	Adjustable from 1" to 22" dia. or length	Allows evenly spaced slots, discs, holes, concentric designs	Fits many B&D routers; No. 76-231 fits others
	Craftsman	9GT25179 Multi-Purpose Router Guide	15	Circles to 24" dia.	Edges, contours, full-circle cuts, trims or bevels laminates; has trammel point	Fits most Craftsman routers
	Porter-Cable	5043 Magic Router Edge Guide	40		Edges, grooves, slots, dadoes	For precise, accurate work; fits all Porter-Cable routers except No. 514
		39120 42210 42225 42160 Standard Edge Guides	16 to 23			Different numbers fit all Porter-Cable models
Hinge template	Black & Decker	U58129 Hinge Mortising Template Kit	130	2½" to 5½" hinge sizes on doors to 8'	Standard adjustments for standard doors eliminate measuring	Complete kit; includes bit, guide, corner chisel, sturdy metal case
	Craftsman	9GT2575 Butt-Hinge Templates	8	3½" and 4" hinge mortises		Templates only; requires guide bushings (extra)
		9GT2564C Butt-Hinge Template-Clamp Set	59	Square or rounded mortises up to 5" long on doors to 7'	Includes three-section template clamp	
	Porter-Cable	59380 Hinge Butt Template	164	3" to 6" hinges on doors to 7'	Includes three templates, gauges, etc.	
		59381 Hinge Butt Template Kit	195	Same as above	As above with bits, case, guide, etc.	
	Vermont American	857 Hinge Mortising Template Set	6	3½" and 4" butt hinges		Templates only; requires guide bushing (extra)

Attachment	Brand	Model/description	Approx. price ($)	Size/capacity	Special features	Comments
Letter-sign set	Black & Decker	76-233 Router Guide	18	2½" and 1¾" alphabets		Bushings for B&D routers included
	Craftsman	9GT2573	15	1½", 2½" alphabets		Two bushings included
		9GT2572C Rout-A-Signer	38	Makes letters from ¾" to 4½" high	Has work clamping device, work support; has template storage carousel	
	Vermont American	855 Router Letter Template Set	18	1½" and 2½" alphabets		Two bushings included
Miter base	Vermont American	375 Portable Saw and Router Guide	68	17½" wide by 3¾" high	Base swivels for any-angle edging or slotting	Also accepts portable circular saws
Panel decorator	Craftsman	9GT25472C Door and Panel Kit	80	Panels to 36" × 36"	Includes 7 corner design template sets and arc attachment	Requires guide bushings (extra)
		9GT25191N Decorout-or	95	Panels to 21" × 42"	Includes 4 templates in 2 styles	Can do planing with optional cutter bit
	Wing	M-100 Router Template	133	Panels to 24" × 36"	Includes 4 corner-design templates	10 other templates and arc designs; 84" × 84" extension bars available
Panel guide	Black & Decker	73-515 Cutting Guide	29	8' length panel	Allows grooving and edging against 8' straightedge	Also use with sabre or circular saw
		79-010 Router and Shaper Guide	22	Any-length panel	Designed to be used with B&D's Workmate work stand	
	Vermont American	376 Panel Crafter	40	Panels to 24" o.c.		Also use with sabre or circular saw
Pantograph (reducing)	Black & Decker	76-232 Design Maker	37	40%, 50%, 60% reductions	Includes 40 sheets of patterns for letters, numbers, designs	Requires workbase or workbench mounting
	Craftsman	9GT25187C Router Pantograph	33	40%, 50%, 60% reductions	Includes stencils for 5 letter styles, 10 line drawings	Has capability for limited 3-D carving
		9GT25183C 2-D Router Pantograph	16	42%, 50%, 58% reductions	Includes 1 set of letters and 2 line drawings	
	Vermont American	850 Router Pantograph	23	42%, 50%, 58% reductions	Old English- and modern-lettering sheets, assorted drawings	Requires workbase or workbench mounting
Pin router	Craftsman	9GT25153N Pin Router	180	20" × 27" worktable, 12½" throat, 3⅝" stock-thickness capacity	Has depth gauge and depth stop; 1 template and 10 designs included	Worktable mounts to work surface
	Shopsmith	505806 Overarm Pin Router	595	29¾" × 17¾" table, 14⅞" throat, 11" stock-thickness capacity	Adjustable column, precision depth stop, steel base	Accepts routers with 3" to 4½" body dia.
Spindle lathe	Craftsman	9GT2525C Router-Crafter	75	3" square × 36" long legs, posts, spindles	Optional drive adapter allows full-length cuts	
	Vermont American	852 Router Lathe	65	3" square × 36" long legs, posts, spindles		
Table	Black & Decker	76-400 Router Table	40	17¾" × 13¾" × 10⅜" high	Jointer-planer-type fence, dust-collector outlet	Molded-plastic top
	Central	666A 3-in-1 Table	85	22" × 18" × 35"	Converts to 10" high table model	Has extensions to make 34" long; use also for circular and sabre saws
		690 Quick Change Artist Table	103	22" × 18" × 35"	Tools are attached to insert plate for top loading into table; same as above	Use also for circular and sabre saws

Pin router is named for its guidance: a pin that protrudes from the table directly under the router bit (top photo); the router mounts on an overarm. You tack a template to the back of your work, then place the template over the pin. As you move the work, the pin rides the template grooves and the router duplicates them in your workpiece (photo above). Pin routers can also cut dadoes, rabbets, and edge bevels against pin or fence, and they allow inlay work, mortising, and laminate trimming, as well.

Spindle lathe guides the router as it travels over slowly rotating stock while the cutter mills the desired shape. Indexing head and cable-feed mechanism let you rout straight grooves, flutes, and spirals, or trace templates.

Letter-sign sets let you make professional-quality signs. Plastic letter and number templates snap into holder and guide router bushing. Shown left to right: Vermont American set, Black & Decker set, and Craftsman Rout-A-Signer.

Router pantograph has adjustable-position arms that let you trace a pattern with a stylus while the router creates a reduced-size duplicate. You can use supplied letters and patterns or make your own. Neat work requires practice.

MANUFACTURER AND SUPPLIER ADDRESSES

Beall Tool Co., 541 Swans Road N.E., Newark, OH 43055; **Black & Decker Manufacturing Co.**, Towson MD 21204; **Central Quality Industries, Inc.**, Polo IL 61064; **Craftsman Tools** (Sears, Roebuck and Co.), Sears Tower, Chicago IL 60684; **Dupli-Carver**, 4004 W. 10th St., Indianapolis IN 46222; **The Hirsh Co.**, 8051 Central Park Ave., Skokie IL 60076; **Hobbi-Carve** (Kurt Manufacturing Co.), 1720 Marshall St. N.E., Minneapolis MN 55413; **Kimball Woodcarver**, 2602 Whitaker St., Savannah GA 31401; **Leigh Industries Ltd.**, Quesnel, BC, Canada (sold in the U.S. by Constantine, 2050 Eastchester Rd., Bronx NY 10461, and Woodcraft Supply Corp., Box 4000, Woburn MA 01888); **Marlin Industries**, 3537 Old Canejo Rd., Suite 104, Newbury Park CA 91320 (catalog $1); **Porter-Cable Corp.**, Box 2468, Jackson TN 38301; **The Rustic Shop**, 7431 Artesia St., Buena Park CA 90621; **Shopsmith, Inc.**, 750 Center Dr., Vandalia OH 45377; **Vermont American**, Box 340, Lincolnton NC 28092; **Wing Sales and Distributing Co.**, Box 1360, Payson AZ 85541.

Attachment	Brand	Model/description	Approx. price ($)	Size/capacity	Special features	Comments
Table	Craftsman	9GT25456 Router Table	18	18" × 13⅛" × 11"		Stamped-steel top
		9GT25444	50	Same as above	Jointer-planer-type fence	Die-cast-aluminum top
		9GT25443	60	Same as above	Jointer-planer-type fence, dust-collector outlet, roller guide	Same as above
	Hirsh	TRST 2	30	18" × 13" × 11"		Molded-plastic top; can also be used as sabre-saw table
		TRST 3	45	18" × 13" × 14½"	Has front-mounted off-on switch	Same as above
	Vermont American	396 Deluxe Router & Saber Saw Table	34	12⅜" × 18⅝" × 10⅝"	Two fences, trammel bar	Stamped-steel top; use also for sabre saws
		395 Economy Router & Saber Saw Table	30	13¹/₁₆" × 18" × 10⅞"		Plain flat top, no miter gauge
Threader	Beall	Beall Wood Threader	129	Cuts ½", ¾", and 1" dia. threads	Includes matching taps for female threads; includes cutter bit	Can be ordered for one size thread only at prices from $58 to $67; add other(s) later
3-D duplicator	Craftsman	9GT25189L Router-Recreator	120	3-D up to 8" cube, signs & plaques to 10" × 24", spindles to 24" long		Includes shelves, mounting blocks, stylus rods
	Dupli-Carver	T-110	299	18" tall × 10" dia.	Optional $49 adapter allows spindle-gunstock carving to 8" × 36"	Includes ⅝-hp router and bits
		F-200	799	40" tall × 14" dia.	Optional $99 adapter allows spindle-gunstock carving to 8" × 60"	Unit is floor model; includes router
		F-480	999	40" tall × 20" dia.	Optional $109 adapter allows spindle-gunstock carving to 8" × 66"	Same as above
	Hobbi-Carve	H-2001	149	10" wide × 12" long × 2" deep	Uses 2-level work area with tracing stylus on lower level, router on top level	Mounts on 24" × 32" or larger work surface; patterns must be flat-backed
	Marlin	CM-610	494	8" × 28" × 3" deep capacity		Machine base not included
		CM-614	543	12" × 28" × 3" deep capacity		Same as above
		CM-624	592	22" × 28" × 3" deep capacity		Same as above
2-D duplicator	Kimball Wood-Carver	K-3	2,250	12" × 28" engraving area	With ball-tip stylus for duplicating pictures, logos, line drawings	Includes 1-hp router motor
	Rustic Shop	Guide-All II Model 2	99	20" × 32" base	Mirror-image templates are moved under top-mounted stylus; router under table cuts work	Larger optional base sizes are available
Universal base	Vermont American	859 Router Roller Edge Guide and Guide Bushing Kit	15		Adapts most routers for common guide bushings and for laminate-veneer trimming	

master drill-press jig

A drill press can be your most versatile wood-shop power tool. But for each job you need a special setup. This master jig—actually a basic table and eight accessories—will outfit your drill press for drilling, drum sanding, routing, shaping, and other woodworking chores. All will be done more easily and accurately since you won't have to improvise setups. Furthermore, you'll be able to use your drill press in otherwise-impossible ways: for drilling and sanding pivot-guided circles, for example, and for pin routing, routing grooves parallel to a curve, and V-block work. Some of these jobs can't be done any other way.

Though you'll probably have little reason to remove the basic table from your machine, it takes only seconds to do so. The table sits solidly on the tool's own table and gets ample anchorage from a C-clamp or two.

Here, the jig is shown mounted on a 15-inch drill press with a fairly average-size (11 by 14 inches) table. A smaller or larger table won't affect how the jig is built, but a few areas—

Main table for the master drill-press jig rests on the tool's regular table and is secured with one or two C-clamps. Two drawers provide storage for accessories you build. Here jig is equipped with the straight fence, which makes it easy to drill holes equidistant from the stock's edge, as shown in left photo. Other uses for the fence are shown on following pages.

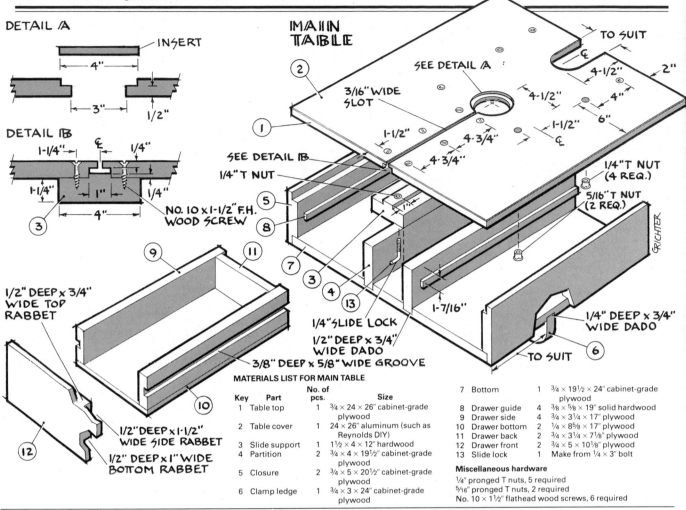

DETAIL A

INSERT

4"

3"

1/2"

DETAIL B

1-1/4"

1/4"

1-1/4"

1"

1/4"

4"

NO. 10 x 1-1/2" F.H.
WOOD SCREW

MAIN TABLE

SEE DETAIL A

3/16" WIDE
SLOT

TO SUIT

4-1/2"

2"

4"

6"

1-1/2"

4-3/4"

4-3/4"

1/4" T NUT
(4 REQ.)

5/16" T NUT
(2 REQ.)

SEE DETAIL B

1/4" T NUT

RICHTER

1"

1-7/16"

1/4" SLIDE LOCK

1/2" DEEP x 3/4"
WIDE DADO

3/8" DEEP x 5/8" WIDE GROOVE

1/4" DEEP x 3/4"
WIDE DADO

TO SUIT

1/2" DEEP x 3/4"
WIDE TOP
RABBET

1/2" DEEP x 1-1/2"
WIDE SIDE RABBET

1/2" DEEP x 1" WIDE
BOTTOM RABBET

MATERIALS LIST FOR MAIN TABLE

Key	Part	No. of pcs.	Size
1	Table top	1	3/4 × 24 × 26" cabinet-grade plywood
2	Table cover	1	24 × 26" aluminum (such as Reynolds DIY)
3	Slide support	1	1½ × 4 × 12" hardwood
4	Partition	2	3/4 × 4 × 19½" cabinet-grade plywood
5	Closure	2	3/4 × 5 × 20½" cabinet-grade plywood
6	Clamp ledge	1	3/4 × 3 × 24" cabinet-grade plywood
7	Bottom	1	3/4 × 19½ × 24" cabinet-grade plywood
8	Drawer guide	4	3/8 × 5/8 × 19" solid hardwood
9	Drawer side	4	3/4 × 3¼ × 17" plywood
10	Drawer bottom	2	1/4 × 8 5/8 × 17" plywood
11	Drawer back	2	3/4 × 3¼ × 7 1/8" plywood
12	Drawer front	2	3/4 × 5 × 10 1/8" plywood
13	Slide lock	1	Make from 1/4 × 3" bolt

Miscellaneous hardware
1/4" pronged T nuts, 5 required
5/16" pronged T nuts, 2 required
No. 10 × 1½" flathead wood screws, 6 required

INSERTS

1/4"

SOLID

DRILL AND COUN-
TERSINK FOR NO.
4 x 3/4" F.H.
SCREWS

4"
DIAMETER

DIAMETER
OF GUIDE
TO SUIT
DRUM

SPECIAL INSERT FOR
PATTERN SANDING

FOR DRUM SANDING
(INSIDE DIAMETER TO
SUIT DRUM)

Inserts fit four-in. hole in main table; they're used for drum sanding and other operations. Make them from ¼-in. tempered hardboard (diagrams above). And make plenty—the more you use them, the more jobs you'll discover for them. Cut holes in some inserts to accommodate sanding drums of various sizes, rotary files, and burrs.

Inserts with holes let you use the full width of the sanding drum. Move the work against drum's direction of rotation, and keep it moving slowly but steadily to prevent indentations. (For inside curves, put work in place before lowering and locking drum.)

For pattern sanding, attach a disc the diameter of the sanding drum to an insert and align it perfectly with the drum (center). Tack the pattern under rough-cut work and sand (right). Pattern will ride against the disc, which will serve as a guide.

Surface or edge sanding with a sanding drum is done by passing work between straight fence (sketch, right) and drum. Slots on base of fence let you locate it to fit work. Make light cuts and keep work moving. Feed against drum's rotation.

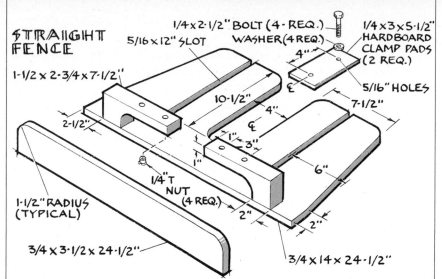

STRAIGHT FENCE

1/4 x 2·1/2" BOLT (4 · REQ.)
WASHER (4 REQ.)
1/4 x 3 x 5·1/2" HARDBOARD CLAMP PADS (2 REQ.)
5/16 x 12" SLOT
1-1/2 x 2-3/4 x 7-1/2"
10-1/2"
4"
5/16" HOLES
7-1/2"
2-1/2"
4"
1"
3"
1"
6"
1/4 T NUT (4 REQ.)
1-1/2" RADIUS (TYPICAL)
2"
2"
3/4 x 3·1/2 x 24·1/2"
3/4 x 14 x 24·1/2"

Straight fence keeps you accurate on drilling, routing, sanding jobs. First make base and fence. Attach fence with glue and nails; be sure it's vertical. Make brackets and, after installing the four T nuts, attach each bracket with glue and a two-in. flathead screw (up through base). Bolts through clamp pads fit T nuts in main table.

Straight-line routing can be done against fence. (But be sure to substitute a router chuck for the standard chuck.) Make the pass so the cutting action will tend to force the work against fence. Feed from left to right. Use highest speed and feed slowly.

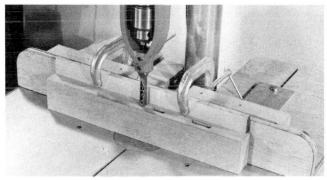

Mortising can be done against the straight fence if you equip your drill press with standard mortising bits, chisels, and adapter. Use a slim piece of wood and C-clamps as a hold-down to keep the work from pulling up when you retract the chisel.

the opening for the column, the placement of the clamp ledge, and the hole for the circular inserts—must be tailored specifically for your machine.

Making the Basic Table

Cut the plywood top and aluminum cover to size (see diagram), and bond them together with contact cement. Mark the long dimension with an accurate center line. Precisely on the line, cut the opening for the drill-press column, using a saber saw. The width of the opening and the radius of the arc must suit the diameter of your tool's column.

Put the top in position on your drill-press table, and use the drill to make a small hole on the center line. This will mark the exact center of the circular cutout that receives the inserts used with sanding drums. Use a fly cutter or a hole saw (or a saber saw) to form a three-inch-diameter hole. Then, working with a portable router equipped with a template guide, form a four-inch-diameter, 1/4-inch-deep concentric recess (see diagram) around the perimeter of the three-inch hole.

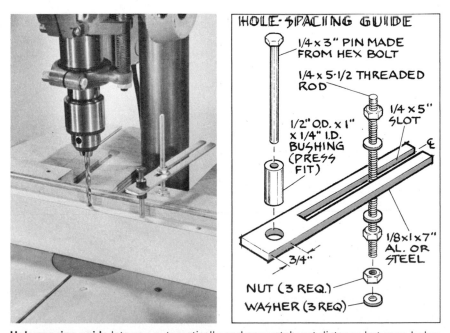

HOLE-SPACING GUIDE

1/4 x 3" PIN MADE FROM HEX BOLT
1/4 x 5·1/2 THREADED ROD
1/4 x 5" SLOT
1/2" O.D. x 1" x 1/4" I.D. BUSHING (PRESS FIT)
1/8 x 1 x 7" AL. OR STEEL
3/4"
NUT (3 REQ.)
WASHER (3 REQ)

Hole-spacing guide lets you automatically and accurately set distance between holes. Author used 1/4-in. guide pin, so all starter holes must be 1/4 in. (They can be enlarged later.) You could use smaller pin and bushing or prepare an assortment. To use guide, drill first hole, then set gauge and pin to spacing needed. Thereafter, inserting pin in drilled hole will automatically position work for next hole. Guide adjusts vertically and laterally, and it can be put in any of the T nuts on the straight fence's brackets.

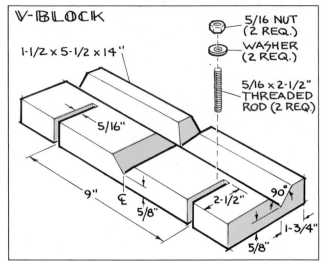

V-BLOCK

1-1/2 x 5-1/2 x 14"

5/16 NUT (2 REQ.)

WASHER (2 REQ.)

5/16 x 2-1/2" THREADED ROD (2 REQ.)

5/16"

9"

5/8"

2-1/2"

90°

5/8"

1-3/4"

5/8"

Drill accurate holes through rods and tubes by placing them on this V-block, which attaches to the main table of your master jig. This one has enough built-in adjustments so you can be precise in aligning the drill bit with the center of the V. The V-block is secured with threaded rods that fit T nuts in the main table.

This forms a lip to hold the inserts. Or you can outline the four-inch recess with a fly cutter and remove the waste with a chisel. If you do it the latter way, outline the recess before you make the three-inch hole.

Providing for Add-ons

Carefully locate and drill the holes for the four ¼-inch and two ⁵⁄₁₆-inch T nuts. (Bolting on various accessories.) In each case, first drill a ¹⁄₁₆-inch pilot hole all the way through. Enlarge this from the top to the bolt size that will be used and from the bottom to accommodate the outside diameter of the T nuts. These T nuts do not have to be installed flush, but be sure to use the pronged type.

Next, use a table saw to form the slot in the table top and the groove below (see diagram detail). A very useful slide rides in this groove. Be sure the saw is aligned so you will cut exactly on the center line. First form the ³⁄₁₆-inch-wide slot by making repeat passes. Then, with the blade projecting ½ inch above the table, shape the one-inch-wide groove— again with repeat passes.

Shape the slide support as diagrammed, and after flush-installing the T nuts for the slide lock, attach the support beneath the table with glue and six No. 10 by ½-inch flathead wood screws. Be precise when countersinking the screws; they must not project above the table surface.

Cut the partitions, closures, and bottom to size. Assemble the parts on the drill-press table so you can mark the exact locations of the dadoes in the bottom for the partitions and for the clamp ledge. Attach the drawer guides with glue and brads, then assemble all parts with glue and finishing nails. Follow this sequence: First install the clamp ledge on the bottom, then attach the partitions by gluing and nailing into the sides of the support. Finally, add the bottom and closures.

A point about the clamp ledge: On

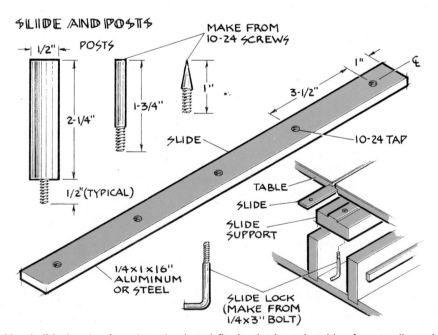

SLIDE AND POSTS

POSTS

1/2"

MAKE FROM 10-24 SCREWS

1"

2-1/4"

1-3/4"

1/2"(TYPICAL)

SLIDE

1"

3-1/2"

10-24 TAP

TABLE

SLIDE

SLIDE SUPPORT

1/4 x 1 x 16" ALUMINUM OR STEEL

SLIDE LOCK (MAKE FROM 1/4 x 3" BOLT)

Metal slide (made of steel or aluminum) fits in slot in main table of master jig and accommodates posts that guide work for various jobs. Smaller posts are made from 10-24 screws; the ½-in. post can be made on a metal-turning lathe, or you can cut a ½-in. steel rod to length, mount it in a drill press, file one end, and use a die to form the threads. The slide is held in position by an L-shape slide lock.

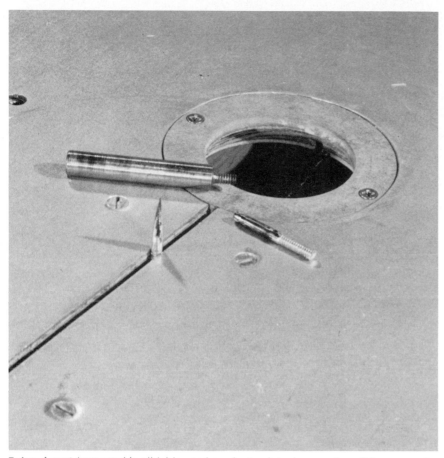

Pointed post (mounted in slide) is used as pivot point when work can't have a center hole. Use the straight post when it can; ½-in. post is shown in use on next page.

Drilling holes around a circumference is easy when you mount the work on a post on the slide. Just center the drill bit on the line, lock the slide in position, and drill.

some drill-press tables, the front edge is not 90 degrees to the table's surface. In such a case, use the clamp ledge only as a positioning guide; use a C-clamp or two at the back edge of the table to provide anchorage for the jig.

The drawers hold the accessories and necessary hardware. Their design is pretty basic—not the kind of thing you'll find on heirlooms—but adequate. Be sure that the drawers will slide easily. Bore 1½-inch fingerholes through the drawer fronts. (Knobs or pulls might snag clothing.)

Workmanship Is Critical

Be persnickety when constructing the master jig. With careful layout work and construction, you'll produce a long-lived and accurate piece of workshop equipment. Carefully sand all parts before and after assembly. Set finishing nails slightly below the surface of the wood, and fill the holes with wood dough. Treat all surfaces with a couple of coats of sealer. Polish the aluminum cover with very, very fine steel wool, then frequently apply paste wax, rubbing it to a polish. Also, wax all wood surfaces against which work must bear or move.

The photos show some uses for the master jig and its accessories. The diagrams tell you how to make all the parts.

In general, follow the standard rule: When your cut must be deep, take the time to achieve full depth by making repeat passes. Remember that sanding should be part of a *finishing* operation—don't attempt to sand when you should use the saw.

When using your drill press for routing or shaping, use chucks that are specifically designed for those operations. A three-jaw chuck, for example, is not designed to take the side thrust that routing produces.

Keep your hands away from cutting areas regardless of the operation. Even a drum sander can do damage. Always wear safety goggles and, when needed, a mask.

Master Drill-Press Jig Accessories

The diagrams shown here include two guards for the jig (page 147). Make and use them. But remember that they can't think for you. Keep your hands away from cutting areas, wear safety goggles, and, when needed, wear a mask—*By R. J. De Cristoforo. Illustrations by Gerhard Richter.*

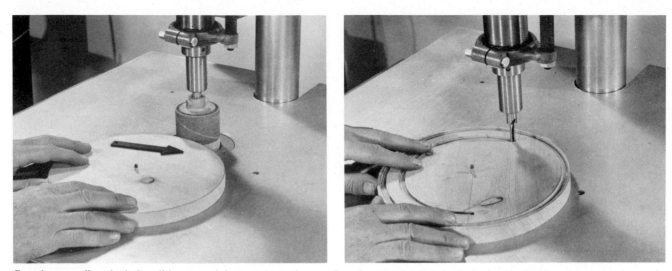

For pivot sanding, lock the slide so work just contacts the sanding drum and rotate it clockwise. A circular table insert is cut to fit the diameter of the sanding drum. Use the same technique to cut circular grooves or rabbets in a disc.

Use the ½-in. guide post to sand parallel curves. First sand (freehand) the edge that rides the post, then sand the second edge by moving the work between the post and drum. Routing a groove parallel to a curved edge is also done with this post.

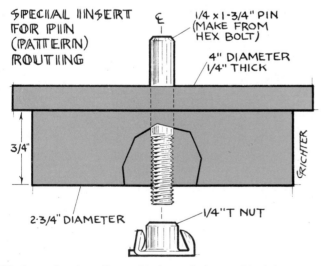

SPECIAL INSERT FOR PIN (PATTERN) ROUTING

1/4 x 1-3/4" PIN (MAKE FROM HEX BOLT)

4" DIAMETER 1/4" THICK

3/4"

RICHTER

2-3/4" DIAMETER

1/4" T NUT

Pin (or pattern) routing guide is made from a blank insert—a four-in. disc cut to fit the hole in the main table of the jig. You lock the blank insert in the hole tend use the drill to form the center hole. A T nut holds the pin in the insert, as diagramed.

Pattern for pin routing duplicates what you want to rout in the work. It is tack-nailed, as shown, to the bottom of the work. Then the work is flipped and moved so that the pattern rides against the guide pin. You can incise designs or raise a panel..

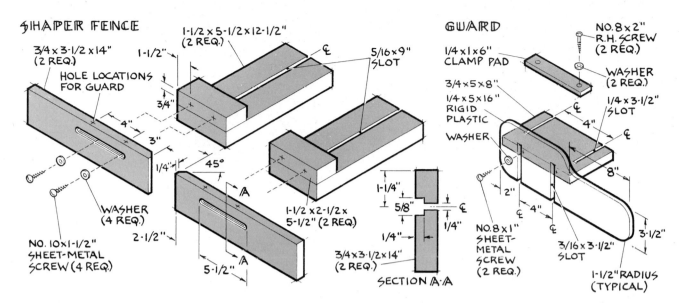

SHAPER FENCE

3/4 x 3-1/2 x 14"
(2 REQ.)

HOLE LOCATIONS
FOR GUARD

1-1/2 x 5-1/2 x 12-1/2"
(2 REQ.)

1-1/2"

3/4"

4"

3"

1/4"

45°

5/16 x 9"
SLOT

WASHER
(4 REQ.)

NO. 10 x 1-1/2"
SHEET-METAL
SCREW (4 REQ.)

2-1/2"

5-1/2"

1-1/2 x 2-1/2 x
5-1/2" (2 REQ.)

A

A

1-1/4"

5/8"

1/4"

1/4"

3/4 x 3-1/2 x 14"
(2 REQ.)

SECTION A·A

GUARD

NO. 8 x 2"
R.H. SCREW
(2 REQ.)

1/4 x 1 x 6"
CLAMP PAD

WASHER
(2 REQ.)

3/4 x 5 x 8"

1/4 x 5 x 16"
RIGID
PLASTIC

WASHER

1/4 x 3-1/2"
SLOT

4"

8"

2"

4"

3/16 x 3-1/2"
SLOT

3-1/2"

NO. 8 x 1"
SHEET-METAL
SCREW
(2 REQ.)

1-1/2" RADIUS
(TYPICAL)

Shaper fence works like commercial units: Each half is adjustable to control depth of cut. Each can be moved laterally to minimize the opening around the cutter. Slots in fences and lips around them can be cut either with a router or by drilling overlapping holes. (Use a 5/8-in. bit set to cut 1/4 in. deep. Chisel out the slot; on its center line, drill overlapping holes with a 1/4-in. bit.) Acrylic guard, an essential safety feature, mounts on the in-feed fence and moves in and out to accommodate different work thicknesses.

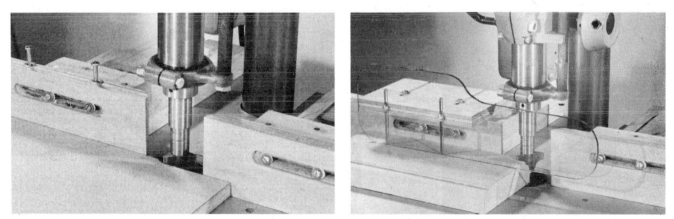

When entire edge of stock is removed (left), out-feed fence is moved forward to equal depth of cut. Thus, work is supported before and after it passes the cutter. In-feed and out-feed fences are in line (right) when the cutter is removing part of the edge.

GUARD

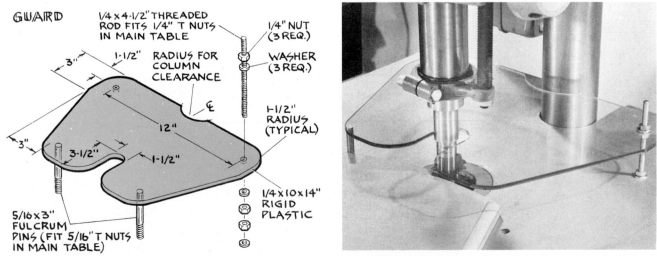

1/4 x 4-1/2" THREADED
ROD FITS 1/4" T NUTS
IN MAIN TABLE

1/4" NUT
(3 REQ.)

WASHER
(3 REQ.)

1-1/2"
RADIUS FOR
COLUMN
CLEARANCE

3"

12"

3"

3-1/2"

1-1/2"

1-1/2"
RADIUS
(TYPICAL)

1/4 x 10 x 14"
RIGID
PLASTIC

5/16 x 3"
FULCRUM
PINS (FIT 5/16" T NUTS
IN MAIN TABLE)

Freehand shaping is done when straight fences can't be used. Fulcrum pins, made from 5/16-in. bolts, fit in T nuts in the table and provide support for the work. Depth of cut is controlled by collars that mount on the shaper adapter along with the cutter. To start the cut, brace the work against the left-hand pin and advance it carefully into the cutter until the edge rests against the depth collar. At this point you can swing the work clear of the pin or continue to use it for support. Make—and use—the guard.

tilting jig for your drill press

For years I've found it difficult to drill accurate holes at an angle with my drill press. The problem was worse when I had to bore a series of angular holes in a circle. I was tempted to buy a tilting drill-press vise with a swivel base but quickly gave up on that idea after checking the prices.

I solved the problem by building a tilting jig. To my delight, it works perfectly. The job of building it was made easier with a new circle-cutting device: the Industrial Hole Cutter from H.I.T. Products (Box 6906, Hollywood, Fla. 33021; $30). You could make the curved cuts with a router, but you'd need an accurate guide.

The base is made of ¾-inch plywood, 11 by 11 inches (or an inch or two larger than your drill-press table). Using the hole cutter (or a router), cut two interrupted circles (four slots each). The inner circle should be four inches in diameter; the outer circle, 6½ inches in diameter. The pivot point of the circle is the center of the base. The four slots cut along the inner circle are approximately 1⅝ inches long, and those on the outer circle are about 2¾ inches long. These eight slots must be rabbeted ⅛ inch deep on the upper side of the base using a ¼- or ⅜-inch rabbeting bit. The slots will be exactly ¼ inch wide, enabling you to attach the jig to your drill-press table using ¼-by-two-inch carriage bolts.

Make the ¾-inch-plywood tilting table exactly the same size as the base. Cut an eight-inch hole out of its center. The hole must be perfectly round. Next, cut an eight-inch disc out of ¾-inch plywood; cut the same slots as you've cut in the base.

Rabbet the slots on the underside of

Tilting jig positions the workpiece so you can drill holes at any angle. Work attaches to disc, which swivels 360 deg.

the disc; ¼-by-two-inch carriage bolts can be put into the slots to clamp work or to hold jigs to the table.

Now dado a ¼-inch-wide groove on the underside, ¼ inch deep and ¾ inch from one edge of the tilting table. The dado is used to hold a 12-inch threaded rod. Next, cut a piece of ⅛-inch hardboard the same size as the table, with a seven-inch hole in the center. Glue and screw the hardboard piece to the bottom of the tilting table covering the ¼-by-¼-inch groove. (This keeps the disc from falling through.) Now cut a saw slit through the plywood and hardboard from the edge of the table across the dado cut to the edge of the hole. Insert a 12-inch threaded rod in the dado groove with a hex nut on one end and a wing nut on the other. By tightening the wing nut, you will squeeze the table tight enough around the disc to lock it at any position.

Cut two identical quadrants from ¾-inch plywood. Make one straight side

10¼ inches and the other 9¼ inches long, as shown in the sketch.

The curved slot in the quadrant is necessary to adjust the angle of the tilting table. This slot should be ¼ inch wide and 7¾ inches from the same pivot you used to cut out the quadrant. The slot starts and ends ½ inch from the two edges.

The base and table are attached to one another with a full-length piano hinge on the edge opposite the threaded rod. The quadrants are attached to the table so that the center rod of the piano hinge is aligned with the center of the pivot holes that were used to cut the quadrant's slots. Screw two hanger bolts into the base, positioning them so that they protrude through the slots of the quadrants. Wing nuts and washers on these hanger bolts will allow you to lock the quadrants to the base at any angle from zero to 90 degrees—*By Howard Silken.*

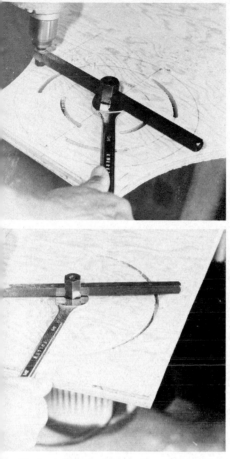

Circle-cutter accessory for any portable drill lets you cut the quadrants, as well as the holes, slots, and disc. The special bit cuts like a saw. Make the jig of five pieces of ¾-in. plywood and one of ⅛-in. hardboard (see sketches).

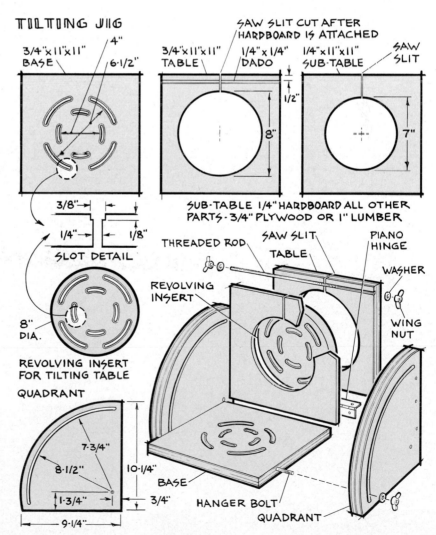

TILTING JIG

3/4"x11"x11" BASE   4"   6-1/2"

3/4"x11"x11" TABLE   SAW SLIT CUT AFTER HARDBOARD IS ATTACHED   1/4"x1/4" DADO   1/4"x11"x11" SUB-TABLE   SAW SLIT

1/2"   8"   7"

SUB-TABLE 1/4" HARDBOARD ALL OTHER PARTS - 3/4" PLYWOOD OR 1" LUMBER

3/8"   1/4"   1/8"

SLOT DETAIL

8" DIA.

REVOLVING INSERT FOR TILTING TABLE

QUADRANT

7-3/4"   8-1/2"   10-1/4"   1-3/4"   3/4"   9-1/4"

THREADED ROD   SAW SLIT   PIANO HINGE   TABLE   WASHER   REVOLVING INSERT   WING NUT   BASE   HANGER BOLT   QUADRANT

pour yourself a parking pad

A driveway is a little like a clothes closet—no matter how big it is, there's never enough room. Solution: for your shirts, add another shelf; for your car, try a parking pad. It's an additional parking spot for company or your own cars, and it's also a perfect work area.

The parking pad I constructed is 18 feet square and six inches thick. I found that I could save a considerable amount of money by doing the preparation myself, as shown in the accompanying photos (next page).

On a project this size, however, it is best to buy premixed concrete from the pros. They'll know the right mix and aggregate size for the compressive strength you'll need—at least 3,500 psi.

On the finished pad (below) I used crusher-run gravel as fill between the drive and slab. The fence is not just a finishing touch—it's also a necessary marker during the snow season—By Ray Hill.

Preparation is as important as using the right concrete. Begin by leveling ground (1) with a shovel and rake. Then tamp soil with tamper. Spread two to three inches of crusher-run gravel (2) and tamp down again. (Moisten the earth slightly before tamping; it helps compact the gravel and earth more solidly.) After ground is prepared, set up 2 × 6 form boards (3). Stakes hold boards in place. Author used a mason's line to place the first form board in position. The other three boards were positioned using a square and level. Reinforcing wire (4) is cut with bolt cutters and should cover entire pad area. Weight the wire down with heavy rocks as shown. Wear gloves to protect your hands. Just before concrete is poured, wet the area thoroughly (5). Start pouring concrete in one corner (6) and spread it evenly. Routinely raise the reinforcing wire up as you work (7)—the weight of the concrete tends to push it against the ground. The idea, of course, is to keep the wire centered within the pad for strength. After concrete is poured, use a bull float to level it (8). Push the float forward, with the leading edge raised slightly, as is being done here. Then pull it back toward you, again with the leading edge raised. Repeat the passes with the bull float until the pad is smooth. No other floating is necessary. Before concrete hardens, use a trowel to cut the concrete away from the form boards (inset). Then round off the sharp edges with an edging trowel. Finally, spray curing compound over the still-damp concrete, and let dry.

plumb in an automatic washer

If you live in an older house without provision for an automatic washing machine, you can add it. The job couldn't be easier than with Genova PVC drain-waste-vent pipe and CPVC or PB hot/cold water supply tubing.

Select a washer location convenient to a vent stack or building drain where you can pipe the waste water from the washer. Give second consideration to nearness to a point where you can tap a hot and cold water supply. You must also consider what floor space is available. An upstairs location may prove step-saving and it has the advantage that water can drain away by gravity. On the other hand, a basement location often is selected because the space is there.

In a basement laundry, unless your sewer runs below the basement floor level, waste water must be pumped out. Not many public health codes will permit the use of a sump pump for this, even though that's the way it's often done. While an ordinary sump pump system will handle laundry wastes all right, bacterial action takes place in the sump pit, sometimes making for a smelly basement. Moreover, a periodic sump cleaning becomes a nasty job. The proper way to pump out laundry wastes from a basement is with a sealed sewage-ejector.

Connecting a Drain

Since an automatic washer's drain pipe is least flexible, make that run first. You may wish to add a laundry tub at the same time you plumb in the washer. It must be connected to a drain and vented the same as a kitchen sink. Use a 1½-inch PVC waste pipe and vent. A laundry tub permits the use of a suds-saving automatic washer. In any case, the washer empties into the tub.

You can also drain a washer directly into what is called a standpipe, a 1½- or 2-inch PVC pipe reaching about 36 inches above the floor and located behind or beside the washer. A P-trap below the floor seals off the DWV system's gases from the house. With a standpipe, a suds-saving washer cannot be used effectively because there is nowhere to store the suds.

If the distance from the trap to the nearest vent is more than 2½ feet (1½-inch pipe) or 3½ feet (2-inch pipe), the trap must be revented, according to most plumbing codes.

The washer's drain pipe can tie into a vent stack using a tee. Tie into a horizontal drain by dropping in from above via a 45-degree elbow and a wye inserted in the horizontal pipe. One drawing shows the use of a Part No. 61231 saddle tee. If your vent stack is a 3-inch Genova in-Wall Schedule 30 one, this easy method may be employed. In any case, the fittings you use to make the connection depend on what kind of pipes you are connecting to.

Water supply. A pair of ½-inch CPVC or PB hot and cold water pipes are run to the wall behind the washer. This is probably an ideal use for PB's flexibility. Either way, the system should end in a pair of threaded hose bibbs. Ahead of them you'll need two extra-large air chambers made of ¾-inch CPVC tubes 18 inches long and capped at the top. These oversized chambers prevent damage to the water supply system when fast-acting washer solenoid valves snap shut after a fill cycle. A water-hammer arrester will also do the job.

The drawings show the components of a CPVC and a PB system with two types of drain hookups. They are guides to the parts you will need for your hookup. A basement system would be most similar to the attic-type hookup, which is supplied with water from above—*Richard Day. Art courtesy of Genova, Inc.*

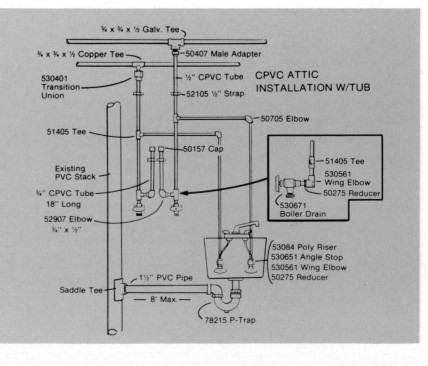

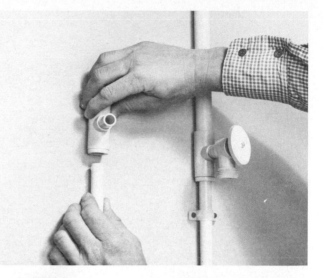

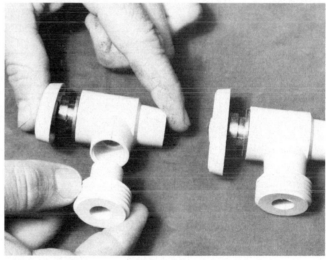

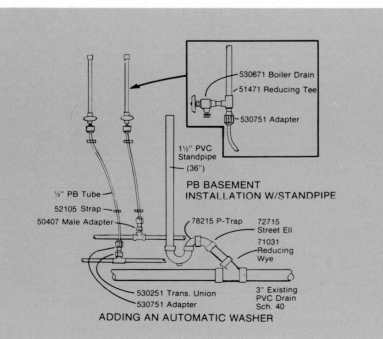

530671 Boiler Drain

51471 Reducing Tee

530751 Adapter

1½" PVC
Standpipe
(36")

**PB BASEMENT
INSTALLATION W/STANDPIPE**

½" PB Tube

52105 Strap

50407 Male Adapter

78215 P-Trap

72715
Street Ell

71031
Reducing
Wye

530251 Trans. Union

530751 Adapter

3" Existing
PVC Drain
Sch. 40

ADDING AN AUTOMATIC WASHER

1. The neatest, fastest way to make a hole in the floor for the washer's standpipe is with a hole saw. Chucked in an electric drill, this one cuts a 2" hole, clean as you please. (Other sizes are available.)

2. Drain hose from the washer slips inside the PVC standpipe and discharges waste washer water to the house drainage system. To keep system gases from escaping, a P-trap is installed below the floor.

3. Behind-the-washer supplies for hot and cold water are solvent welded of CPVC tube and fittings. A pair of ¾" × ¾" × ½" reducing tees with reducing bushings permit ½" supply tubes, ¾" air chambers.

4. Lacking Genova Part No. 530671 washer hose valves for washer supply hose attachment, you can make them from Part No. 530661 ½" angle stop valves and Part No. 53128 male hose adapters solvent welded in.

how the modern home plumbing system works

Where does the water come from; where does it go? Your home plumbing system is two separate systems, really—water supply and water disposal. Both are made up of several hundred feet of pipes and fittings that join them. Water in the water supply system is under pressure—some 50 pounds per square inch (psi). Thus, water supply pipes can be fairly small in diameter, yet still carry enough water. Water in the disposal, also called the drain-waste-vent (DWV) system, always flows by gravity. For this reason its pipes and fittings must be larger in diameter to carry the required flow without clogging or backing up. Both systems are designed to operate safely and quietly.

The systems, water supply and DWV, never are connected to each other. If contaminated water got into the drinking water, it could sicken or kill. Water from the water supply system flows into the drain-waste-vent system, never the other way around—*Richard Day. Art courtesy of Genova, Inc.*

This illustration shows a typical plumbing system for a two-story home with a basement. Adjustments for a one-story home, or a house without a basement, are easy to make. In any layout, it is critical to keep the water supply and DWV systems separate.

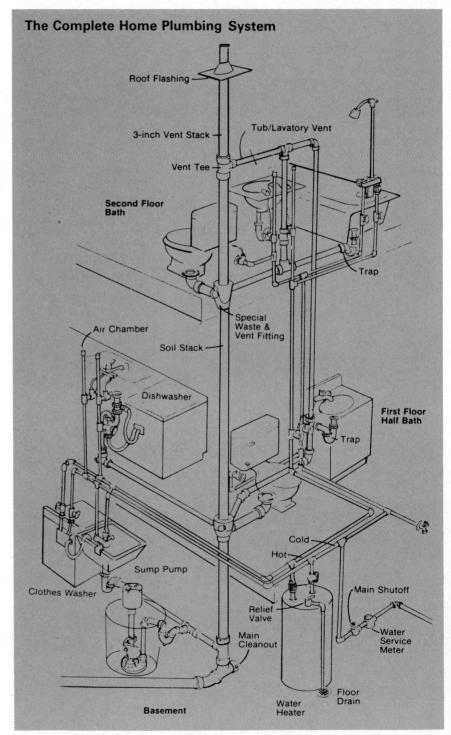

The Complete Home Plumbing System

Roof Flashing

3-inch Vent Stack

Vent Tee

Tub/Lavatory Vent

Second Floor Bath

Trap

Special Waste & Vent Fitting

Air Chamber

Soil Stack

Dishwasher

First Floor Half Bath

Trap

Cold

Hot

Sump Pump

Clothes Washer

Main Shutoff

Relief Valve

Main Cleanout

Water Service Meter

Basement

Water Heater

Floor Drain

electrical plans and blueprints

Usually, the best way to plan any involved job is to first "put it down on paper," and this is essential when planning an electrical wiring job. You can save hours of working time, plus many dollars worth of materials, by having a good working drawing or blueprint that shows where each receptacle and light fixture is to be installed, as well as where and how the wires will be run to each of these. For instance, you'll know whether to go through the walls or under the floors with your wires. Most local authorities will require that you make up some sort of wiring diagram to submit to the electrical inspector. Such a drawing helps show that you intend to follow local codes and makes it easier for both you and the inspector to insure that the job will be done properly.

Reading and Understanding Blueprints

Let's start with the blueprints used in the construction of a new house. Regardless of whether you're planning to wire a new house or an addition, or to rewire an older house, electrical wiring blueprints or homemade wiring diagrams are made up basically the same way. Many people think of house blueprints as mysterious sets of drawings that only an engineer or experienced contractor could understand. And sometimes, if they're poorly done, they can be just that! Actually, an or-dinary set of house plans from a good reputable company or architect is fairly easy to understand by the average do-it-yourselfer, provided he does one thing: learn the abbreviations and symbols used for the various materials in the house. In a typical blueprint wiring diagram, the locations of the wiring devices are marked with the electrical symbols and abbreviations established by the American National Standards Association.

It's much easier to use these symbols and abbreviations than to try to pictorially represent each item, or to write in its name. The symbols shown on the following page are the standard electrical symbols found on all electrical wiring blueprints or diagrams.

Learn the symbols or keep the chart handy when studying your house blueprints so you can understand fully what goes where. When making up your own blueprint or drawing to submit to an electrical inspector, use the symbols as well. They'll speed up understanding for everyone.

In addition to the symbols shown, letter abbreviations may be placed in or near the symbols. These are some of the most common for house and farm wiring:

> **DT** —Dust-tight
> **EP** —Explosion proof
> **R** —Recessed
> **G** —Grounded
> **RT** —Raintight
> **WT** —Watertight
> **VT** —Vaportight
> **WP**—Weatherproof

Making Your Own Wiring Plans

After studying the details of the house wiring blueprint, it's easy to appreciate how important a good plan or drawing is for the installation of a complete wiring job in either an old or a new house. Naturally you won't be interested in making a drawing as elaborate as a blueprint done by a professional architect, but you should

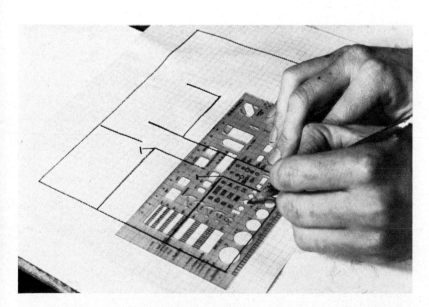

A template like this one helps speed up the task of drawing a wiring diagram.

Electrical reference symbols

The electrical symbols are those suggested for use on drawings as prepared jointly by the American Consulting Engineers Council and the Construction Specifications Institute and as published in CSI Document 16015 (June 1973). Reproduced with permission of the Construction Specifications Institute, Washington, DC 20036.

Electrical Abbreviations

(Apply only when adjacent to an electrical symbol)

Dust Tight	DT
Explosion Proof	EP
Grounded	G
Rain Tight	RT
Recessed	R
Vapor Tight	VT
Water Tight	WT
Weather Proof	WP

Electrical Symbols
Switch Outlets

Single-Pole Switch	S
Double-Pole Switch	S_2
Three-Way Switch	S_3
Four-Way Switch	S_4
Key-Operated Switch	S_K
Switch and Fusestat Holder	S_{FH}
Switch and Pilot Lamp	S_P
Fan Switch	S_F
Switch for Low-Voltage Switching System	S_L
Master Switch for Low-Voltage Switching System	S_{LM}
Switch and Single Receptacle	⊖S
Switch and Duplex Receptacle	⊜S
Door Switch	S_D
Time Switch	S_T
Momentary Contact Switch	S_{MC}

Ceiling Pull Switch	Ⓢ
Multi-Speed Control Switch	Ⓜ

Receptacle Outlets

Where weather proof, explosion proof, or other specific types of devices are to be required, use the uppercase subscript letters. For example, weather proof single or duplex receptacles would have the uppercase WP subscript letters noted alongside of the symbol. All outlets should be grounded.

Single Receptacle Outlet	⊖
Duplex Receptacle Outlet	⊜
Triplex Receptacle Outlet	⊕
Quadruplex Receptacle Outlet	⊕
Duplex Receptacle Outlet— Split Wired	⊜
Triplex Receptacle Outlet— Split Wired	⊕
250-Volt Receptable Single Phase Use Subscript Letter to Indicate Function (DW-Dishwasher; RA-Range, CD-Clothes Dryer) or numeral (with explanation in symbol schedule)	⊜
250-Volt Receptacle Three Phase	⊜
Clock Receptacle	Ⓒ
Fan Receptacle	Ⓕ
Floor Single Receptacle Outlet	⊟
Floor Duplex Receptacle Outlet	⊟
Floor Special-Purpose Outlet	⬟ *
Floor Telephone Outlet-Private	◁

Circuiting

Wiring Exposed (not in conduit)	——E——
Wiring Concealed in Ceiling or Wall	——

Wiring Concealed in Floor	— — — —
Wiring Existing**	- - - - - - -
Wiring Turned Up	———o
Wiring Turned Down	———●
Branch Circuit Home Run to Panel Board	→→ 2 1

Number of arrows indicate number of circuits. (A number at each arrow may be used to identify circuit number.)***

---

* Use numeral keyed to explanation in drawing list of symbols to indicate usage.

** Note: Use heavyweight line to identify service feeders. Indicate empty conduit by notation CO (conduit only).

*** Note: Any circuit without further identification indicates two-wire circuit. For a greater number of wires, indicate with cross lines, e.g.:

—⊢⊢⊢ 3 wires;

⊢⊢⊢⊢ 4 wires, etc.

Neutral wire may be shown longer. Unless indicated otherwise, the wire size of the circuit is the minimum size required by the specification. Identify different functions of wiring system, e.g., signalling system by notation or other means.

Panelboards, Switchboards and Related Equipment

Flush Mounted Panelboard and Cabinet *

Surface Mounted Panelboard and Cabinet *

Switchboard, Power Control Center, Unit Substations (Should be drawn to scale.) *

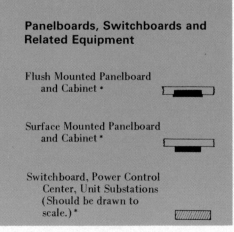

Flush-Mounted Terminal Cabinet (In small scale drawings the TC may be indicated alongside the symbol.)*

Surface-Mounted Terminal Cabinet (In small scale drawings the TC may be indicated alongside the symbol.)*

Pull Box (Identify in relation to wiring-system section and size.)

Motor or Other Power Controller (May be a starter or contactor.)*

Externally Operated Disconnection Switch*

Combination Controller and Disconnection Means*

* Identify by Notation or Schedule

Power Equipment

Electric Motor (HP as indicated)

Circuit Element, e.g., Circuit Breaker

Circuit Breaker

Fusible Element

Single-Throw Knife Switch

Double-Throw Knife Switch

Ground

Battery

Contactor   C

Photoelectric Cell   PE

Voltage Cycles, Phase   Ex: 480/60/3

Relay   R

Equipment Connection (as noted) ▲

Lighting

	Ceiling	Wall
Surface or Pendant Incandescent Fixture (PC = pull chain)	TYPE / WATTS	SWITCH / PC / CIRCUIT
Surface or Pendant Exit Light	⊗	⊗
Blanked Outlet	Ⓑ	Ⓑ
Junction Box	Ⓙ	Ⓙ
Recessed Incandescent Fixtures	⊡	
Surface or Pendant Individual Fluorescent Fixture	⊙▬	

Surface or Pendant Continuous-Row Fluorescent Fixture (Letter indicating controlling switch)

Fixture No.
Wattage

Symbol not needed at each fixture

*Bare-Lamp Fluorescent Strip

Residential Occupancies

Signalling-system symbols where a descriptive symbol list is not included on the drawing.

Pushbutton

Buzzer

Bell

Combination Bell-Buzzer

Chime   CH

Annunciator   ◇

Electric Door Opener   D

Television Outlet   TV

Electrical symbols

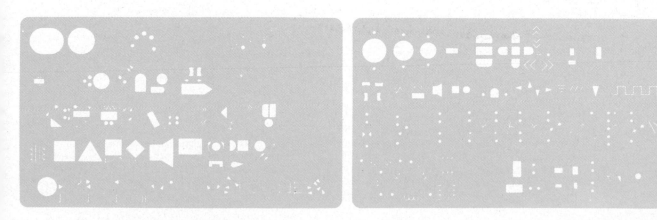

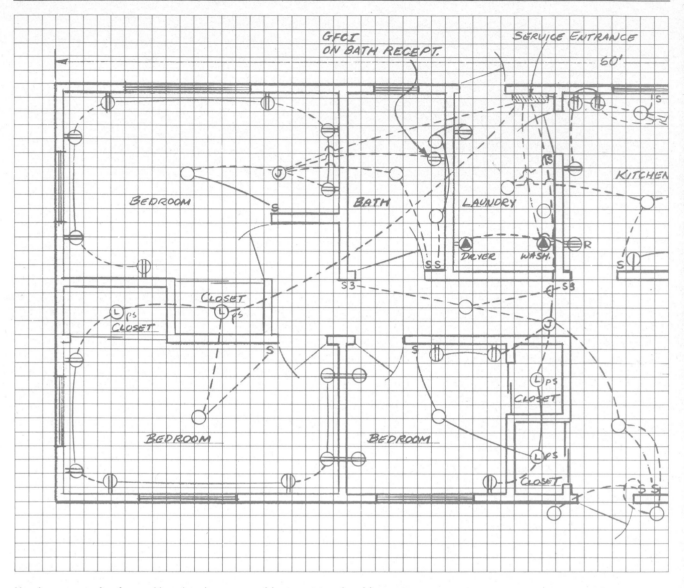

Here's an example of a working drawing you could present to a local inspector.

strive to make an "accurately sized" plan of the house to be able to determine exactly how much wiring materials you will need.

Use architectural paper which has small squares lined on it. Allow each line to represent either 1 foot or ½ foot, depending on the size of your house and whether or not you can get the entire floor plan drawn on the paper. The larger size drawing will make it easier to figure the amount of materials needed. Measure the outside of the house; then measure the inside of each room; and roughly draw these walls in position on the graph paper. Also mark significant features such as doors, windows, fireplaces. Once again symbols don't have to be fancy, just simple indications of what they represent. Mark the intended locations of light fixtures and other hardware.

Mark the position of the various fixtures using the standard symbols and abbreviations.

If you wish to speed up the chore, you can purchase a small plastic template from an art supply store which allows you to trace silhouettes of most of the electrical symbols. With all electrical units marked in place, you can determine the best way to run the wires with the least amount of effort and materials. It's a good idea to make the initial drawing on the squared drawing paper, then use pieces of thin tracing paper over this to mark the lines indicating the wires for the various circuits. You'll probably end up changing these circuit lines several times before finally deciding on the best locations anyway. Once you have decided where each item is to be located, make up a final drawing.

Now, by counting the squares, you can determine how many feet of wire will be needed for each run. Remember you must also figure the height of the walls for each run of circuit wire down to a receptacle. Add 18 inches for bends in ceiling and floor plates, as well as about a foot for each connection at an outlet box. By adding all these figures together, you can come up with a fairly accurate estimate of the amount of wire you will need.

After placing the items in position on the drawing, according to code with regard to the number of receptacles or lights, you can tally up what you'll need. You can then show this to the electrical inspector; he will probably suggest some better ways to run wire or to place fixtures.—*Monte Burch. Blueprint by Richard Meyer. Template illustration courtesy of Chartpak, Inc.*

wall and ceiling fixtures

Y ou will seldom encounter complications in mounting wall or ceiling fixtures as most of them are designed to fit standard outlet boxes. In general, both wall and ceiling fixtures may be mounted either by means of a threaded "fixture stud" attached to the center of the box, or by a mounting strap with boxes that lack the stud. The stud is favored for heavier fixtures.

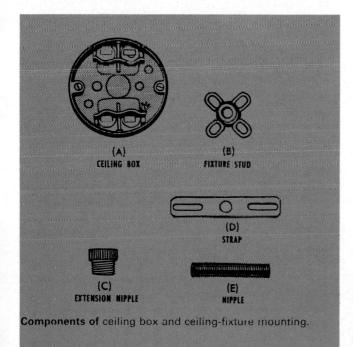

Components of ceiling box and ceiling-fixture mounting.

(A) CEILING BOX

(B) FIXTURE STUD

(C) EXTENSION NIPPLE

(D) STRAP

(E) NIPPLE

Fixtures in New Work. In new work (home construction) the boxes are mounted in the framing before the walls and ceilings are covered. Standard metal hangers are then used to secure the boxes to studding or joists. A wide variety of these hangers is available at hardware and electrical supply dealers. Some are designed to hold the box firmly to a single stud; others are adjustable to permit spacing the box at any desired distance between studs or joists. As the house framing is exposed, installation of the boxes is very simple.

Fixtures in Old Work. In old work a number of different methods and devices are used to simplify installation. Switch and outlet boxes, for example, can be mounted without fastening to the wall framing at all. The plaster or wallboard is used as support. One type of box used in this way is fitted with a folding clamp on each side. It is inserted in the hole cut to fit it and pushed in so that the front brackets seat firmly against the outside of the wall.

The side clamps, flat against the box, slide into the hole easily. To lock the box in place, the screws that open the clamps are turned in, spreading the clamps and drawing them snug against the inner surface of the wall.

Another device that can be used on standard boxes is made of thin sheet metal and sold under such trade names as "Hold-It." In form it might be compared to a T with two vertical legs instead of one. The box is pushed into the hole made for it and brought up snug against the outer wall surface (stopped there by the brackets or ears at the ends). Then the sheet-metal fasteners are slipped in on each side of the box, tipped at an angle with the cross of the T inside the wall. Next, they are set straight (so the T cross is vertical inside the wall if the box is set vertically) and pulled outward by the legs until the cross member is seated firmly against the inner surface of the wall. Then the protruding legs are bent over the edges of the box to lock it in place. From there on the box is handled in the usual manner.

Ceiling Boxes. To mount a ceiling box an "old-work hanger" is used. This is simply a metal bar or heavy strap with a sliding stud on it. As a first step, cut a hole in the ceiling to match the size and shape of the box to be installed. The cable may then be snaked through the hole and connected to the box. (The box must be a type with a knockout or hole for stud-mounting.) Next, slip the bar or strap of the hanger up through the hole and slide the stud so that half the hanger extends to each side of the hole.

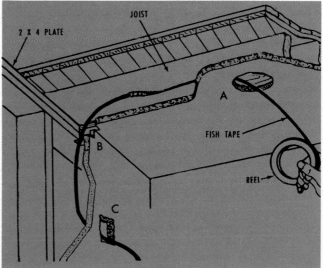

JOIST

2 X 4 PLATE

A

B

FISH TAPE

REEL

C

To lead new wiring from ceiling (A) to wall (C), it is necessary to remove small section of plaster at B where wall and ceiling meet so 2-by-4 plate can be notched to pass cable. After cable has been led through, plaster can be patched to conceal hole.

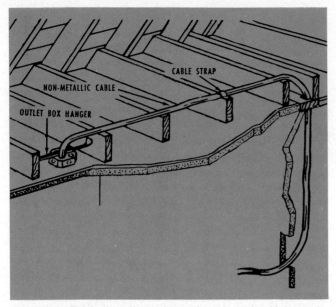

If attic is unfinished, wall-to-ceiling wiring is easier. Hole can be bored from attic into wall; outlet box and hanger are easily mounted from above. Use plywood panel for working platform in unfloored attic. Nonmetallic cable is shown here, but BX or conduit may be used, depending on local requirements.

The stud should be centered in the hole. Then push the box up into the hole so that the stud extends downward through the stud hole in the center of it, and turn the nut loosely onto the stud. Make sure the cable is not cramped against the inner ceiling surface, then tighten the stud, and the job's done. The bar should run crosswise of laths in plaster ceilings.

If the ceiling box is to be mounted in a ceiling with an unfinished attic above it the job can often be done simply by using a new-work hanger. Cut the hole in the ceiling first, then mount the hanger to hold the box in the hole, working from above in the unfinished attic. A few boards or half a sheet of plywood can provide a working platform across the ceiling joists if there is no flooring in the attic.

Mounting a New Fixture in an Old Box. If you are simply mounting a new fixture on an old box, the work is much simpler. An examination of the existing fixture will quickly tell you whether it is mounted with screws or a stud. If you can arrange to have a helper in removing or mounting fixtures, the job will be easier and faster. If not, have some heavy but soft iron wire on hand, like that used in coat hangers. This can be bent to form a double-ended hook to hold the fixture while you disconnect the wiring.

All such work, of course, must be done with the current definitely off. You can turn it off at the main switch or unscrew the fuse that supplies that particular circuit—if shutting off power throughout the house would involve serious inconvenience. But do not merely shut off the wall switch supplying the fixture. There is too much danger of someone inadvertently turning it on again while you're working on the wiring.

Form one end of the wire hook before you remove the stud nut or screws holding the fixture in place. If you have a helper, of course, he can hold the fixture while you disconnect it, eliminating the need for the hook. Once the fixture nut or screws have been removed, lower the fixture carefully to provide room to disconnect the wiring. Almost always you will find a hole or clamp in the box over which the hook can be anchored. Do not anchor it over the wires.

The lower end can be slipped through the stud hole or the screw holes of the fixture canopy and bent upward for a firm hold. This prevents the fixture from slipping or dangling in such a way as to place a strain on the wires before you can disconnect them.

If the wires are connected with solderless connectors, the job is fast and easy. If the wires are spliced, soldered, and taped, clip them close to the splice on the fixture side of the splice, leaving just enough fixture wire to grip with pliers. With the fixture disconnected and out of the way, you can use a soldering iron to melt the solder on the splice while you pull off the remaining fixture wire with pliers. As the fixture wire is usually the flexible multi-strand type, the solid wire from the box may have little or no distortion in the bared end-portion, making it usable again without clipping. Try to save as much of its length as possible for ease of work when you resplice.

Wiring the Fixture. Merely connect the white wire to the white, black to black, as in regular outlet wiring. In connecting the new fixture use solderless connectors if you want to speed the job and simplify any future changes.

Because of the wide difference in fixture design, you may need a different length nipple for the new one if the mounting is by means of stud and nipple. Often, however, you will find that the "hickey" which joins the nipple to the fixture stud in the box will provide enough adjustment.

Fixture Repairs. If a fixture fails to light when switched on, the trouble may be either in the fixture or the switch. Often a defective switch can be spotted by the sound it makes. The click (if it's a snap switch) may sound dead. If the switch controls more than one fixture, however, and the others light, the trouble is in the individual fixture. If in doubt, try replacing the switch first. It's an easier job than removing a fixture that may not be in need of repair.

The commonest causes of fixture troubles are in switches mounted on the fixtures themselves, and in the bulb sockets. Naturally, if one or more bulbs fail to light in a multi-bulb unit, check the bulbs first, trying them in another lamp or fixture. Next, *with current off* at the fuse or main switch, check the center contact at the base of the socket, using a flashlight. If the contact is blackened, scrape it clean with a sharp-tipped screwdriver. Then try a new bulb in it. Often corrosion at this point is the cause of the trouble. With current on again, the bulb should light if the contact was at fault.

If the bulb still does not light, the trouble is either a broken wire or a loose connection at the socket terminal screws, or possibly a defect in the socket itself. With current off, you can remove the socket from its base (if standard) by pressing it at the point indicated by the word "press" stamped on the shell of many popular brands. If the terminals are tight, disconnect them and substitute another socket as a test.

With current on, if a bulb lights in this socket you have located the trouble and can then buy a new socket to match the fixture, if the test socket was borrowed from a lamp or from the workshop gadget box. If the test socket bulb does not light, the trouble is in the fixture's wiring. (Neon-glow test lights are sometimes used to check the various parts of fixture wiring, but socket substitution is safer as no live terminals are exposed when the current is on.)

If wiring must be replaced, particularly through curved ornamental tubing (as in many chandeliers) it is best done by firmly twisting the bared ends of the new wiring to those of the old, so the old wiring pulls the new wiring through. As you pull the old wiring out of one end of the tube, you pull the new wiring in the other end, and finally all the way through.

Fixture Mounting

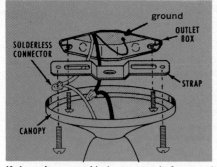

If there is no stud in box, strap is fastened to threaded ears, and fixture is then fastened to strap.

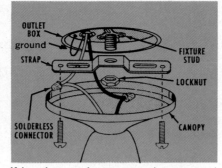

If box has stud, strap may be mounted with threaded nipple and locknut. Fixture is mounted on strap in usual way.

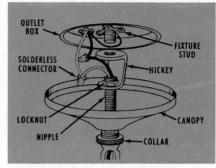

Ceiling drop fixtures are usually mounted from stud, using two nipples joined by "hickey." Both hickey and collar can be adjusted to draw fixture canopy snugly against ceiling.

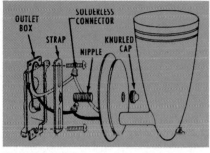

Wall fixture is attached to rectangular box by means of strap and nipple.

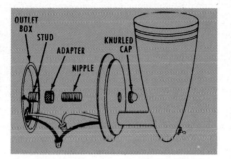

Outlet box with central stud requires only adapter and nipple to attach wall fixture.

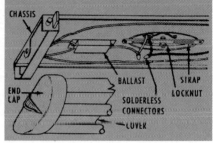

Fluorescent fixture can be ceiling-mounted with stud, nipple, and strap.

Soldering Electrical Work. If a splice must be soldered or heated with a soldering iron to separate it, you can use an old-style soldering iron heated by a blow torch. Naturally, the current to the wiring being repaired must be off. Certain types of electric soldering irons which have no electrical contact between current supply and heated tip can be used with an extension cord to another circuit in the house that has not been shut off. Before doing any electric soldering by this method, however, *be sure* to check with the manufacturer of the soldering iron as to its safety in this type of use. The reason: when a fuse is unscrewed to shut off current to a house circuit only the hot wire (black) is "broken." The white ground wire is still connected to the power source. Any contact between the white wire of the fuse-out circuit and the black (hot) wire of any other circuit would cause a direct short.

Facts About Lighting

For general overall lighting in a room, the ceiling fixture can provide shadowless light in working areas such as kitchen or workshop. This is achieved by using several fixtures spaced apart to flood a given area with light from a variety of angles. The principle is simple: a shadow cast by light coming from one direction is illuminated by light coming from the opposite direction. The effect is especially easy to achieve with several large fluorescent fixtures. Other fixture types with various additional features such as dimmer switches offer a light range from a mere candle glow to full illumination. Others have a three-way switch, enabling you to have focal downlight, candlelight, or a combination of both. Some models have a concealed spotlight to dramatize a centerpiece on a formal dining table. With all these features to choose from, providing good lighting is easier than ever.

Since the ceilings in today's homes are considerably lower than those in older ones, many people think that chandeliers are out of the question, except perhaps over a dining table where there would be no danger of bumping your head. Such is not the case. The new fixtures have been designed with this in mind, and modified versions that still retain traditional design (where it is desired) are available. Some new designs are conceived so that they fit snugly against the ceiling, and proper proportions in the scaled-to-fit models make their use practical in the smallest homes.

Other types are mounted on ceiling tracks. This allows you to have the overhead light at more than one location, according to your needs.

The Science of Lighting. Good lighting does not mean just enough light. It means also control of glare, which can make reading, sewing or other tasks difficult, and irritate the eyes. Proper distribution of the illumination is also important. Unshaped lamps do not produce good lighting by any means. Use lamp bulbs of ample wattage with a proper shade to focus the light without allowing direct light to assail your eyes.

When your lighting, by experimenting with various lamp wattages and shades, seems comfortable, and your eyes do not tire after extended use with the lamp, take a reading with a photo light meter, and make a note of that reading. Make the reading on a piece of ordinary gray cardboard. Then when you want to duplicate your successful formula in another part of the house, all you have to do is try different bulbs until the meter reading is the same as before. The reason for using the gray cardboard is that different colors on walls and ceilings have different reflective factors, but the neutral gray assures you of getting the same effect each time. This is an especially good procedure for desk and reading lamps, but is not as important in over-all illumination—*By George Daniels.*

kit for emergency plumbing repairs

The temperature kept dropping. By morning it had sunk to 22 below, colder than it had been in years. The Lloyds awoke, ready to spend a quiet Sunday buttoned in the bosom of their suburban home. But Cindy Lloyd soon discovered there was no water pressure anywhere in the house.

"Must be a frozen pipe," George said as he bundled up to go out and check. He was back shortly, stomping snow off his feet. "Someone unplugged my heat tape," he accused. "Pipes in the crawl space are probably frozen solid. They should be thawed soon, though."

Soon, however, they heard a disheartening sound coming from the crawl space: the steady trickle of running water. "Blasted pipe's split, I'll bet. Gotta turn off the water," George muttered as he hurried outside.

"Shall I call a plumber?" Cindy shouted.

"Guess you'd better," he yelled back.

But the only plumber she could reach was on his way out to a long list of emergency calls. The other plumbers were already gone. The Lloyds weren't the only ones with frozen pipes that morning.

George Lloyd ended up taking his family to a motel, where they spent two nights before the pipes were repaired. The repairs, at overtime rates, plus the motel bill and meals cost the family $300.

You can keep this from being your story by putting together an emergency plumbing-repair kit. I've designed one that's so simple to use you won't mind doing the repairs yourself (see table). The kits contain CPVC-plastic adapters, tubes, and couplings. These can be used to replace sections of ½- and ¾-inch house piping. The parts are assembled with solvent-welding cement, which you also include in your emergency kit.

Why CPVC? First, this tough, heat-resistant thermoplastic is rated to withstand a pressure of 100 psi at 180 degrees F. Second, solvent welding is super-simple; no pipe threading or sweat soldering is required. Another advantage is that CPVC will halt the electrolytic action that transfers metals within a plumbing system, especially in hard-water areas. (Spots from which metal is transferred can get thin and leak.) Your system will be even better after the repairs than it was before.

You'll need two sizes of repair kits—½- and ¾-inch—because most houses have both sizes of water-supply pipes. Choose either the kit for copper or CPVC pipes or the one for threaded-metal pipes, depending on the kind of plumbing your house has. Parts for both types are shown in the drawing as well as listed in the table. The tubes and fittings can be purchased at a good hardware store or home center. The kits will cost about $12 each to put together. (A service call from a plumber: about $35 plus per-hour charges.)

I show parts made by Genova. If you use another brand, be sure it offers

EMERGENCY PLUMBING-REPAIR KITS

Pipe Type (House)	Pipe Size	Parts	Fits Pipe Removed (Min.-Max.)	Tools Needed
Threaded galvanized-steel or brass	½-in.	1 ½-in. by 10 ft. tube* 2 ½-in. CPVC couplings 2 ½-in. transition unions Solvent-welding kit	4¾-in.–10 ft. 4 in.	Pipe wrench, hacksaw, and pliers or open-end wrench
	¾-in.	1 ¾-in.-by-10 ft. CPVC tube* 2 ¾-in. CPVC couplings 2 ¾-in. CPVC transition unions	5½ in.–10 ft. 4¾ in.	
Sweat-type copper or solvent-welded CPVC	½ in.	1 ½-in.-by-10 ft. CPVC tube* 2 ½-in. Genogrip adapters (or equivalents) 4 ½-in. CPVC couplings Solvent-welding kit	1⅜ in.–1½ in. (using just adapters and couplings) 2⅝ in.–10 ft. 1½ in.	Hacksaw or tubing cutter
	¾ in.	1 ¾-in.-by-10 ft. CPVC tube* 2 ¾-in. Genogrip adapters (or equivalent) 4 ¾-in. CPVC couplings	1⅞ in.–2 in. (using just adapters and couplings) 3½ in.–10 ft. 2 in.	

*Cut to convenient storage length—couplings included for 40-in. lengths

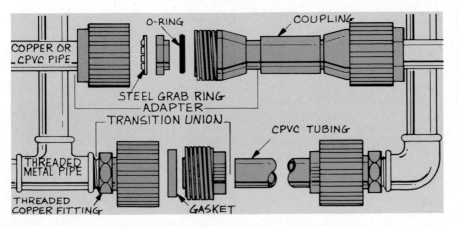

To repair copper or CPVC pipe (top) you need adapters and coupling. For longer repairs you need CPVC tubing. Transition unions for threaded pipe accept CPVC tubing directly.

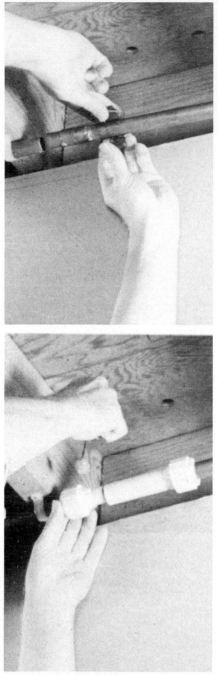

To repair a leaking copper or CPVC tube, cut out the defective portion with a hacksaw or tubing cutter (top). Next, slide an adapter onto each tube end and tighten, following package directions. Slip a coupling onto each adapter, then cut CPVC tubing to bridge the gap. Slip it into the couplings, then solvent-weld all the CPVC slip joints as shown above.

transition unions to go between the plastic and metal piping and take up differential thermal movements. Tape or wire the parts of the kit together and put them in a handy place. The kit is for repair of pipes and tubes only. If there's a faulty fitting, it will have

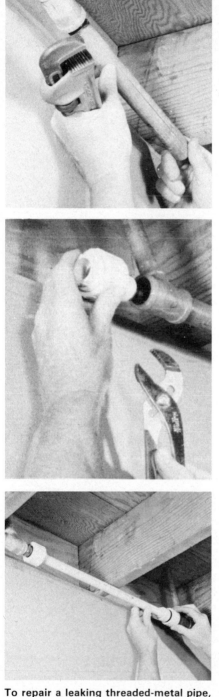

To repair a leaking threaded-metal pipe, saw through the defective pipe, then remove both ends with a pipe wrench (left). Next, thread on the transition unions, using one at each end of the remaining metal pipe (center). Tighten with pliers or an open-end wrench. Use pipe dope or TFE tape on the male threads. Now measure the distance between the gaskets inside the two transition unions and deduct one inch. Cut the CPVC repair tube to that length, and solvent-weld it into the transition unions (right). Let the welds cure two hours.

to be replaced, of course.

The parts of the emergency kit you should use depend on the required length of your repair. A short repair in copper or CPVC—up to 1½ inches long in a ½-inch tube and up to two inches in a ¾-inch tube—can be done with just the two adapters and one CPVC coupling between them. An adapter is pushed onto each cutoff end of tubing (see photos) and tightened a bit beyond hand-tight. It helps if you coat the tube ends with petroleum jelly or silicone lubricant for easier sliding. Each adapter comes with a plastic grab ring inside and a stainless-steel version on the blister card. Discard the plastic ring (it's meant for flexible tubes), and insert the steel one.

With ½-inch copper or CPVC tubing, repairs of lengths between 1½ and 2⅝ inches cannot be made: They fall between lengths that the parts will fit. With ¾-inch tubing, you can't make a repair between two and 3½ inches. Make your cutouts short or long enough to avoid these "blind spots." There are also minimum repair lengths for both sizes of tubing. They're listed in the table. Beyond these lengths, two CPVC couplings are used, one at each adapter. A length of CPVC tubing cut to the proper length slips into the couplings to bridge the gap (see illustrations).

A look at the table shows that the shortest repair you can make in ½-inch threaded-metal pipe is 4¾ inches; in ¾-inch threaded pipe it's 5½ inches. You make the repairs by threading a transition union onto each end of the good pipe and connecting them together with a length cut from the CPVC tubing. Longer repairs simply call for a longer connecting tube.

The table also lists the sizes of repairs the kits will handle. The maximum length with each kit is just over 10 feet. By adding more CPVC tubing and couplings to link the tubes, longer repairs can be made. Because 10-foot CPVC tubes are too long for convenient storage, you'll probably want to cut them into shorter lengths. I've listed the parts in the table assuming you'll cut the tubing to 40-inch lengths. If you want shorter lengths, add more couplings—one for each saw cut you make—and you'll still be able to make a 10-foot-long repair.

By keeping the parts of the kits together where you can find them, you'll be able to fix a leaky pipe at any time. The repair should last as long as your house plumbing does. And if you make a copy of this article to put with your emergency kits, it will remind you how to use them.—*By Richard Day.*

renewing a pool deck

When this 40-foot pool was installed on the steep slope behind Ken Herrington's home in California, a plywood apron was suspended around it. For a cool, neat-looking walking surface, Herrington covered the plywood with outdoor carpet. The very month his five-year warranty expired, Herrington tells us, the carpet deteriorated rapidly: "So I ripped it up and let the exposed plywood dry completely."

A still older deck, stretching 62 feet across the back of his house, had been connected to the pool area by steps and smaller deck sections. This was all of redwood, now badly in need of refinishing. Herrington considered the major chore of sanding off the weathered surface—difficult because of all the surface nailing.

He then decided to tackle the renewal of all his deck areas as a single project. First he covered the plywood

pool deck with 30-pound building felt. Then he nailed 1×2 cedar sleepers every six inches over the felt, at right angles to the pool edges.

When planks are nailed on top of these slats, there's a space beneath for drainage. At the sides and far end, the pitch of the apron encourages rainwater to run off the outside of the deck, instead of into the pool.

Before nailing the planks across the sleepers, however, Herrington painted the bottoms, edges, and ends with a polymer wood stabilizer made by the Flecto Company (Box 12955, Oakland, Calif. 94604) called Varapel (any good quality deck paint will work).

Some of the advantages of Varapel are that you apply it as it comes from the can (you don't thin it or use paint thinners to clean up your brushes); and that special resins penetrate deep into wood-cell walls and fibers and, on subsequent curing, reinforce the nat-

ural wood structure, increasing its water resistance.

After finishing off his pool deck by brushing two top coats on the face of the new planks, Herrington decided to coat all the old weathered decks with Varapel, as well. His only preparation was to reset all popped nailheads. Where nails weren't holding planks flat, he drove in new spiral nails.

Herrington offers two tips for working with Varapel: "Sometimes, when lumber goes through a planer, the resins become burnished and slick in spots. Roller coating such new wood won't make the paint adhere as well as brushing. If you see any slick spots, it's best to sand them rougher before you paint.

"When you come to clean your brushes, first try warm water and soap. But if the paint is stubborn, switch to lacquer thinner—*By Al Lees. Photos by K. L. Herrington.*

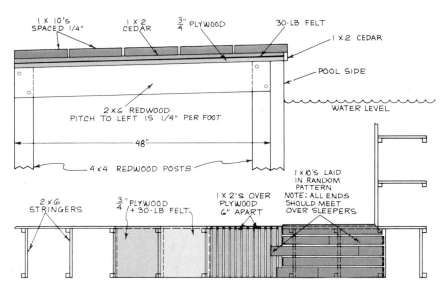

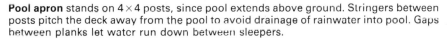

Edge strip is nailed to ends of sleepers, flush with their tops. First plank is then laid over strip as shown in sketch.

Pool apron stands on 4×4 posts, since pool extends above ground. Stringers between posts pitch the deck away from the pool to avoid drainage of rainwater into pool. Gaps between planks let water run down between sleepers.

Three spiral nails used in project (l-r): paint-dipped stainless (because of higher cost, on four rows nearest pool only), galvanized, and aluminum. All hold well.

Brushed on weathered, unpainted wood, Varapel can cover in one coat, for effect seen at left where previous day's coat has cured. We topped this with second coat.

Cedar planks (1×10) are laid on sleepers with ¼-in. gaps. After trial positioning, lift and paint planks before nailing.

Stepped decks were sound, so were just painted to match new pool apron. Roller speeds application on weathered wood.

preframed window replacement

According to the Architectural Aluminum Manufacturers Assn., there are more than three-quarters of a billion windows in U.S. homes. So how come you got the ones that leak air? Well, you're not alone.

Most homes still have single-pane windows that cost, it's estimated, from $20 to $100 a year in heat loss through conduction and drafts. But you can cut that loss in your home by 50 percent or more, claims the AAMA, with new double- or triple-glazed windows. And window replacement can be simplified.

Preframed aluminum windows are available in a variety of sizes and styles through local lumberyards or home-improvement centers. Basically, you measure the frame, carefully remove the old window, and install a replacement window system of matching size. There are no structural changes, so no carpentry is needed; you may not even need to repaint. And since the new window is installed from inside the house, you won't need scaffolding and the job can be done at any time.

These photos show the simple procedure. The only tools you'll need are hammer, screwdriver, broad chisel, ⅜-inch drill, square, plumb, light hacksaw, and caulking gun. Result: easy-to-operate airtight windows that save money and add to the value of your home.

Remove molding and inside stops with a chisel and save for reuse. Remove spring balances, pull out bottom sash (above), and cut weight cords. Pry out parting stops at top and each side of the window frame, as shown above. This will allow you to slip out the top sash.

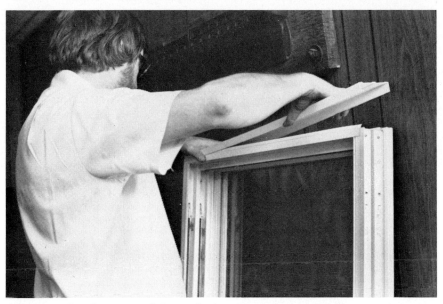

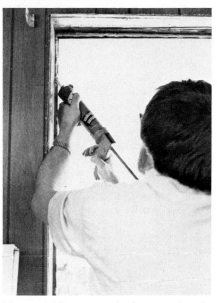

After removing the new sash for easier handling, place the header expander on top of the frame. Or if the windows have fins, then trim the fin at the proper serration.

After a trial fit, remove the frame and caulk against the blind stop at both top and sides.

Push the window frame against the caulked blind stops, and drive the first screw. Be sure you have the proper screwdriver at hand.

If the frame has alignment screws, adjust them until both sides are plumb. If not, add shims at the center of both jambs until square.

Once the frame is square, complete the installation with additional mounting screws. Then you place both sashes in their tracks.

Apply caulking all around the window framing as an inside seal. This, along with the blind-stop caulking, will prevent any air leaks.

If an expander header is used, lift it to the top of the opening. Drill mounting holes, and insert wood screws to anchor the header.

Replace the inside stops and molding, which were previously removed. Use care with the hammer—or you may not yet be finished.

new compact bench tools

Back in June 1980, I wrote a piece on what was then a brand-new trend in stationary power tools: compact, self-contained, bench-top tools. That article was one of the most widely read power-tool stories ever published in POPULAR SCIENCE. Clearly, people are fascinated by these little workhorses.

And with good reason: Most homeowners can't justify the cost of full-size tools, nor can they find the space to house them. The compacts solve both of these problems. These sleek, lightweight packages can be stored between uses, yet can be pulled out, plugged in, and put to work in seconds.

Since the first group of compact tools came out four years ago, a second batch has come crowding into my shop. Most major power-tool makers—Skil, Black & Decker, Sears, and Benchmark Tool Co.—now offer one or more compact bench tools.

I've been working a number of representative tools hard for the past several months. Some were disappointing; others were surprisingly good. Take a look at the following reports and you'll see which are which. Be sure to note the spec tables. They'll help you decide which tools have the power and capacities to handle the jobs you have in mind. The prices will tell you if the tools fit your budget, and the storage sizes let you see how much space they take up between jobs.

Band Saws

What's the ideal bench-top tool? Look at Skil's 10-inch band saw (p. 175, top; left) and Black & Decker's model 9411. Each is light, compact, and easy to store. And neither one suffers much in comparison with full-size saws. Both tools do everything you could expect of a band saw. (Although I didn't test it, Sears offers a saw essentially the same as Skil's. It's the Craftsman 10-inch band saw [catalog number 9HT 2442N]; $190.)

I used these saws to cut a variety of

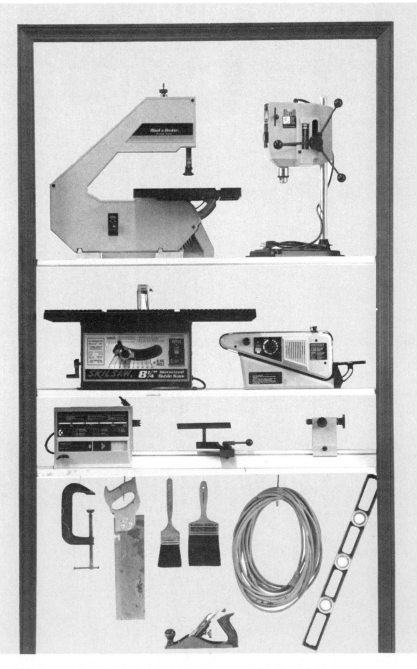

Bench tools in a closet include (clockwise from top left): Black & Decker band saw, Shopcraft drill press, sander, and wood lathe, and Skil table saw.

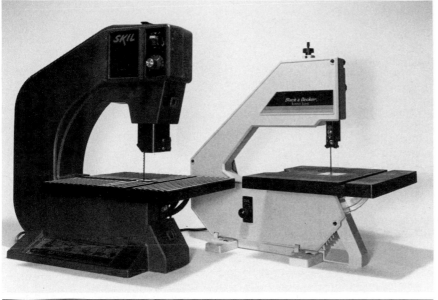

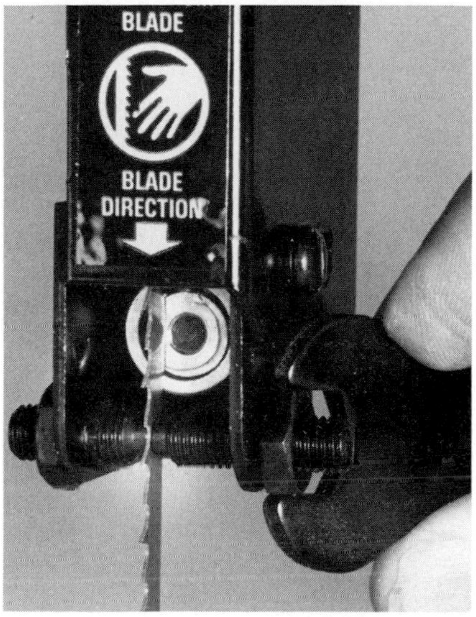

Model	Approx. cost ($)	Power (amp)	Max. thickness (in.)	Throat (in.)	Variable speeds?	Storage size (in.)	Weight (lbs.)	Blade capacities (in.)
Black & Decker 12½"	180	3	4	12½	Yes	22¼ × 14⅛ × 24¼	23	¼ and ⅜
Skil 3104	195	4.2	4	10	Yes	24 × 15 × 24	26	⅛ to ½

curves and straight lines in hardwoods and pine. Each tool cut as accurately as any band saw I have ever tested, slicing cleanly through pieces up to four inches thick. Both saws have surprisingly large tables for good work support. Each has variable speed and takes metal-cutting blades without any modification—something my full-size saw can't do.

But these saws do differ from full-size tools. Overall construction is lighter: Pulley wheels are plastic instead of metal, for example. This keeps both price and weight down. In exchange, you probably give up some long-term durability and a certain smooth "Cadillac" feel that only comes from tools with a lot of mass. And

while most full-size saws will handle stock at least six inches thick, these saws only can manage four-inch stock.

Finally, adjusting the blade guides on these saws—something you must do every time you change blades—requires some fussing with screwdrivers and tiny wrenches in tight spots. On the Black & Decker, for example, blade guides are threaded studs that you lock by tightening a nut (photo at right). My big band saws are much less tedious to adjust. But overall, these are small sacrifices well worth enduring if you want an economical, lightweight, compact tool.

Though each is a fine tool, the saws are not interchangeable. Black & Decker's, for example, has a roller

bearing for a blade backup; the Skil band saw uses a solid, flat plate. The bearing should run cooler and give longer blade life.

The Skil saw is heavier and more powerful, however, and I would probably choose it over the Black & Decker for work on the heavy end of the spectrum. It will, for example, saw stock at its maximum four-inch-thickness capacity quite nicely. Feed the Black & Decker four-inch stock, and it starts to struggle a bit: The frame seems to flex under the strain, and the blade begins to chatter and cut erratically. The Skil also takes a wider range of blade sizes—from a light ⅛ incher for ultra-fine scrolling to a ½-inch skiptooth blade for re-sawing.

While the Skil (and the Craftsman) would be better for heavier work, the Black & Decker is much quieter, lighter, and more relaxing for medium- and light-duty work.

Sander

The Shopcraft four-inch belt sander is a tool in a class by itself. Never have I seen a belt sander with all the features this one has.

Instead of traveling around the usual two rollers, the four-by-36-inch belt winds around an unusual arrangement of three rollers (photo at right).

This arrangement creates three separate sanding surfaces. One is the conventional long, flat surface top. The second, also a flat surface, is vertical and mated with a small, tilting worktable.

The third sanding area is a readily accessible, drumlike surface on which

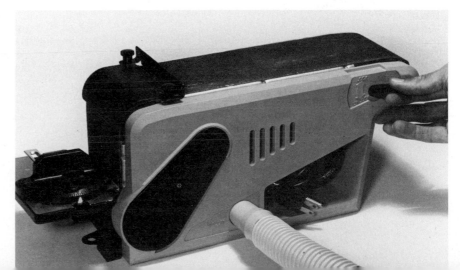

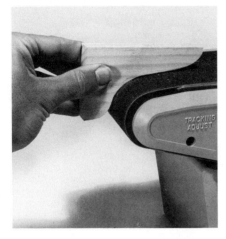

Model	Approx. cost ($)	Power (amp.)	Belt size (in.)	Work-surface size (in.)	Belt speed	Storage size (in.)	Weight (lbs.)
Shopcraft 4" Belt Sander	149	3.2	4 × 36	4 × 9½	150–500 feet/min.	7½ × 18½ × 8	13¾

the belt tracks around the tension roller. This is quite useful for sanding small curved or odd-shaped pieces (photo above).

These three surfaces, combined with the Shopcraft's compact size and light weight, make it a very interesting

tool. And several extra features boost its versatility. It has a variable-speed motor, quick-release belt-change lever, and a belt-tracking knob. Convenience features include a vacuum-cleaner dust-pickup port and a handy cord-storage compartment.

The speed of the sander ranges from 150 to 500 feet per minute. That's slower than what I'm used to. (My portable four-inch sander runs at more than twice that speed.) One result of the slower speed, of course, is that this tool cuts more slowly than other belt sanders. But another result is that it gives you good control. It won't grind away wood faster than you like, and it can be used on plastics without causing so much heat to build up that they begin to melt and gum up the belt.

The slow speed is also ideal for sharpening. With most grinders and belt sanders, you need a feather touch or you'll burn the edge of the tool you're sharpening. Not so with the Shopcraft. I used it on my best chisels and found that it cut quickly but created almost no sparks. And the sander never let the edges overheat.

If you have trouble cutting clean miters, you'll appreciate the vertical sanding surface and its worktable. The table takes an accessory miter gauge that makes it easy to sand up to four-inch-wide miters dead true and smooth. By using the miter gauge with the table tilted, you can even sand compound miters.

My rating? The Shopcraft sander is a clever, useful tool in a clever package.

Lathes

Anyone who has a shop wants a lathe, the ultimate fun tool. But a full-size lathe can eat up a lot of space—and several hundred dollars. The Benchmark Tool Shopcraft Wood Lathe (at top in photo) and Sears Drill-Powered Wood-Turning Attachment are two ways to circumvent these problems.

Sears seems reluctant to call its wood-turning attachment a lathe, and in some ways I have to agree. The attachment uses your electric drill as its power source. Secured by a worm-screw hose clamp, the drill can be easily removed for other work. But the limited capacities of the tool just about restrict it to making miniatures such as candlesticks and pepper grinders.

The attachment's performance depends entirely on the quality of the drill that powers it—and most of the drills I see these days have a fair amount of chuck wobble. That's OK for drilling holes, but it causes chattering and rough cuts when you're turning wood. This chatter is further compounded by the fact that the tool weighs less than 10 pounds. Still, at $25, you might consider this tool to introduce a youngster to wood-turning, or even to satisfy your own desire to do a little small-scale turning. Just be aware of the limitations. The tool is adequate for light work up to 16 inches in length—the maximum possible. And it has no provision for faceplate-turning work of any kind.

Shopcraft's seven-inch wood lathe is a big step up in capacity and price. It

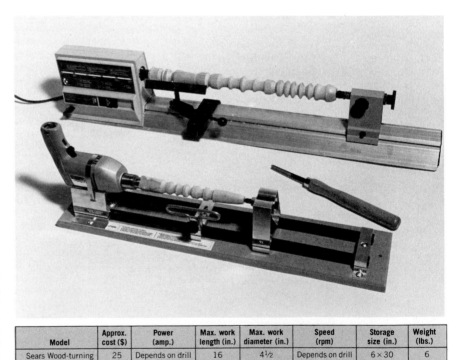

Model	Approx. cost ($)	Power (amp.)	Max. work length (in.)	Max. work diameter (in.)	Speed (rpm)	Storage size (in.)	Weight (lbs.)
Sears Wood-turning Attachment	25	Depends on drill	16	4½	Depends on drill	6 × 30	6
Shopcraft 7" Wood Lathe	170	3	27	7	700–1,800	42 × 5⅛ × 8	23

has built-in variable-speed power, handles stock up to 27 inches in length, and can be used with a faceplate. Its 27 inches between centers is just enough to turn most table legs, and with the faceplate you can turn bowls up to seven inches in diameter.

A sliding switch-speed selector gives you continuously variable turning

speeds from 700 to 1,800 rpm. That's adequate, but for fine finishing cuts on spindle work under four inches in diameter, I'd like to see a top speed closer to 3,600 rpm.

For the smoothest-possible work, I found it best to fasten this lathe to the heaviest available work surface. Vibration is the enemy of good work, and although the lathe itself runs quite smoothly, most workpieces are slightly out of balance. Combine that lack of balance with the light weight of this lathe (20 pounds), and the result is chatter and whip—unless you couple the lathe to a lot of mass.

Once the lathe is anchored, though, it's a lot of fun to use. It has plenty of power and lets me make tricky shearing cuts as smoothly as with my big, gap-bed Rockwell lathe. Heavy cuts tend to tax the light structure of the Shopcraft, causing the work to flex and chatter, but heavy cuts aren't good practice anyway.

Adjustments are convenient. You can move the tool rest and advance the tailstock spindle easily, without fumbling around for wrenches. The necessary knobs and levers are permanently in place. Moving the tailstock, however, requires an Allen wrench.

Another convenience is a spindle lock on the headstock that makes spur-center and faceplate changes easy. And though the instruction book doesn't mention it, I also used this lock for indexing 60-degree intervals. To do this trick, you must work carefully because the lock is a bit sloppy.

In my opinion, the Shopcraft is a good compromise between utility, price, compactness, and portability. It will handle most turning jobs in the light-to-medium class, and when you're finished you can slip it under your bench or hang it from a nail on the wall.

Drill Press

A drill press should be able to drill holes accurately, of course. But I expect mine to do much more than that. I'm just as likely to chuck a wire wheel, sanding drum, contour sander, fly cutter, or rotary rasp into my full-size drill press as I am to chuck in a twist drill bit.

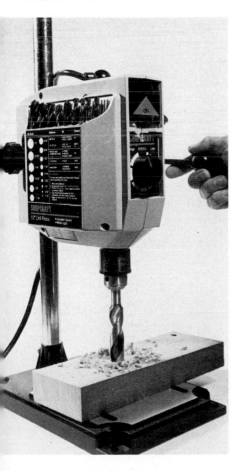

Model	Approx. cost ($)	Power (amp.)	Max. thickness (in.)	Throat (in.)	Speed (rpm)	Storage size (in.)	Weight (lbs.)	Chuck size (in.)
Shopcraft 1/2" Drill Press	100	3.2	12¾ chuck to table	4⅞	300–800 rpm	10¾ × 10¾ × 21	15¼	½

The Shopcraft ½-inch drill press is one of the few compact drill presses I've seen with the kind of full-size versatility that satisfies me. It has the power, the variable speeds, and the ½-inch chuck it takes to handle just about anything you throw at it.

When you look at the spec table for this compact press, it may seem impossible that it can manage most of the tasks of a standard-size tool. But like most compact drill presses, the Shopcraft can do a few tricks to overcome its limitations and even surpass the big boys in some ways.

Its throat, for example, is just 4⅞ inches. That's not much reach compared with the almost eight inches my floor-model drill press has. But with the Shopcraft, I was able to drill a hole in the center of a full sheet of plywood. How? By placing the entire press right on the plywood. Then I could drill a hole down through the center hole in the baseplate.

Another example: The maximum-thickness capacity of this press is listed at 10¾ inches. But I also overcame that limitation. Mounting the drill press near the edge of the bench let me swing the head out over the floor and drill into the end of stock over 40 inches in length.

About the only thing this little press won't do is drill holes at an angle; neither the base nor the head tilt. If you want to get around that problem, you'll need a tilting drill-press vise. Or you can build an accessory tilting table.

After I'd satisfied myself that this press would handle routine drilling jobs, I brought out my four-inch fly cutter and slipped it into the chuck. A fly cutter is a good test of a drill press. It takes a lot of low-speed torque to turn it, and if the press is out of square or the chuck wobbles, the cutter will chatter or bind up. I had no such problems with the Shopcraft: The cutter produced a smooth, even cut.

If you like to do quality work, the ½-inch chuck is a real boon. My best bits—Forstners and high-quality brad points—all have ½-inch shafts. Over the years I've tested a variety of compact drill presses, but this is the only one I've seen yet that could take these special bits.

How does this tool compare with Black & Decker's electronic drill press, the revolutionary tool I tested for PS in July 1981? The Black & Decker, with its computer-chip brain, has the edge in sophistication. It gives you push-button speed control, plus LED readouts of depth or revolutions per minute as you drill. It can shut itself off instantly if the bit binds, and it has more torque than the Shopcraft.

On the other hand, the Shopcraft has that versatile ½-inch chuck, and the Black & Decker has just a ⅜-incher.

Table Saws

The table saw is the heart of any wood shop, but both the Skilsaw 8¼-inch motorized table saw (p. 178, left) and the Black & Decker eight-inch table saw (p. 178, right) required lots of adjustments to make them work properly.

I don't expect a compact bench tool to have the power, capacity, or convenience features of a full-size tool. But I do expect it to make smooth, accurate cuts. The two saws I tested couldn't do so in the form in which they were shipped from the factory.

Both saws have the power and capacities to handle most work with one- and two-inch nominal lumber. But neither saw worked properly without modifications.

Let's start with the Skil. Flip it over on its back and look inside. What do

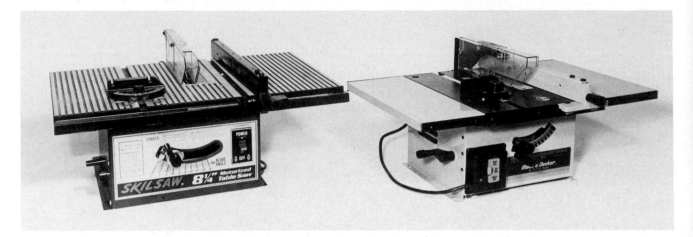

you see? A portable Skilsaw with its plastic handle sawed off. A Skilsaw is a fine tool for its purpose—primarily rough carpentry—but it is not built to the tight tolerances needed to give you the kind of smooth cuts you'd expect from a table saw. The blade arbor on my sample had so much end play—a full 1/32 inch—that the blade was free to wander back and forth in its kerf. Smooth cuts were just about impossible with this saw.

First, I tried the standard combination blade that came with the saw. This blade produced the ragged, rough-cut plank in the left-hand pair of samples shown in the photo. I tried better, more-carefully-ground combination blades. Then I tried carbide-tipped combination blades. All produced unacceptable cuts. Finally, by switching to a hollow-ground planer blade, I produced the smooth board shown in the left-hand pair—but only with a great loss of cutting speed.

Rough cuts weren't the only problem with the Skil. To make smooth, accurate crosscuts and miters, a table saw's miter-gauge slots must be dead parallel with the blade. On my saw they were a full 1/16 inch out of line. On most saws you can shift either the table or the blade to achieve parallelism, but not on the Skil.

In addition, the splitter assembly on the blade guard could not be aligned with the blade until I filed its adjustment slots oversize. The miter gauge came with no pointer and fit very loosely in its table slot (about 0.017-inch side play), further contributing to rough, inaccurate miters.

How about the Black & Decker? I unpacked the saw, spent 50 minutes putting it together, set it on my bench, and flipped the switch. The saw got up and walked across the table. Poking around beneath the saw, I quickly found the problem. The blade arbor had been improperly machined. In-

Model	Approx. cost ($)	Power (amp.)	Blade size (in.)	Max. work thickness (in.)	Max. rip (in.)	Table size (in.)	Storage size (in.)	Weight (lbs.)
Black & Decker 9419	160	7.5	8	1¾	13¼	26½ × 15½	26½ × 19 × 14½	36
Skil 3102	190	10	8¼	2	12	27 × 16	27 × 19¾ × 13½	37

stead of fitting snugly on the ⅝-inch shaft, the blade was riding on a necked-down section (see photo at right, top). As a result, the blade was mounted some 1/10 inch off center and was dangerously out of balance.

According to Black & Decker's Tim Miller, a few other saws with improperly machined shafts have slipped onto the market. "Those parts came from a vendor who wasn't working up to our quality-control standards, and we now have changed to another supplier," he told me.

To make the saw usable for testing, I ground about ⅛ inch off the back of the arbor bushing. This let the bushing slide far enough up the shaft to make room for the blade on the ⅝-inch arbor (right, middle photo).

Once I had done that, the saw performed well enough. It had none of the end-play problems that plague the Skil. Its miter-gauge slots are easily adjusted parallel to the blade, and the splitter assembly and guard worked well.

But as the right-hand pair of sample cuts shows, there was still a great difference in cutting quality according to blade selection. As with the Skil sample, the rough plank was cut with the combination blade supplied with the saw, and the smooth cut was made with the hollow-ground planer blade.

If I had to pick one of these tools, I would choose the Black & Decker saw, but only after making sure that its arbor was properly machined.

Moreover, a table saw is such an important part of a shop that I think you'd be happier spending the extra money for a full-size table saw. If you need to save space, mount the saw on a cabinet and store all your other compact tools in that cabinet.

If you insist on a bench-top table saw, you might also consider the Sears Craftsman 7½-inch table saw that I wrote about in 1980. In my tests, its blade tracked straight and true, producing acceptably smooth cuts.—*By A. J. Hand. Photos by the author.*

kit-built thickness sander

I don't have a thickness planer in my shop. When I needed wood planed to thickness (or rough wood smoothed), I took it down to the local cabinet-and-millwork shop where, for a reasonable charge, they ran it through one of their planers. It was inconvenient, but it saved me the $1,200 to $3,200 cost of the tool.

I seldom do that anymore. Not that I broke down and bought a planer. Instead, I made a tool (from a kit) that

Working parts for DynaSand drum sander are covered by hardwood-ply dust hood and belt and chain guards (p.177). Sanding drum (above) is wrapped with abrasive strip, the end secured with spray adhesive. Paper coil is pattern for strip.

can do most of the jobs a planer can and even do them better. It's called a drum sander (but it's unrelated to the small sleeves you chuck in a drill press for smoothing curves). On this drum sander, the sanding head is a large cylinder around which you wind a strip of sanding cloth, spiraling it around to completely cover the drum (see photo). The work is laid on an adjustable table and fed under the rotating abrasive-covered drum. The drum-sander kit I bought is called the DynaSand Thickness Sander. It's made by Kuster Woodworkers (Box 34, Skillman, N.J. 08558).

Actually, it was one of those trips to my local cabinet shop that set me on the trail of DynaSand. That day the proprietor, Paul Moser, did my job on a new tool—a 36-in.-wide belt sander. Instead of knives dressing the wood, an abrasive belt did the work. My ¾-in. mahogany was quickly reduced to the ⁹⁄₁₆-in. thickness I wanted. And the quality of the work was first-rate.

Wide-belt sanders and their cousins, abrasive planers, are replacing knife planers, belt sanders, and stroke sanders in cabinetmaking shops and furniture factories, Moser told me. The reason: They will sand wood to very accurate dimensions. Any kind of grain, including end grain, can be surfaced, and the flaws that planers often leave are virtually eliminated.

But wide-belt sanders are not manufactured for the home workshop. The tool in that cabinet shop is driven by a 24-hp motor and costs $20,000—obviously not for me.

A drum sander, however, will perform the same sanding operations as a wide-belt sander. And the price is affordable. DynaSand kits are available in three drum widths: 12, 18, and 24 inches. The kits contain the necessary special and industrial parts you are not likely to find in hardware stores. You have to supply the wood, plywood, and plastic laminate for the frame, table, and belt and chain guards; and a drive motor for the drum. The basic kits are for

manual feed. A separate kit converts the sander to power feed—an option you can add later if you prefer.

My first step was to decide which size would be best for my shop. The 12-in. size may be great for model builders and musical-instrument makers, but it doesn't have the capacity for furniture making. I looked back over 10 years' woodworking projects to see if I could justify the additional cost and space required for the 24-in. model instead of the 18. The glued-up work I did in that period that was more than 18 inches wide consisted of two workbench tops, one trestle table top, and two settle ends. And only the settle ends were less than 24 inches wide. Thus my choice was obvious: Go with the 18-in. model, which would handle almost everything, and continue taking the wider stuff to the cabinet shop.

Putting It Together

The instructions that come with the kit specify 1½-inch hardwood for frame and legs. I used maple; oak would have been another good choice. Dimensioned patterns are provided for all parts. Joints are mostly half-lapped, so making the parts was easy. Accuracy is important, however. Clearances are tight, and if the sander is going to work well, it has to be assembled square.

You do the initial assembly with glue only so you don't put frame-assembly screws where they'll be in the way of mechanism screws you install later. When I did install the frame screws, I used enough to hold the frame together as if there were no glue.

The gear motor that drives the feed rollers is mounted on a platform extending from one side of the frame. I did not use the Kuster pattern but substituted a design of my own; mine uses less wood and is better secured. It also provides a mount for the motor and vacuum-cleaner switches so that they face the in-feed end of the sander. The drive for the sanding drum is located near the bottom of the sander on a hinged board. The weight of the motor provides belt tension, which can be adjusted by moving the motor on the board.

The table is critical. It must be flat, rigid, and smooth. It is made of two layers of ¾-inch plywood, reinforced with hardwood side rails and surfaced with glossy plastic laminate. I used furniture-grade birch plywood; marine ply would be a good choice, too, but A-C-grade (exterior) fir plywood is absolutely out. The plywood must be flat initially; you should be very picky about this.

The table-raising mechanism consists of threaded rods mounted to the frame at each corner and driven synchronously by sprockets and drive chain. Threaded blocks attached to the table ride the rods. Each turn of the rods (by a single crank) raises the table ¹⁄₁₀ inch.

The six-inch-diameter sanding drum is mounted on a one-inch shaft in self-aligning pillow blocks. Care must be taken to center the drum in the frame. In-feed and out-feed rollers are on steel shafts that rotate in phosphor-bronze bearings. The bearings lie in slots in the wood frame, pressed down by hefty coil springs. The springs are retained in square aluminum holders and held down by aluminum channels screwed in place. To avoid strain on the small-cross-section parts of the frame in which the screws go, I drilled loose-clearance holes 1¼ inch deep then drilled deeper pilot holes for ¼-by-three-inch lag screws. The feed rollers are also driven by sprockets and drive chain.

To power the sander, Kuster recommends a ¾- to two-hp-drive motor, depending on the size of the sander and the intended use. I purchased a Sears medium-duty, ball-

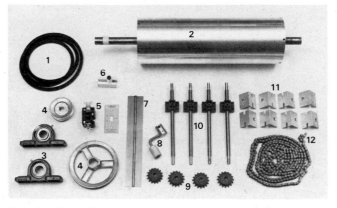

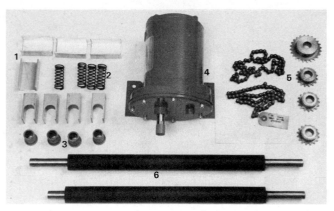

Parts for 18-in. thickness-sander kit from DynaSand (above, left) include: V-belt (1), six-by-18-in. aluminum drum on steel shaft (2), pillow blocks (3), pulleys (4), motor-starter switch (5), roller-chain tensioner (6), piano hinge for motor board (7), table-adjustment crank (8), sprockets (9), threaded rods with traveling blocks (10), brackets (11), and roller chain (12). Optional power-feed kit for it (right) contains these parts: aluminum spring holders and caps (1); springs (2); phosphor-bronze bearings (3); 1/4-hp, 15-rpm gear motor (4); roller chain and sprockets (5); in-feed and out-feed rollers (6).

bearing, capacitor-start, one-hp motor, which can run on either 115 or 230 VAC.

Guards on the sander are very important. The danger from the belt is obvious, but the danger from the slow-moving chain drive is worse. With 50 foot-pounds of torque driving it, anything caught in the chain is going to get mashed in the sprocket unless the chain breaks or a set-screw lets go. You also have to build a hood over the drum to keep sawdust from blowing all over your shop and, more particularly, to keep sawdust off the feed rollers so their traction will not be impaired. I connected the dust hood to a Sears 12-gallon wet-or-dry shop vacuum, which I bought especially for this sander since it will be the most prolific sawdust producer in my shop. Patterns are given in the instructions for making the guards and the dust-collector hood, but I beefed up mine beyond what Kuster called for.

Another change I made was to file flats on the roller shafts for the setscrews. It is unlikely that one of the screws will let go, but if one did, you could have a board shooting out the in-feed end of the sander.

To assemble sander frame, you attach base to legs with glue and screws (above, left). Legs are attached to upper sander frame with bolts only. Assembled sander (right), minus guards and dust hood, reveals motor on hinged board. Chain for table-raising drive passes through slots in leg and corner posts. Note chain tensioner behind V-belt. Feed rollers are connected with sprockets and chain.

Gear motor for feed rollers is mounted on a platform attached to sander frame (above left). Threaded rods of table-raising mechanism, attached to sander frame at top and bottom, pass through threaded blocks, which are attached to the table. Chain and sprockets drive all rods at once to control table height uniformly. Dust-collector hood (right) doubles as a guard for the sanding drum when the top is in place. Baffle (being inserted) keeps dust away from the in-feed roller.

The abrasive used on this drum sander is three-inch-wide abrasive cloth—the same material sanding belts are made of. It can be purchased from Kuster and others in 60, 80, 120, and 180 grits on 150-foot rolls for about $43 per roll.

I have used my DynaSand to surface a wide variety of work, including fir end grain, using 60- and 80-grit abrasive. The depth of cut that can be made depends on the width of the work piece, the direction of the grain, the wood density, and grit and condition of the abrasive (how worn and how clogged it is). It also depends on the horsepower of the sanding motor, the speed of the drum, the feed speed, and (with power feed) the ability of the feed rollers to push the work against the drum. DynaSand does a great job dressing standard thickness S2S (surfaced both sides) lumber to intermediate thicknesses. It can handle stock up to 17½ inches wide and four inches thick. Pieces can be as short as 10 inches and as thin as ³⁄₁₆. Thinner pieces should not be run through because the feed rollers will rub on the table surface. Shorter and thinner pieces can be dressed if they are fastened to support boards.

The weakness of the Kuster DynaSand is its wood construction. Wood simply is not as rigid as steel. This has been a problem in some of the sanders: sanding is heavier for about five inches at each end of boards.

This is caused by the table flexing under the feed roller loads. There is some deflection as the wood goes under the in-feed roller, then increased deflection (and decreased sanding) as the wood passes under the out-feed roller, then sudden increased sanding as the wood clears the in-feed roller.

The problem is in the plywood used in the table. It is a random problem; some pieces of plywood deflect more than others.

The cure is to bolt pieces of steel channel under the table end-to-end. You can run the channel all the way to the end (short of interfering with the chain) and give away an inch of thickness capacity, or you can keep it short of the bottom framing. I suggest using three ¼-by-1½-by-three-inch pieces of channel.

Attach the channel near the ends only, using two ³⁄₈-by-2½-inch flathead machine screws with self-locking nuts at each end. The large diameter will spread the load over a decent wood area.

Unless the back of the channel flange is ground flat, you should insert a three-by-five-inch metal shim across the center of the bed.

The Kuster DynaSand drum sander is not interchangeable with a home-shop planer. While it can be used to dress rough lumber, it is slow at it—even with 36-grit abrasive. On the other hand, DynaSand will surface wood with the grain or across the grain, and even handle end grain without danger of leaving chip marks, gouging, grain raising, or "washboarding"—always potential hazards with a planer. It can smooth knots and the wildest grain. And it will let you reduce ¾-inch wood to a veneer.

The 18-inch DynaSand kit with power feed costs $585. With motor, wood, and hardware the total cost is about $825. Prices of other kits: manual feed—12-inch ($245), 18-inch ($295), 24-inch ($345); power feed—12-inch ($490), 24-inch ($640).

Kuster has introduced a line of Ultra-Sand thickness sanders similar in design to the DynaSand line. Instead of being wood-framed kits, they are ready-to-run with welded tubular steel frames and steel shrouds. Prices are $800 (12-inch), $1,100 (18-inch) and $1,400 (24-inch), all less main drive motor. Prices do not include freight—*By Thomas Jones.*

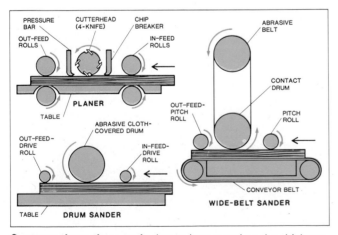

Compare these three tools that reduce wood to the thickness you want: planer, wide-belt sander, and drum sander. Cross sections show how each works.

index